RESCUE
FEMINIST

An Indian fairy tale of equality and other myths

SALONI CHOPRA

notionpress.com

INDIA · SINGAPORE · MALAYSIA

Notion Press

No. 8, 3rd Cross Street,
CIT Colony, Mylapore,
Chennai, Tamil Nadu – 600 004

First Published by Notion Press 2020
Copyright © Saloni Chopra 2020
All Rights Reserved.

ISBN
Paperback 978-1-63745-360-5
Hardcase 978-1-63745-361-2

Cover Photo Credits: Deep J Panchal.

Dedicated to:

My army of Indian womxn who have always stood by me and given me the opportunity to empower them through my words.

The women I grew up with, my mum and nani, who perpetually remind me of my patriarchal boundaries, while *simultaneously pushing me to cross them.*

And, of course, my brother, who taught me to question my conclusions, and be aware of my assumptions.

CONTENTS

WITH LOVE, SALONI

Random notes and opinion pieces, mostly because I couldn't write a "real" book.

It took me a while to figure out what I wanted to write about. Two years, multiple international trips trying to figure out a way to share something with you, but I was stuck somewhere forgetting what the truth is—I was trying too hard to be someone else; someone that was a real "writer." I wanted to write in abstract about womxn's journeys; I wanted to write poetry, talk about love in magical ways, and give you the kind of advice no one has ever given before. *I wanted to be good.* Inspired by my favourite writers, poets, and people I thought were wonderful, I wanted my first book to be... *perfect.*

In the journey of trying to be perfect, I wrote 300 words in 700 days. Most days that I tried to write this book, I'd stare at my screen for an hour, Instagram for another hour, out of the window for two hours—and in the end, frustrated, four coffees and three wines later, I'd end up writing a long post on Instagram about something that mattered to me.

Enter.
Send.
Post.

There, that was my two years spent working on my book. I'd curse myself because I'd written something for Instagram and posted it immediately, whereas I should've been working on chapters… *Maybe I wasn't meant to write a book*, I thought. Instagram was it for me. Why didn't I have anything to say here, yet so much to say there?

As ridiculous as it sounds, it took me this long (when I say *this long*, I mean it. I started writing this particular introduction in Melbourne in November 2018 and finally finished it in Spain, in August 2019) to realise that I was trying too hard to be *perfect*—the opposite of what I tell you to focus on becoming. I wanted to write things that I didn't relate to or feel anything about, in the abstract, things that sound good on paper, forgetting that the reason anyone ever reads my words is because I'm honest about my journey and my views. Because my story… has been relatable to you. My words, a comfort. So, when what comes naturally to me is to write this book and talk to you about how I got where I am today, then why was I trying so hard to do everything but that?

> *"The best time to plant a tree was 20 years ago.*
> *The second-best time is now."*

So, here I am, ready to accept that I don't have to be perfect. Ready to share my imperfections with you. I don't have to have all my ducks in a row—my ducks are running wild and free—and I don't have to talk about love in unrealistic romantic ways… I'm going to talk to you about the things I've learnt as a feminist in the last decade. Things that have moved me, broken me, built me up again, and saved my life. Writing this book has often felt like something is choking me. Time and again, I've had to face my deepest fears, and I've honestly lost count of my anxiety attacks, but maybe that's all the more reason for you to keep reading.

Because it's always good to begin right at the start, let's get a few things straight. Over the last two years of writing this book, I have been confronted by my own thought processes, my self-conflicts, and often my own unintentional ignorance. While editing this book and rereading my chapters every day, I noticed that I kept talking about men and women. Men and *women*. I noticed that often when I spoke about relationships, I assumed them to be heterosexual, and when I spoke about women, I wasn't actively thinking about the non-binary community or even trans women. That began to bother me because in many instances in the book, I talk about how much the words we choose matter—why the language we use is so important. So, I went back and changed all the *women* in my book to *womxn*, because I wanted to create a space for us all, which includes diverse perspectives. If *women* are oppressed, so are the LGBTQ and non-binary communities, and *far too many* human beings in our society today would choose to identify as a womxn in her own right, and not a mere extension of a man, including cis womxn.

Not so long ago, I was on a flight, sitting next to a little girl who was watching a fairy tale, and I wondered… *in our brave new world, what kind of a womxn would she have the opportunity of becoming?* I wondered if she'd be rebellious, or would she be taught to take up more space? Would she be asked her sexual preference? Would she know that fairy tales weren't really about what *all womxn* wanted from life? I looked at her and couldn't help but wonder—was there a parallel universe where Cinderella was an independent and outspoken womxn, who neither came home before midnight nor needed a fairy godmother? Maybe in that world, this little girl will never grow up to be the damsel in distress, neither will she be cursed and locked up in a castle with the voice and hair of an angel, and birds won't sing along with her, nor will she think that in order to be loved, she must be the colour of snow. Maybe the princess will be the hero of her own story, and her adamant desire to fight for her rights is what will rescue her from this world, and in the process of saving herself, she'll save many more princes and princesses, by setting examples and breaking stereotypes, and storybooks wouldn't then shy away from telling stories about a prince who was rescued by a feminist.

I'm going to talk to you about what feels right to me, when it feels right to me, and hope that it is everything you're ready to hear, while knowing that it's absolutely okay if you're not. You don't have to agree with everything I think or I'm about to say, as long as you agree to let me remind you to think for yourself again.

With love,
Yours, Saloni.

CHAPTER 1

MEN, WOMXN, AND OUR APPLES

I'm going to try and do this under 2000 words.

First, just because I stand for one issue, it doesn't mean that I don't stand for other issues. Yes, things related to womxn are highly sensitive for me, and I spend most of my time discussing women's rights, especially the ones that, according to me, are *most basic*—but that doesn't mean I don't care about LGBTQ, poverty, environment, mental health, animals, education, violence, and other important issues.

We, as individuals, are affected by different things at different levels of intensity, and caring excessively for one doesn't have to take away from the other. That's the most beautiful part about being human to me, that we can coexist in this world, affected by so many different things that we care about, and do our own part to change/create awareness about it all. We have the ability to organically segregate, divide, and balance our causes—how amazing is that?

Here I am, talking about womxn and our right to our bodies, while someone else is trying to raise awareness about cancer. Another person about climate change and the impacts of recycling. Someone else about animal rights, and *you*, you may want to help refugees or the LGBTQ community or children or men's health. It is so important for each of us to continue doing our part towards the things that affect us the most, and do our best at it. Even a business is doing their bit by employing thousands of people and helping them grow individually and have a life in society, while also helping our economy—something many of us might not be able to do. So, even when you think that someone isn't doing *anything*, they're doing their part by simply *existing*. The assumption that you can exist and not be part of change is the problem because you're still changing this world when you're choosing to be complacent. Ask yourself if that's the kind of change you wish to be a part of.

We're all doing something that helps us grow together and just because we care about one thing more than the other or often are affected by one issue more than others, *does not mean we don't care about anything else.* Imagine if *everyone* only cared about recycling and no one did anything about poverty, or only about gender and sex but neglected the health care industry, or catered to the needs of animals but not education. We would never exist, would we?

Secondly, when someone is talking about a problem in society, *pointing out another problem doesn't solve anything.* I think they now call it *"whataboutism"*—I'm learning a thing or two from the younger lot. For example, if I say, *"Women are oppressed and don't have equal rights in society,"* and you reply with, *"But what about false rape cases?"* sure, and what about AIDS? What about plastic and noise pollution? And also, what about India-Pakistan? You see, *whataboutism* deflects, and it's highly entertaining for trolls, but it doesn't solve anything. If you're going to use one problem to deflect from the other, you're just wasting everybody's time.

It actually breaks my heart to see that far too many people who *do* stand for men's rights don't actually do anything productive towards men's rights at all... instead they waste so much of their time attacking women's rights. Every time someone wants to talk about women, you'll see 20 people get up and say *"but what about men!"* In the end, those people are solving nothing. I've learnt more about *men* from reading *Invisible Women* by

Caroline Criado Perez than I have on anti-feminism blogs on the internet. What does that achieve?

Let's talk about men's rights while focusing on *men*, shall we? In fact, if there's anything I've learnt over the years of discussing *women's rights*, it's that if we let women have equal rights in this world, we would be fixing *so many of the issues* related to men. But unfortunately, far too many people in this world consider standing up for women as a threat to men—and it is a threat; it's a threat to their current status quo and rights, but that's not necessarily a bad thing, is it?

Here's a stolen example from my brother: Imagine a scenario where as soon as you (a man) were born, society gave *you* four apples, but when I was born, they gave me just two apples, even though neither of us did anything to deserve less or more. However, we go on to live our lives happily together, oblivious of what these apples are even for, let alone each other's unfair apple division. One day, I finally realise that you have more apples than me, and I want the same amount as well because it turns out that having fewer apples from the day I was born makes my life so much harder and far more restricted than yours, and I demand it because I deserve the same things as you. When you were younger, you thought so too, but we grew up with completely different lives and now you're not so sure anymore. But *some sections of our society* fight to make a new rule: *you must share just one of your apples with me in order to have fairness.* I am then suddenly a threat to you and your apples, aren't I? If you have to let go of something that's been only yours and share it with me, that's a threat to your power, your ownership, isn't it?

My demand for equal rights is a threat to you because so many of the privileges you were simply born with are being taken away/shared with others. It's normal for you to feel momentarily attacked because you've been so used to living life with more apples than me, but should I be sorry for demanding the same equality as you? No. Should I give up? No. Should I be violent or arrogant? No. Is it your place to tell me I'm not allowed to ask for this change? No. Should you insult, assault, threaten, rape, or murder me when I disagree with you? **No.**

In an ideal world, we would find a way to live together and share our apples with each other, with respect. Men would understand that they were unfairly privileged, to begin with, and help other people understand why it's okay to share their apples with other people that were never given enough for no fault of theirs, but simply because of the gender or sex they were born into.

In this instance, the apples are your rights. *Yes, plot twist.*

Going back to men for a second, mental health is a huge problem when it comes to men's issues. Suicide rates are higher, there's more pressure on men to be the bread-earners of the family. There's less talk about depression. Men are expected to be strong and very often encouraged to lack sensitivity.

There is inequality in gender and sexes. If womxn were given the right to education and equal pay, if roles were divided equally, if womxn were also expected to be bread-earners (which would mean they'd have to have the same education and opportunities), eventually, the pressure to be the term *"man of the house"* wouldn't exist; it would be shared equally. However, until we have the capacity for more schools, young boys would have to compete with womxn for their class seats, and men would compete with womxn for jobs, and chores would be divided because womxn wouldn't be doing most of the unpaid labour anymore, and that is when womxn become a threat to all that men have had and also haven't had to give up until now.

This notion that womxn make babies and cook food and raise children and look after the house and give good blow jobs but are shy and introverted yet cry a lot because they're hormonal hence hysterical, while men are strong and independent and work hard to earn money for a family of 30 people while they sacrifice their own dreams, that men never cry and they can't cook, let alone raise children—these are the stereotypes that are harming womxn, men, *and* non-binary communities.

There are womxn that want to work. Some that don't ever want to compromise their careers in order to have babies. Ambitious and independent womxn. There are also men that are sensitive and caring and daydream about raising their kids and being stay-at-home dads instead of having full-time jobs. There are non-binary people that can be and are mothers. Let all people flourish by giving them equal opportunities to do all or none of the above. If anything, yes, **be** a threat to the current stereotype of *men's rights*. Stand up for equal rights for all. Let human beings decide what they are, and how they wish to identify themselves. TALK about the issues that you are most passionate towards. Talk about men's health, talk about gender roles, and genderqueer rights, or if you wish to, talk about womxn's rights. Talk about the children growing up *right now* that are so confused because they do not even have role models in our society that they can look up to. Because we're still struggling for their rights to be who they are. Talk about the animals that can't fight for their own rights or this land that we abuse every day. *Talk about anything that you truly care about.*

But the next time you're *talking* about the issues that *you* are most affected by and someone wants to throw *whataboutism* in your face, remind them that they're not doing justice to either of the causes and are simply wasting your time… or hand them this chapter.

Tell me below what you care about the most, and how are we going to bring change?

My Notes

My Notes

———

CHAPTER 2

INSERT FATHER'S NAME BELOW
_____ BASTARD

Jesus. I hope you're ready for this. It's going to get a *little* ugly.

Everyone everywhere wants to know your father's name. I get 20 messages a day on Instagram asking me who my father is, and I'm not at all surprised because from casual patriarchy to the deep-rooted ones in our legal system, *everyone wants to know your father's name.* I have never, ever been asked my mother's name with the same authority and importance.

"But, you didn't fill out your father's name…"

It's almost mandatory, it's an expectation. A passport or a birth certificate without a father's name? Impossible.

Try getting away with it in school. I remember as a kid, my brother and I would fight to have our mum's name on all school documents and certificates—because why the fuck not? Growing up with a single mother, she was really our only parent. I may as well have not come from sperm because there was definitely no positive input of any sperm raising this *awesome* woman here.

Then as you grow older, past the school battles, try getting a police verification for passport purposes done without your father's name—my most exhausting procedure yet.

Why does your mother's surname not match yours?

She uses her maiden name, sir.

Why would a married woman do such a thing?!

Because my parents are not together.

What do you mean "not together"?

I mean they are divorced.

Oh, so she's not even with her husband… *slow chatter in Marathi around the station* Fine, get a divorce certificate.

Umm, sir… I think she doesn't have one. She was young, and he didn't give it to her, but why don't I just give you documents that prove she's my mother so we can skip this part?

No, no, so it's not even a real divorce?

It is, of course, but he never gave her the hard copy document. But regardless, I do have documents that say *she's my mother.* My passport. The house papers. Birth certificate. Which one can—

That won't work. Show us the marriage certificate.

Sir, they had gotten married in a small city… as I said, she was young… this can be very triggering, so unless it's extremely important, I'd rather not ask her… We have photos, if you want to see the album? My grandparents were present too… I mean, do you really need this document? She's my mother, as it says so *in my birth certificate…*

You mean to say your mother never married this man, she never divorced this man, but here you are...

I didn't say that, SIR. I said that I don't think she has some of the documents. I said I don't want to cause her pain. Her name is already on my passport as MY mother.

What kind of a woman is this? What is this upbringing, huh? No wonder you are back answering.

How have I—I'm telling you she's my—

No, no, you fake Indians... ruining our culture and this country. You go live in the West instead of polluting here.

My biological father was (**is**) an awful, awful human being. He didn't give her any alimony, child support, or even help her to physically raise us in any way. He lied, cheated, and he was abusive. He never gave her documents when they were actually needed, he threatened and manipulated her, and he never respected any of us. Yet, our society won't ever ask *"what kind of a man is this?"* They won't applaud her for raising us alone. They won't genuinely ask why she doesn't have any documents, does she need help, is she alright... no, but they will judge.

*A bastard. You're a bastard child, then. Your parents were never married. But your mother had you. *laughs**

Yes, sir. A bastard, to a *bastard*—because he must truly be the only reason why the word *"bastard"* was even turned into an abuse, an insult, and then the rest of us suffered the consequences forever.

That exchange above was somewhat what happened. Mixed with Hindi and Marathi and lots of slangs and underhanded comments, often suggestions and gestures and indications about my character as well as my mother's without actual name-calling. No, I didn't give my last big monologue as well as I wrote it, and they did not call me a bastard to my face, nor do I think I am one, though I couldn't care less. But they may as well have called us *sluts* with how they spoke about us. Absolutely no question of the kind of man this *so-called father* was that married my mother, dominated her, had kids practically everywhere in the world for all we know, left them all, never gave her the right papers without her having to beg for them, and took zero legal responsibility towards his children—yet, everybody wanted to know my father's name, because without his name after mine, *who even was I?*

But a woman that chose to get away from such a man as fast as she could, a woman that asked for nothing in return legally except for him to never trouble her or her kids again, a woman with a lot of strength and courage, who did as best as she could for her kids and raised them to the best of her capacity, a woman so young who worked day and night and made her career so she could give us the life she always wanted us to have, one where we'd never feel the absence of a father—this wonderful, beautiful, strong, sensitive, superwoman is who the world chooses to judge as they destroy *her* character. For something that wasn't her fault, to begin with.

What an amazing world we live in. Honestly, I'd rather be a bastard than to be accepted by this patriarchal society.

Growing up without a father, especially one like mine, was probably the best thing that could've ever happened to me. So, the next time someone wants to know my father's name… I'd rather smile and say "actually, I'm a bastard." Because it would be easier to let them think I was born not knowing who he was than to explain why I hated him so much. Yet, I don't go around saying that, because I've recently also understood that calling myself a bastard automatically means that this society yet again judges the mother, not the father.

Anyway, while we're here with so many pages to go and so many more things to discuss, I guess I wanted to get this topic over and done with, get it off my chest, maybe? I hope to God that if the man that contributed his sperm to your birth is as awful as mine was, *I hope he left*—because every now and then, when I think about what our lives would have been like had he stayed, it scares me to death. It's petrifying, and no one should have to ever deal with that.

So, hello, for those of you that don't know me yet, I am a Saloni Chopra—daughter to my mother, who happens to also be a Chopra.:)

My Notes

My Notes

CHAPTER 3

TOXIC LOVE & QUICKSAND

Let's be completely honest for a second. India is such a big male-dominated society that it is almost impossible to move here and not have a humongous life-changing, if not threatening, crash into patriarchy. So much so that you're eventually experiencing a lot of road rage and rash driving around the stereotypes of women and the expectations they are held up to every-single-day.

I was 19 when I moved here. Oh boy, was I a naive (little) girl! And shockingly, it didn't end there... I stayed naive for another five years. *Add another three years to actually understand the problem and then acknowledge that this problem was not me.* This is why when I look around me and I see girls as young as 19 or 20 years old talking about equality and human rights, I'm so blown away. Then they tell me they're inspired by *me* and I laugh a little at the irony of how ignorant I was when I was their age (and much older).

Anyway, the teenage me was all set to move to Melbourne to study fashion design at RMIT... and then suddenly realised that she wasn't going to be doing that anymore. A year later, she found herself in Bombay. Clustered, hot, polluted, noisy, and dirty Bombay. Also, the same Bombay that this small woman with big dreams fell head over heels in love with. Busy, filled with life, chaotic, and dreamy Bombay. A city where you could barely stop to catch your breath on a crowded road. I could get lost in the streets here… I could go anywhere I wanted in autos and not feel motion sick because of how airy they were. There were people *everywhere!* I could sit alone in my room in silence and yet never feel lonely because when I looked outside the window even at 1 am, there were people having chai and talking about their families and sometimes talking about something they had no business being in whatsoever, and I wasn't going to realise why that was very bad for a few more years, but I loved it. I loved the vibe this city had. The constant chaos, constant… *life*.

For a girl that grew up with no friends in a tiny little city called Adelaide, where everyone knew each other and you couldn't go into the city without bumping into the first boy you ever kissed, your kindergarten crush, your current crush, the boy that hasn't answered your call in four weeks, the popular girls that hate your guts, the racist kids, friends of your parents, and your math teacher that thinks you're sick because you skipped her class three days in a row, *all the while having zero friends*—living in Mumbai where nobody knew who I was, and I never bumped into anybody, and I could maybe, possibly make friends, was a dream come true for me. Here, I bumped into myself.

Back in Adelaide, I don't think I'd ever even spoken to my own neighbours… and here I was, smiling at everyone I saw in my building (until, of course, I learnt that smiling was either creepy or a sexual invitation to strangers and also that, eventually, none of these people were going to like me).

But hey, I basked in that honeymoon period for years. Smiling, laughing, making friends with uncles and chatting up paan wale bhaiya and smoking my first cigarette and getting drunk every weekend with so many new people that wanted to get to know this new girl from *Australia*.

I was now an adult, in a world so buzzing that even I couldn't hold my shit together. I met some amazing people that are my best friends till date, some that stayed until they needed, to teach me a thing or two, and others that were simply passing through.

I have never been afraid of acknowledging that I was extremely ignorant while growing up. I'm well aware of that. My life revolved around my world, my problems, my stories, my sufferings, me. I was a privileged brown girl living in a first world country with her problems, and some memories of abuse she couldn't seem to let go of. Not all of my problems were silly; many were the kinds I wouldn't wish upon anyone, some should've never been real problems but became so due to the standards of beauty we set so high for women, others because children are often neglected or raised in unintentional environments where no one's at fault, but everybody is to blame... I didn't learn that for years either. Then there were problems that I was told were very *common* for a teenager. Possibly hormonal or mental—I guess it's officially too late to know now.

I don't necessarily like to look down upon my problems as a kid because I know if this was us talking about another person's childhood, then I'd be really sympathetic, and I'd understand their issues, but somehow when it comes to my own memories, I'm much harsher to myself. I go into an awful zone of *"Gosh, Saloni, you stink of privilege and yet here you are, whining"*... Well, I hope it's clear to you now that we *all* have issues. Even those of us that think we can write books!

With most of my childhood blocked out (I have very little memory from 6-16; it's like I was in and out of a coma) and very little to regret, when I moved at 19 years, I was ready to begin my life. At first, I wanted to be a fashion designer, but after having started a three-year degree and realising within the first three months that this wasn't meant for me because I hated six out of eight subjects, I dropped out and instead started working on movies—*assisting* designers. Soon enough, two projects down, I learnt that designing, overall, wasn't for me either.

It happened while I was standing outside a famous actor's van with 20 hangers. He'd just lectured me on not getting his favourite navy blue and white ankle-length CK socks and *how dare I get the black & white ankle-length (you never see his socks in the movie, ever)?* I stood there in the sun with his 15 hangers and a particular linen kurti that I had already ironed three times and it still hadn't been worn by him. I could see that soon I'd have to run for the 4th ironing, and I wondered *what was it that I was doing with my life.* I knew I grew up wanting to be a designer, but was that simply because it's what my mother did? Because she was a designer, so I thought I wanted to be one too? It must've been... because I don't remember designing clothes for anyone else but myself. I would sketch dresses for hours, on tissues and paper and any plain surface I could find, dresses that *I* wanted to wear. Dresses that I thought would look good on me. But to make clothes for *other people?* Never even thought of *that* as a profession. I thought maybe fashion designing meant making clothes for myself—narcissism has evidently been the only consistency in my life.

Yet, here I was... somehow.

You'd think that a girl who'd learnt in 2011 that she wanted to act and not be a fashion designer would then focus on acting. Of course not. I told you, some of us are just really slow at change, and life... I kept working on movies as an assistant director or a stylist up until 2014; that was when I finally thought, *why not try something I actually like for a change?*

Throughout the mistakes and the multiple unsure decisions, all I knew for sure was that Bombay loved me. And I loved it back immensely. My Bombay.

I've always said I have a love-hate relationship with this city; much like all erotic but toxic love stories, there was tension between us. It drove me crazy on some days when I swore I'd leave it, I swore I was done for good, and other days, it made me fall so deep in love—this city was meant for me. To me, Bombay was like quicksand, it sort of just sucks you in, and as long as you stay calm, you stay alive. But if you panic, it will swallow you whole.

This city gradually also made me aware of who I was... who I *am.* It showed me things I liked and disliked, made me more aware of what pushes my buttons and how much I was willing to take before I break.

This city made me dig deeper into my heart and ask myself questions about the kind of womxn I wanted to be. What did I want to stand for? What did I believe in? Who am I, and was I going to fight for it?

This city made me a feminist.

Do you have a special relationship with a city, a place, or even a moment?

My Notes

My Notes

CHAPTER 4

LOVE, ESTEEM, IMPORTANCE

Quick game:

Put each of these in one of the three categories.

1. "I don't think I deserve to be loved by someone forever."

2. "I don't think everyone would love the kind of person I am, but surely there are people out there that would love me for who I am."

3. "I think everybody should love me, be nice to me all the time regardless of what they're going through because I am loveable and I deserve everybody's attention."

If you're going to read the rest of this book (low-key hoping you say yes), then you're going to have to know the difference between these terms, because I will tell you *a lot of times* that you are absolutely gorgeous, and loved, and you deserve *the world,* that you're *beautiful,* you are *enough*—and you *are* all of those things… but it's important to know what that means first.

Unfortunately, there are far too many people in this world that confuse self-love with self-importance, and I don't think we need any more humans with self-importance and entitlement. They're the reason that the rest of the world feels neglected, insecure, and not *enough* to begin with.

Self-esteem and self-love often go hand in hand for most people.

Number 1 is an example of someone who lacks self-esteem and thinks that they're not good enough for anyone in this world because *they think* there are too many things wrong with them—perpetually comparing themselves to others, letting the world get to them, and believing that they're *not enough*. Most of us feel like this very often in life, especially womxn but also many men. The words I write are usually for you... *yes, I see you,* and I can't believe you let the shittiness of this world make you feel like something is wrong with *you.*

A lot of people with self-esteem issues have low confidence, history of bullying or harassment, abusive childhoods, body image issues, maybe more than that or maybe none of the above. You and I can't always pinpoint *why* a person lacks self-worth (hence, therapy), but whatever the cause, I just want to tell *as many people as I can* that this world's ridiculous expectations of *who you should be* doesn't mean you lack something. You are *enough* as you are.

What does that mean?

It means you have all the things the world thinks you lack, and if you don't have them, then maybe you don't need them. And if you need them, but for whatever reasons haven't been able to have them even though you've tried, know that you're still enough. You've got the potential to do *anything* you wish to do. If you're not harming anyone or hurting people and are simply living your life on your terms, then stop letting the world get to you. *Self-esteem is an individual's subjective evaluation of their own worth. To me, you are worth all the love this world has to offer.*

A big chunk of our world tries to force *different* people into *one little box* that isn't designed for all of us. So, when people don't *fit,* the world tells them they're too much or too little and that they lack something. *When I say you're enough, I'm talking to you.*

<u>*Number 2* </u>is an example of a person that probably has self-esteem and maybe loves themselves too. As I said before, both seem to go hand in hand for me, but the difference is that I think we as people often fluctuate. You might lack esteem but love yourself, and other times you may lack self-love but know you are worth more. I want you to remember to *value* yourself, even when you are caught in a rut of toxic human behaviour that makes you feel shit about yourself. You are beautiful—I am talking to *you, you self-loving often slipping human.*

As for the people that fit into <u>*Number 3*</u>: you still have time… I guess. Yes, the world should be kind, the world should be polite, but the world doesn't *owe you anything.* Everybody is fighting their own battle, and everyone has things they need to get on with. If you think that people owe you something just because you were born into this world with privilege, then I'm sorry but you're in for a disappointment. When I say *you are enough,* I am most certainly not reconfirming your delusion of *"hell yeah, I'm enough, why hasn't my fucking coffee come yet, waiter?"* No, sorry, risky territory.

"Am I enough? Can I ever be enough? Yes, I can be. I am enough" is a great place to begin.

"I know I am enough. A lot of people may not be right for me, and maybe I'm not right for them, but I'm not going to let their expectations of my body, my life, or my achievements bother me. I will filter out toxic people because I am enough" is just perfect.

"I am enough. In fact, I am more than enough. Why should I change anything for any of them? Why should I listen to what they're saying or care if I'm hurting them? I am enough, and I never need to change anything in order to love" is *self-centred.* Do you know what you're doing when you think like that?

You're harming and tampering the space I'm trying to create for people in the 1 and 2 categories, the ones that *need* to occupy more of the space you've forcefully taken up.

Being enough doesn't mean everybody will love you. Being enough doesn't mean that you never have to be better as a person, or give and receive love, or change, compromise, sacrifice, listen, adapt, evolve, have patience, apologise, or be empathetic. *You can be enough and still have to occasionally do some or all of the above.*

Being *enough* just means that you shouldn't let people walk all over you, or make you feel bad about yourself, or allow them to make you feel like you don't *deserve* to occupy the space that you take up in this world.

Self-respect, self-esteem, self-love, identity, self-worth are all extremely important, and they're not *self-importance.* You can exist, knowing that you deserve it all, as does everybody else.

I want you to remember that you're enough, and so are others.

You are beautiful, and so are other people.

You should go and occupy all the space you want in this world, as long as you let others do the same for themselves.

Expect the kind of empathy, generosity, and kindness in return that *you* are willing to offer.

You are as capable of loving as the love you are willing to give.

You deserve the kind of respect you give to other people.

You should *stop* doing things that cause you pain, and allow others to do the same.

Set your boundaries, and respect theirs.

While a lot of this is tricky and often complicated, I think in the end we all have to look in the mirror and ask ourselves if we want to be treated the way we treat other people. If other people are treating you with disrespect and a lack of kindness, then that's when I need you to know: *you are more than fucking enough to walk away from abuse. You don't have to put yourself down in order to be loved or accepted.*

You will figure this out with time, I promise.

Just remember to be humble and to love yourself enough to know when you deserve better.

I know it's easier said than done… this whole book is about you and me, our mistakes, and different ways that we can begin to love ourselves, so I guess we are all learning, right?

Self-love, self-esteem, or self-importance: which one do you relate to the most, and why?

My Notes

My Notes

CHAPTER 5

IN 2020, WE DON'T BURN OUR BRIDES, WE SET FIRE TO THEIR SOULS

My not-so-radical-feminist best friend recently made me realise something I hadn't really considered before. I knew the *feeling...* I'd just never aligned these fragments of feelings to create a straight line of thought before. I tend to talk a lot about gender inequality and the unfair ways in which womxn are treated in marriages and families; it's painful, it's jarring, and it's suffocating. But there's maybe more to it.

Going back in time, between the 1940s to the 1990s, there was a huge practice of dowry death and bride burning in India. According to statistics, in 1990 there were 5800 dowry deaths in our country, and by 1991, CNN ran a story saying that every year police received more than 2500 reports of bride burning.

While dowry deaths, bride burning, marital rape *(What? A crime? No way!),* and torturing the daughter-in-law are still commonly practised in different parts of the country, the statistics have definitely dropped. Dowry is now often publicly condemned, and we don't as commonly see families burning their brides either.

Don't be fooled though, it's still happening—it's just not happening in the same numbers. Women are now also being educated, they have jobs, careers, and *opinions*, so couples share more common responsibilities than ever before.

Welcome to the new, educated society, where there's high hopes of equality.

Don't make yourself too comfortable here though, because what I realised while talking to my not-so-radical-feminist friend *(it's a whole other thing I could write a chapter on. Oh wait, I did – Chapter 21)* is that even though we aren't burning brides or demanding dowry, we've found newer ways of torturing brides, and yes, it's exactly what it sounds like.

With time, people change and with changed people come changed habits and behaviours. We now live in a society where because we cannot openly burn a womxn when we think she's not good enough for our son, isn't fertile, or doesn't bring enough dowry, we simply find ways to set their souls on fire.

When a girl with a good job, a stable career, a plan, a voice, and opinions of her own enters a man's family—let's not forget even with all her progressive attitude—she doesn't hold the power in that dynamic. I see men talking about how they are far more resilient towards family drama, and how if a woman's family didn't approve of them, it really wouldn't bother them the same way. *"I wouldn't care,"* he says. Little does he realise, this resilience is nothing but a privilege that he's given with how men are treated in society.

Men don't feel the need to be accepted by a womxn's family—that's not a thing to be ticked off in their checklist. Clearly, if her family doesn't like *him*, something must be wrong with *them*. No boy is raised being told he has to learn to be a good husband or else his in-laws will be ashamed of him, or a girl won't marry him, or the typical *"how will you live in their house if you don't know any housework, you'll bring shame to us, what will her mother say, what kind of man have I sent into their home?"*

And when a man talks to his mother, he rarely gets lectured on calling his in-laws every second day, and how he *must* appreciate them and stay in touch with his partner's parents regularly and keep them happy in order to keep peace at home—that's never a usual conversation because, to be honest, *"do you regularly talk to her parents, beta? Work is not everything, call your in-laws too, you're losing sight of priorities, son"* is not even a point of conversation.

Having a job, dreams, money in our accounts, and short denim shorts doesn't change the fact that we as womxn are still conditioned to seek desperate approval from a man's family. What they think *matters*—because they are *his parents.* So, when a woman enters the family of a man, she's usually seeking their validation because that's what is embedded into her head from the beginning. And the family in question, however modern, may pretend like they don't know that, but they *usually* know. They know they hold the power, and they're not afraid to show it.

It starts with little things at first. It's about her clothes. *"Why does she wear such clothes? Red is really not her colour. Why did she upload a photo in a bikini on the beach, and how could her gown at the party be so backless?"* For some, it may even be as orthodox as sleeveless tops and jeans. Clothes are usually a very important aspect. Next comes her ambitions. Most modern families want an educated, working, ambitious girl for their son because *both of them should work,* instead of just the man paying the bills. Very often, we want a womxn that brings money to the table because let's face it, life has only gotten more expensive and raising a family is the job of two, not one. So, you'll meet a lot of *"we're not old fashioned, we want an educated daughter-in-law, we allow her to work."*

But this ambition is conditioned. If she's as ambitious as him, then that's not okay. God, that's worrisome. *"Does she not know?"* When she's working late nights to be promoted and he has to eat take away food, that is when the families object to *her* priorities—not his. *"Was she taught nothing?"* If she puts her career above the desire of having a child, that's a big red sign. *She's not family orientated, she's not wife material, or it's her upbringing.* God forbid if her parents are divorced… then it's probably the lack of a father figure in her family—*you see, that is why she's so characterless, there was no man present to control her.*

Lastly, if she is opinionated and has a strong sense of self, she's brainwashing and controlling their son. *She trains him and tells him what to say, she has a problem with everything, he wags his tail to her, she is clearly bullying him.* We've all heard them—often within our own families. We, collectively as a society, absolutely *do not* feel very comfortable around strong, opinionated, vocal womxn; they shake the system.

So, as a man's family, ideally what we're looking for is a timid, kind, polite, caring, working womxn who can take care of the house, respect the parents, dress very well but always as per their culture, have no desires or ambitions of her own that break the barriers they've set in place for the womxn of their family, satisfy her husband but not enough to distract him, is well educated, with a degree, but a stronger sense of maternal love, and very little self-respect. Welcome to the life of a progressive Indian womxn.

In the 21st century, we're not burning our brides as often anymore, but we are ripping them apart, piece by piece. We give birth to womxn, only to condition them into being independent young womxn with dreams and desires, then we not-so-subtly teach them to be good homemakers and mothers. We let them play with fire, unaware of how it's going to destroy them. We carefully place them in places and situations where they seek approval in a toxic environment. We spit on their ambitions, curb their dreams, limit their bodies, abuse their ability to express themselves, restrict their growth, control their clothes, insult their pain and tell them to tone it down, demand their respect, and remind them of how they'll never be good enough for our families and our sons.

There are multiple types of abuses that don't leave bruises and burns, the kind that damages more than just your physical body; it burns your soul in ways where you no longer have an identity of your own. So, you sit there on that sunny afternoon, reading about a shocking orthodox era when brides were set on fire, and you let the sun warm you a while longer as you finally realise where this constant internal burning sensation comes from. It finally makes sense. You don't feel so crazy anymore. You don't feel like you're losing your mind from the different kinds of suffocating encounters every day. It all makes sense, like the end of a *Black Mirror* episode. Except, this is not some dystopian future, it is the present—*your* present.

And so you hope that the drowning, burning, missing parts of you will find the courage to live long enough to shake the system and let their earth quake.

When you finally have a daughter, maybe you'll break the cycle and tell her that the question isn't if a boy and his family will one day want her or not, the bigger question should be, what does *she* want from her life? Maybe instead of trying to squeeze womxn into limited, rigid boxes, we should raise them to wander and wonder—*in what shape do they actually fit?*

I have a little exercise for you. Ask your parents what they want in a son-in-law or a daughter-in-law. Write them down and compare below.

My Notes

My Notes

CHAPTER 6

THE CHAPTER THAT DOESN'T REALLY LEAD TO ANYTHING. HELLO, THERAPIST

It's not that I hate families… okay, I hate families.

But it's not some sort of malicious hate; it's more of a *"fuck-you-humans-all-I-ever-wanted-was-you-and-you-never-wanted-me-back-so-I-hate-your-guts"* kind of hate. I wasn't born hating families… No, there was once a time when all I ever wanted was a big fat family (minus the fat-shaming and the wedding).

I grew up in a very small, protective family where everyone talks to everyone, and things are forcefully discussed, and no one is satisfied until we dissect every word the other person has said every week, and we just have to talk—like all the damn time. Even if it didn't make you happy. Communication was what kept our family together. Even when you don't want to hear it, when you wish your mother will just for once not tell you that your skin looks dull or your hair looks like shit, be assured that she would say it, and she'd say it because to her, this was her way of expressing her love. Maybe it sounds fucked up to some of you, but my mother considers her honesty the best of her gifts to the people she loves. To date, she says, *"Because the world is full of lies, I'm never going to lie to you, ever,"* and sometimes I'm like, *"Yeah, okay, mother, turn it down a notch though."* There's a difference between honesty and brutality, and then she says, *"I will die before I am fake with you!"* And then I say, *"Well, maybe there's a difference between telling someone they are useless and telling them they could be more useful! Ugh."* And as you can guess, turning down a notch is not a quality any of us possess in the family, myself included.

My family of four. Five. Okay, six.

My brother, our four-legged sibling Oscar, my grandmother, my mother, and then in the extended family, there's my mama and my mami, and their two four-legged children. Even with the cousins around, there's only a few of us that can actually do all the talking because barking doesn't count… so, I call it a *small family.* I obviously have other relatives, but this is it. This is my daily life, these are the humans that can annoy and bother me enough to push every button in my system, and then some more.

So, growing up, obsessing over *Hum Saath Saath Hain* as a little NRI kid, I was obsessed with big families. I wanted to grow up and find a beautiful boy with parents and like five siblings, and they would have their own soulmates and together they'd have all their children, and I'd sit there wondering about all the different relationship *titles* I would be to everyone in his family. *Oh, how happy I was in my little bubble.* Waiting for this man with this big family. One day, him and I, and his siblings and their lovers and their children, along with our (definitely adopted) children would play together, and we'd all celebrate Christmas together and wear matching onesies and hide gifts under a tree—never mind that I'm not Christian, dreams are dreams. All year would be perfect, just like this Christmas.

My best friend made fun of me a decade ago. She said, *"Jesus, Saloni. I don't know why you like families. Families are terrible because they consist of human beings, and let's face it, human beings are shit."* I was like, *"Whoaaaaa. No-they-are-not-I-love-humans!"*

Dreams, indeed, are dreams. I didn't realise that as I grow older, what I want in life, the things I stand for, who I am as a person, the kind of an adult I want to grow into—all of that would become a hindrance to this... little dream.

I also had no idea that people, in general, don't care if you are a good person or not, if you love their son or not, if you are kind to strangers or not, if you give a fuck about the environment or not. In the end, all that matters is your tradition, culture, the God you pray to, the caste you belong to, and how much money you make—oh and also what your stars/astrology says!

Come to think about it, one of my ex-therapists (What? You thought I only break-up with boyfriends? Lol, please, I have an EX everything) was right when he said, *"You don't hate families, you just love the concept of one too much. The child within you wants one so badly that the adult in you is bitter about being rejected far too many times."* Which would make me a terrible person because the bottom line is, *I'm bitter,* I thought.

So, life then takes a full circle, and I'm once again proven wrong, maybe people *are* shit.

I remember when I was 19 (I'm always 19 in this book, so maybe, just maybe, I'm fucking with you when it comes to age), I was madly in love with a Muslim boy. I can't disclose his name or else his wife will find out he's cheating on her (wait, what, I didn't even say anything). Let's call him B for Boy. So, B & I, we were so happy together. Our love story was like a movie—we sat and talked about our dreams, and we wrote down our vows on a piece of paper (mostly consisting of the fact that he would cook me food and I would do his architecture practical assignments; he would wash the clothes and I would fold them; I would work when he's studying, as long as he'd play me his guitar every week). Those vows worked for me. They were balanced and fair. It complimented our weaknesses and gave us a chance to express our strength. He would write songs about me and play them when I made coffee in the mornings, and we'd go swim our hearts out in the ocean. He said he wanted me to spend my life with him, and I would giggle with him on his university campus. We were inseparable... we were loud and young, and we would do stupid things on the streets because when you are in love, the rest of the world does not exist... *until it suddenly does.*

Now, at the start, I mentioned he was a Muslim boy, not because I'm Islamophobic, but because this bit of information is very important in this story. When his parents found out he was dating me, they disowned him—genuinely disowned him, like *"if you choose her, pack your bags and leave, don't show us your face again."* So, he then left them; it all happened so quickly. That was pretty much where our happily ever after ended. If we were a movie, you'd know then that this relationship is over, but we still had hope, as lovers do. I would write his mother sad long emails about how much I loved her son, explaining how maybe... just maybe, his God made me too, and she would delete them all without reading them.

Can you believe, for this tiny (very tiny) period of my life, I considered converting my religion (I'm not even religious) for my love? Do not laugh, we both know how *that* would have ended... as an absolute disaster, with me five years later removing my clothes, yelling on the streets, *"HUH? YOU HAVE A PROBLEM WITH MY BOOBS? YOU WANT THESE????"* Um, yeah, let's just not think about me catering to *any* religion in general. Disaster. Anyway, I told him I would consider it because when we are young and naive, our threshold for pain and tolerance for bullshit is so much higher—that's the best time to fuck with someone's dreams, 18-23 years of age. So, he went and met with his mother, shared the idea of me converting for him, and as she cooked food, she casually said, *"That's a great idea! Why don't you convert her and then dump her? That way, there will be more Muslims in the world. You'll be doing a good deed."*

What did I say?

People-are-shit.

This isn't the religion's fault, and it definitely isn't God's fault. God is just casually defamed for no goddamn reason. This is all human beings. I could not believe she said that about me. So, I asked him what if I converted and then they still didn't accept me, what would happen then? He ever so casually said, *"I don't know, I guess I can't exactly promise they'll accept you. I guess you'd then be Muslim, and we would continue to live like this, without them."*

Which further led to them wanting to come over and see where he stays, so he packed up all my shit for a day and said, *"Please, can I make this look like my place while you're at work?"* I had found this house, paid the rent, worked, did his homework as I'd promised, and hell, even if I didn't do any of the above… he wanted to *hide me.* So, I let him. They visited, and there wasn't a sign of me.

Then, one fine day, he asked me to take a day off from work to come to meet his dad at a mall where they were having lunch. He was going to surprise him and just force him to speak to me (another point in this movie where you'd be like *noooope, this is bad)*. I was thrilled. I said *okay* and took a day off from work, travelled for an hour to this mall, reached the restaurant, and watched them eat as I fixed my hair, standing behind a pillar where no one could see me. Then, suddenly, I got a message from him saying he couldn't do it. He didn't have the courage, he said to me in a text. I stood there behind that pillar for almost 30 minutes after, wondering what had just happened.

They then walked past me. He saw right through me as he left with his father. I can't remember how much longer I stood there.

That night, when I went back home, he said he was really sorry for what had happened. I forgave him because, I don't know… don't we all, sometimes?

But in the coming days, with whatever brain I had left within me, I ended the relationship. I believed him when he said he was sorry, but I still needed to end it. I left him… fine, I didn't *"leave"* him exactly. Instead, I packed all his bags, washed and neatly folded his clothes, asked him to call his father and ask them to pick him up so he could go home. So, he obediently did. *I left* sounded so much cooler than *I asked him to leave me, but the mother in me didn't want him to hurt, so I packed his bags.*

He howled his eyes out later and tried to write to me, but by then my potential religious soul was long gone. I was *proudly* whoring around (I'm here onwards owning that word) and also being extremely grateful that I didn't go ahead and convert into someone that I am evidently not conditioned to be. I was like, *"Buddy, God wants me to explore my options, and if anything, maybe you and your mother should blame yourself because technically, you are now the reason for this one less Muslim in this world. Think about that."*

Again, I love that in my retelling of that story, I have erased the parts where I howled my eyes out for months, moved back home to my mum's house, talked to him multiple times, couldn't understand what religion had to do with love, fell in love with him all over again temporarily, felt broken and lost and weak, knew that this would never end well but loved him anyway, and then finally put an end to it when I was too broken to see him again.

We only give up when our bones begin to hurt and our tears have dried up. It's some sort of crazy self-inflicted abuse, where you don't give up until you're numb. Even though it took me a long time to do it, *I left* in the end, because I needed my dignity and self-respect back (yes, that movie had an eat pray love moment. Go home happy, you audience).

As I grew older, I realised that I wasn't like most other people around me. I didn't know before that the way I saw the world was going to be considered rebellious one day... I wanted children, but the only kind I wanted was the adopted kind. From an extremely early age, I knew I didn't want to bring another life into this world; I *only* wanted to adopt (4) kids. With age, I also knew that I didn't really believe in marriage as a concept. I believed in love, but marriages to me didn't mean anything. Marriages could end. Marriage is what every miserable person I knew was doing for the sake of doing. I swear I was just trying to learn from the world's mistakes... I could see enough unhappy people that had their wedding and got married and were awfully miserable—so what the hell for?

I wasn't going to get married because *"a piece of paper can't tie me down"* (oh yes, I did say such things. I was a free poetic bird with the wind in my wings). I was going to fall in love with a man that understood that marriage didn't make relationships last; companionship, trust, communication, and the desire to stay made it last. I wanted the family that I'd eventually go into (remember the boy with a big family?! Focus!) to love and respect me for the person that I am/was, not because I signed a piece of paper. I was also very proud of the person I was... so I knew they'd love me; what reason could they possibly have not to? Adults are rational and smart and accepting, after all.

As a little girl, I'd seen so many divorces and separations that really opened my eyes. I wouldn't actually say they scarred me... not at all. If I were scarred, then I wouldn't believe in love, but I am such a romantic. I just didn't give into concepts simply because the whole world was doing it. I needed answers, reasons, justifications. I had to be convinced. *"Stop trying to be rebellious"* definitely wasn't convincing me; it was making me irritated and edgy. The concept of two people that love each other wanting to officially tie each other down and then call it love made no sense to me.

More than that, the concept of divorce is what really put me off. I couldn't wrap my head around why some random old person who knew NOTHING about the two people was the one making the final decision about their lives. A judge isn't there when you fall in love, when you're vulnerable for the first time in front of each other, your first sexual moments (that would be weird), the first tears, when your soul is naked and your body is covered. They aren't there when you make promises of forever and stay up the whole night fighting and holding each other in your arms— they don't know what you share at all... and yet, this one *stranger* has the right to sit there and tell you that you're *no longer together anymore*. My love story wasn't going to be bound by some documents. No, I knew I didn't want to get married.

So, there we were, let's recap: not getting married, adopting kids, divorced parents, childhood abuse, and a previously broken heart but, of course, a hopeless romantic that wishes for a beautiful boy with a big fat family. You can hold your horses and sit back down because things hadn't nearly gotten as bad as you think they had. Your girl still hadn't discovered *feminism*. Oh, how life was about change for me when I would realise that I was constantly objectified and because the people objectifying me were horrible, I had to cover myself in order to live, and if I didn't obey, it was my fault. Once my little happy bubble burst and I turned into a womxn, I realised that society saw me as a piece of meat more often than they saw me as a human. I realised that I hated wearing bras all day; it felt suffocating (my mother says I didn't particularly like clothes too much as a kid either. Apparently, at every birthday party, I demanded to be undressed before cutting my cake). I also learnt that I wasn't as strong as I thought I was. I was going to be in an abusive relationship, I was going to be insulted, harassed, slapped, choked, further broken, blamed, abused, gaslit, neglected, cheated on… and then be told that it was my fault.

Between 2011 and 2019, my life changed. I went through some more very awful and confronting experiences with men from 2011 to 2014, when I learnt that parents genuinely hated me. They often hated me for things I couldn't control, like my divorced parents or where I grew up. They also hated my views, my character, and my presence. I was *"too rebellious"* for parents—can you imagine how my world crashed? *I loved families.* Why had all families of boys collectively decided to hate me?

I didn't learn to cook as a kid because I was never told: "cooking is a necessity that you need to survive, darling, hence you must learn." Instead, I was told, *"If you cannot cook, then who will marry you? How will you cook for your husband, and what will his parents say? Food is the way to a man's heart."*

So, I would joke, *"But, Nani, who the hell wants the way to his heart, I want to know if his…"* never mind.

I was every boy's forbidden dream—*dangerous, rebellious, daring, and bold.* Boys liked me because I made them want to take risks in life and I challenged their conditioning; men love the thrill. I was also every parents' worst nightmare. I was going to undo every toxic thing they had worked so hard on teaching their son.

But the other thing you realise with age is that human beings (who are shit) are also extremely territorial. They crave and thrive to find something beautiful, love it, capture it, and cage it.

Men that thought they *loved me* because they fell in love with my desire to adopt or my opinions on marriage or my rebellious mind eventually wanted to change me for them. They claimed that it was different at the start when we'd just met, but as their girlfriend or partner... they all said, *"You can't be the same girl anymore if you love me."* When you think about it, these particular men wanted the same things that the women they were running away from wanted, they just wanted it to come from a challenge... like they earned it. They wanted to win a girl and change her before they put their seed inside her. They were never really in love with *me*, maybe they were just bored in their own pathetic lives and so they sought a thrill. I was that dream vacation for them, the one you save up for your whole life and think you could escape to forever... except give yourself a month before you are homesick again. People crave a change, and when they get that change, they crave consistency and they crave routine. In the end, a vacation is exciting, it's what you want twice a year, but a vacation isn't home.

I was never home. I was an exotic vacation you *speak of* fondly forever, like *"man, I wish I could live that life forever... it was so good,"* but you won't because it requires you to take risks and break stereotypes and never *settle*. You won't sell that house, quit that job, break that FD, pack your bags, and leave. It's just too risky.

Not everybody wants to backpack the world forever, not everybody knows what to do with life when they have a 100% control over it either. One day, everybody wants to go home. The important part is, some people are ethical, concerned tourists, who come and experience a place and then leave, without harming or damaging a thing. They care about this place and they don't want to destroy it. Then there are people that litter and pollute while they're there because they couldn't give a fuck, cleaning up isn't their job, and often these tourists are just too loud. They scream and shout and damage the property. They change the way this place once functioned, the reason why it was even an attraction. And like that isn't enough, they pluck things out and take things back with themselves, projecting false concern, as though they're doing it so they can remember the vacation forever. But in reality, they abuse their rights. They don't care about this place, and they're just ruining the natural order of things… they're toxic and destructive.

You know what I mean?

People are… don't make me repeat myself.

2014: by now, my dreams of ever being part of a love story where the guy would have a big family that I would adore, and it would welcome me with open arms, had all died. I knew what my best friend meant when she said people were shit, and families – they hurt each other. Over land, money, control, power, and misogyny, they hurt each other.

It is not *Hum Saath Saath Hain.*

Which is why when I think about parents, families, and mothers… I can't wrap my head around why anyone in their right mind would want to belong to a big family. I have learnt my lesson, and I admit that this is an *I-loved-you-so-much-in-my-head-that-now-I-hate-you* phase of my life. Yes, I have learnt some amazingly important things, but the bigger the family, the more people that exist to hurt and judge you.

If you are in love, or have ever been in love, and are struggling with the family of the man you are dating—I just want you to know that I am sorry. It's hard; it's going to be extremely hard, especially if you're what they call a *rebel*, if you go against stereotypes, if you break the rules of what a *woman is supposed to be.* If you are ambitious, or don't want children, or are comfortable in your body, or are extremely opinionated and demand that you be respected as a human first before a wife, a daughter, or a mother— then you're in for a tough ride. My heart reaches out to you and I am so sorry because, honestly, I don't really have any advice this time. I don't have the answers. I don't have a light at the end of the tunnel to show you. You're going to have to find your own.

All I can do is prepare you instead of sugar-coating this journey for you. By choosing to be a womxn of opinions and desires, you have chosen a very tough path in life, and at every point, you will be questioned, insulted, accused, controlled, rejected. And this fight does not end with falling in love. It doesn't end at marriage either. It's something you'll have to live with forever… make sure you choose someone that loves you for who you are, someone that supports you and agrees with you, someone that takes your side when the whole world doesn't, and is not intimidated by your strength and your strong sense of individuality. Because how far you go, who you become, and how you raise the future generation has a *lot* to do with the kind of person you marry/spend your life with. Choose wisely and know that *this* journey is still going to be tough.

I cannot tell you that the family you enter will love you. I cannot even tell you that they will respect or accept you, or that they won't try to change you, but what I can do is remind you that everything you do today, absolutely *everything*, will matter tomorrow. This was the light at the end of my tunnel—that everything I do matters. It will matter to the generation that will come after us. This effort, this pain, the nights you cry yourself to sleep and feel like you don't belong and you're not loved or respected, the days you spend wondering, *what's wrong with me? Why is it so bad to want to be free as a womxn? Why am I still fighting? Does any of this even matter?*

It matters. It will pay off. It will pay off, and you may or may not be alive to see it with your own eyes, but I promise you with my whole heart that you would have made a difference in this world. Just the way the womxn that came before us, that fought for their rights and hence fought for ours, are the reason why you and I are even here today, speaking up and having the little voice we have. The fact that I can write a book openly as a womxn and talk about my life, talk about a world being *rescued by a feminist is because rebellious womxn fought for these rights.* They fought for our freedom even when they didn't see a light at the end of the tunnel. They cried and stood alone and didn't give up—for us—and the least we can do is thank them for these opportunities, by passing them on to the womxn that will come after us. The least we can do is hope that one day, a little girl in this world will grow up as oblivious as the boys, and she won't cry herself to sleep because they don't accept her voice. She'll laugh and play sports and become anything she wants to be under the sun. And we will all be watching… proudly.

Raise your daughter equal. Raise your son a feminist.

…but if you're waiting for me to end this with a conclusion… that people are not shit, or that they are shit, then forget about it. I won't give you that satisfaction, not today. Today I want you to be hopeful enough to figure it out for yourself on your own. You can go ahead and learn from my mistakes, but that doesn't mean you have to stop making your own, right?

Sometimes, rambling is therapeutic. So, talk to me, tell me your thoughts. Tell me what's bothering you today. How are you… are you okay?

My Notes

My Notes

CHAPTER 7

THE SPERM DONOR

There are plenty of ways in which life comes into this world. Surrogacy. IVF. Intercourse, unfortunately not always planned or with consent, but there are indeed many different ways in which life comes into this world.

A male and a female have intercourse, and if both of them are able to, and she's ovulating, she becomes pregnant. You (if you are female) can also go to the clinic now and get impregnated by an unknown sperm donor, by the way. Because post the steps of *getting pregnant,* everything you do is on *you.* Especially in our society. A female becomes pregnant, and she has a child. A female then becomes a mother. A female brings life into this world. This might offend you, but it is as close to the biological truth as it gets as of now.

I'm glad that couples have now finally started saying *"we are pregnant"* because even though as a male you cannot go through any of the changes that happen to a female's body and mind, it definitely changes the mindset with which we look at pregnancy, as a *society.* Hopefully, with time, we will look at pregnancy as something that happens with the contribution of two people, instead of just the female.

Biologically, from the moment you conceive to when you give birth, bringing a child into this world is *usually* something a female does. You may support her as a partner, but you're not *really* doing anything towards the process after the point of ejaculation. You can keep her happy and make sure she's in a good mental space, sure, but as the non-child bearer, it wouldn't technically matter if you lived, died, left, stayed, drank, or even snorted cocaine every night. It does not *directly* interfere with the process of birth at all. Upbringing, on the other hand, you have an impact on.

There are men in this world who don't even know they have a child because they either left the female or broke up or ran away or simply had a one-night stand and never spoke again. Or sometimes the female herself lies about it or has left him and doesn't tell the man she slept with that he impregnated her. Either/or, for whatever reasons *people* may have, I just want you to remember that if/when females choose *not* to tell the males involved, they may never know. How insane is that? Regardless of whether a male knows, accepts, disapproves—the outcome is the same either way. If the female chooses to go ahead with the pregnancy, then a child enters the world. The male then automatically becomes the biological *father*.

On the other hand, it isn't humanly possible for a female to *not know* she got a child into this world unless she loses her memory. If she's biologically a mother, *she knows*.

The male, if you think about it, is *kind of* like a sperm donor (if you're male, stay with me, this is important).

Vomiting, motion sickness, morning sickness, hormonal imbalances, headaches, cravings, anxiety, weight gain, weakness, pain, stretch marks, postpartum depression, vaginal bleeding, loss of muscle control, blood loss, stitches, expanded vagina—everything happens to the female.

Hence, it would make sense why in a world run by males, they thought that the male makes the female pregnant, and from then onwards, she is like a vessel that he is filling with *water* (replace with *child*). The vessel is just a medium required for humanity to continue, but what's inside has always belonged to the male. Her body. His gene. His *next generation*. His legacy. His *sperm* as well.

Now it's important for me to remind you once again that everything I'm saying is usually an opinion unless stated otherwise… these are my thoughts, and at this very moment, *my thoughts are that the process of bringing life into the world isn't the act of two after the point of intercourse. I think* in an over-dominating heterosexual society, it is the womxn's journey. I won't address LGBTQ human beings here because if anything, they're fighting to erase the gender roles themselves, but we as heterosexuals seem to have got it *all wrong*. Hopefully, if as a straight, privileged man, you are not threatened by my opinion of womxn solely being responsible for a child, because only then can you go on to become a partner that is *supportive*. We can create a society where we condition straight men to be there for the womxn they end up with by actively encouraging them to go for childbirth classes together, learn more about what womxn go through during their pregnancy, make therapy mandatory, have paid paternity leave instead of just maternity leave so that *both* the parents can (and should) take time off to raise their child.

Start creating a culture where men have more *equal* responsibility towards chores and *raising* a child once it is born. Men could do more housework, and we could stop referring to everything they do as *help* because helping simply means that they're going out of their way to provide their services for something that's naturally *not their job*. As though we have accepted that *everything is a womxn's job, and **good** men, well, they help* (I'll talk more about this in Chapter 14).

Let's change how little we hold men accountable for, because we no longer live isolated in heterosexual societies, let alone heterosexual societies where *womxn stay at home and raise a family and men work*. And even the families who do still follow that must acknowledge that cooking, cleaning, raising children, running a house are *real work*. It is unpaid, and that isn't fair, because it sure as hell is *work*. Womxn that identify as housewives/homemakers are *working*, and their jobs are hard, have no particular hours, holidays or days off, no health benefits, no regulations whatsoever, yet they are doing it day after day, year after year—as daughters, sisters, wives, mothers—for absolutely *no pay.*

We want a society with enough children being born, but we refuse to acknowledge that looking after them, raising them, and caring for them is actual work. If *womxn* took a month off from their *unpaid labour,* it would absolutely have an effect on our economy because men with *paid jobs* would no longer have the luxury of just getting up and going to work every day; they'd have children and homes and the elderly to care for. The reason men have a *choice* whether or not to do unpaid work is because womxn *don't.*

I was raised by two womxn, my mother and my grandmother. It is an irony that even after being raised by two strong and independent womxn, I never really knew anything about womxn's rights until I was in my twenties. *Womxn don't seem to talk about their struggles.* My mother is an extremely passionate, sensitive, stubborn, and talented womxn. There's an inside joke between my brother and me—we are convinced that she works for the FBI and her whole life is one big lie because, really, she always knows everything about us, even when we are in different countries and haven't talked in 10 days… *she knows.* She knows *everything. Always.* How strange is that? Oh, and in case she does work for the FBI, here's hoping I haven't blown her cover.

When I started writing this chapter, I wanted to say something to you, except, when I'm hurting, I tend to write down a lot of things… a lot of things that aren't precisely what I wanted to say, but I think out loud until I can finally say it. Thank you for bearing with me.

This chapter is called *"sperm donor"* because, *to me,* that is all that the man who contributed towards my birth was. Actually no, he was much more… much worse. He was toxic, abusive, narcissistic, sexist, and controlling. I wish he had only been a sperm donor sometimes, but he was much more. You may think I'm exaggerating, but I'm not. For most of my book, I try not to discuss him in detail as I don't personally think he's worth wasting pages over (maybe I'll write a separate book called *How Not to Be a Father*), but his terrible choices may have taught me a lot about life, so I use them as lessons.

Except for providing his sperm to my mother, he had absolutely nothing positive to do with my birth or with raising me. He never paid for my education or recreational activities, holidays, health, medicine, clothes, toys, summer classes, tuitions, or birthdays. He never spent a single penny on me, and let's not even talk about his presence.

Everything that I have ever had is because of my mother and my grandparents from my maternal side. My mother gave us everything we wanted, and every time she asked him to contribute, he disappeared. As a little girl, I would call him up and ask him for things I wanted. He would laugh it off and tell me *"later,"* or say yes and then he'd disappear on me for weeks. He once said, *"You only call me when you want something, because you are selfish"*... I must've been 10 years old. Thinking back, I want to laugh, given that *he left us* to go live with his girlfriend and her children one street down from our house and yet he never had any time for us. I mean, *what could a 10-year-old possibly want?* Other than to not find her father inside showers with womxn, but hey, *been there, done that.*

My mother, on the other hand, worked even harder because she wanted her kids to have the whole world. The man that contributed his sperm was never really around and yet here we are... *here I am.* I have come to realise that in our current society, to give birth and raise a child in this world, what you actually need is the *mother.*

As a little girl, sometimes after school, I would look at all the other kids with their fathers, and I felt a little sad because I wondered, *what had I done wrong for mine to have left me?* I wondered if I was a bad child, had I been selfish, maybe I was being punished? It took me many years to grow up and realise that *it wasn't me; it was him.* That day, I thought, *good fucking riddance.*

You, reading this, may have an amazing father and for that, I'm so happy for you; this doesn't apply to you at all. I hope one day every child is that lucky, but a lot of this book isn't for those people that have exceptional lives with the best of opportunities. It's for the people that are looking for something to make sense of... you might even have same-sex parents or parents that do not cater to gender roles at all, and so you may not relate to some of the things I say, which is exactly the kind of change we are fighting for, isn't it? Some of us grow up in a healthy environment, but far too many of us don't—it just isn't the *norm*.

In the last decade of my life, I've realised that a *stereotypical Indian family* consists of a *father* who exists to set the rules, make boundaries, yell at you, scare you, and of course, pay your bills. Except, that system is starting to fail because a lot more womxn today are either already working or *fighting for their right to work*, and children *do not* need to be scared into boundaries; they need quite the opposite.

When I look around me at my friends who have been raised in a family of two parents, I often thank my stars *(however, maybe I have other issues)* because 90% of the people I personally know do not share a good relationship with their fathers. Their *biggest* grudge seems to be that their fathers have never tried to communicate, get to know them, shared a bond, or shown any vulnerability. Fathers seem to be infamous for maintaining decorum in the family, which, if you ask me, is as easily possible with a mother if you respect her. However, far too many people sympathise with their mothers because of the sacrifices she makes but aren't afraid of her and will probably snap back at her because of the good cop/bad cop dynamic and the fear of their fathers.

We don't often realise that in the process of seeing fathers as the bread-earners and the head of the family, we begin to see mothers as the vulnerable, weaker ones, and eventually, we start to glorify their sacrifices, which automatically means that the day she stops making those sacrifices, we would wonder *why she stopped being a mother...* is that even possible?

Making sacrifices for others her whole life has got to stop being equated with being a *mother*.

I genuinely think that children do not need to be raised with fear and constant abuse. What children do need is love and affection. They need to ask a lot of questions and have someone who is willing to answer them, and not to be shunned... Children need communication. Having talked to most of my friends, I've noticed some very common similarities in their family dynamics: *when they're at home with their mothers, they can have fun, let their hair down, dance and do whatever they wish to*—because their fathers are at work. Rules are broken, jokes are told, and feelings are shared up until the father comes home and that's when you must maintain decorum, stop making noise, and wear appropriate clothes. Mum then cooks and makes sure dad gets everything he needs after a tiring day of work. When most of my friends wanted to go for school trips, they asked their mums, and their mums either asked the dad or asked them to directly ask dad. Indicating that in the end, *everything requires his approval.*

He's the man of the house, except at what point did the definition of that term start to mean that he must lack emotions, tears, affection, vulnerability, care, chore abilities, and love? The man of the house is a provider. He brings food to the table. But it may be safe to say that we're now living in a time where both parents can/should/want to do paid work, therefore all the above can as easily be, and often is, brought to the table by the mother. But are we ready for the mother's duties to also be shared by the father?

Why is it that the moment a child rebels or breaks the rules, the first thing we as a society do is blame the mother? *"This is all because of your upbringing. Did your mother teach you nothing?"* Because she's doing the raising, isn't she? What do you think this dynamic of a heterosexual family teaches young children about the kind of men and womxn they should grow up to become?

Far too many people from my own cultural background never speak up or go against the rules set for them by their fathers, due to the fear of hurting mum or putting her in a position of compromise. They don't want their fathers to get angry at their mothers, for something they themselves have done wrong.

For example: If Priya feels controlled and suffocated by her father but she refuses to confront him because if she were to raise her voice and stand up to him, *she would be putting her mother in trouble.*

Think about where the power lies in this dynamic for a moment.

In my house, growing up, these social structures didn't exist. There were relatives and other external structures we had to worry about, of course. I have witnessed a lot of unnecessary patriarchal abuse around me growing up. When I was a child, I once called the police on one of my relatives. I didn't think about the consequences it would have back then. I didn't know that *doing the right thing would have an impact on my mother.* The adults in my family obviously put me to sleep and told the police there was nothing to worry about; *"she's just a child."* As I've gotten older, I have realised that there are many times in life where I'm given a choice—to stand up for what's right and make my mother's life difficult by isolating her from all her relatives or to stay quiet and leave, so she is not punished for my choices. In an Indian household, we are expected to ignore and turn a blind eye to all the abuse men inflict, to excuse it, cover it up, tiptoe around it, in order for the womxn of the house to be safe. Maybe my third book can be called *How to Isolate Yourself from 101 Relatives in Order to Be Successful.*

Apart from the occasional relatives, there was never a father figure in our house, so there were no strict boundaries that made us fear for our lives. There weren't any rigid rules, and we didn't have to be obedient after dad came home. I wasn't told not to wear certain clothes at home, and we didn't have to be careful about how we behaved because our actions wouldn't directly reflect on how a father blames our mother for spoiling us every day. Overall, the rules we followed and the person we respected was our mother. To the rest of the world, she was our mum, but for us, she was mum *and* she was dad too.

When I finally sat down one day, I realised that given the kind of man my father was, him leaving us was *probably* the best thing that happened to our family. He may be the worst man I have ever met, but the best thing he ever did was to leave us alone. He lost, and I won. I won because he didn't leave us with hate and bitterness. He didn't *abandon* us, leaving a void of any kind. Instead, he gave us space to grow, to flourish, to rise above. I was also raised by the most feminist person I know, my older brother. Growing up, I always bragged about what a wonderful young man he is, my role model. He was the first person to have educated me and influenced me, which then indirectly taught me the things I would've needed to know, in order to understand equity and womxn's rights. So, I had a sudden epiphany, *one of the biggest reasons he is a feminist is because he himself was raised by a womxn that always rebelled against society.* He is usually the first to cry in every argument (he'll hate me for telling you this) because he isn't afraid of being vulnerable, of feeling emotions. He cares about people. He is a therapist and a best friend, and he's the most sensitive, smart person I know, *probably* a lot to do with the fact that he was solely raised by our mother. He wasn't raised under perpetual fear of overstepping boundaries. He was raised with curiosity, care, and love. *Our mother* was the father he needed.

When you marry a man, or simply choose to have a child with him, I want you to ask yourself, *"Is he going to be my life partner, or is he simply going to be a sperm donor?"* Do you need him? What does *he* bring to this table? Because in case you're giving birth and not adopting, know that he cannot physically have the child for you, and if he's *threatened* by that, then how will he ever be able to give your family what is needed? What he *can and should aim to be* is a man that supports you and raises a family *with you.*

Ask yourself if he's sensitive, if he's willing to learn to take up equal responsibility, even in the nine months of the pregnancy. Will he leave the things you are forced to leave if that is what you need, in order to survive that journey? Will he join you for your exercise routines? Will he read books about how your body and hormones change, and what he can do to contribute to this life-changing event? Will he clean and cook and look after the house *with you* instead of only doing it when *you can't?* Will he have patience when you don't? Will there be a balance? And when you do have a child together, will he raise it with you, as a parent, or will he simply be the father that sets boundaries and pays for things? Because neither you nor your child *needs* to live in a space where you cannot grow and flourish as human beings. The worst part about how we raise our children is that *they* grow up to *see* the *mother* and the *father* both play certain roles around the house and *that* shapes what they grow up to think of gender roles, equality, and their responsibility.

To conclude: it isn't that we *don't need two parents* or a *father* in a family—that's not what I'm saying. I am saying that I think what we *do not need* is the existing stereotype of mother and father. The patriarchal, sexist, misogynist, masculine father figure that is perpetually distant and lacks vulnerability; the mother that is weak, sacrificing, dependent, extremely sensitive, constantly compromising in order to put her family's needs above everything else, subservient to the father.

It is toxic and it is ruining the way our boys grow up to behave as men; it isn't working anymore. In order to move ahead, we must make changes. Mothers can have ambitions and paid jobs, while fathers should be more mentally and physically present at home and in the process of raising their children.

Times are changing, people are changing, and if our definition of what a *dad* is doesn't adapt with time, then this father figure that we all grow up to will only become more destructive because the environment you raise the child in is what their normal becomes. Redefine normal. Redefine *dad*.

I want you to think about what you love about your parent(s) and/or your guardians. It doesn't matter if you have one or two, or many more. Make a list of their pros and cons, their role in your life, and tell me what could they change/do to make your relationship with them healthier?

My Notes

My Notes

CHAPTER 8

THE DIFFERENT TYPES OF BAD

There was this boy who, within months of dating, turned to me one night and very casually said, *"I'm really worried about my sister. I don't know what to do."* Concerned, I asked, *"What's wrong?"* He then said, *"Oh, nothing yet… but she's growing up and seems really vocal about a lot of things in life. I'm scared she'll end up like you. I obviously don't want that. I'm worried."* He said these words to me even before I had all my clothes back on. You would be surprised, but in that moment, I said, *"Oh, I'm sorry… I hope so too, I guess,"* as though it was my fault. Like I had done something wrong. I swear I felt like I'd done something awful. Like he was the victim here, and I felt disgusted and guilty that I may have caused something bad to happen to someone he cared for, someone I'd never even met in my life. It took me a few days to realise that he was being horrible to me, and another week to actually leave him. I did *not* immediately know that what he had said to me was *not nice*. But when I did pick up on it, I realised that there were an awful lot of things he said that were extremely derogatory, controlling, and passive-aggressive. Immediately, I also realised that I am not alone—so many women must blame themselves and *continue to live with it.*

They don't teach you this in school, nor do they warn you in college, and it's definitely not a conversation you would've had at home… but when it comes to relationships, there are a hundred and one different ways to have a bad one.

There are multiple different ways in which your partner can be toxic, and if you're unaware of the signs, then you're never going to know any better. I had to learn this in extremely toxic environments, because no one warns us about the things narcissistic people do in a relationship, and no one tells you when it's okay to say *NO* and leave. Parents and schools don't prepare you for this.

Growing up, I noticed that what we are constantly learning, intentionally or unintentionally, is that *women make compromises.* Good women solve problems. A great woman keeps a family together, puts her loved ones before herself. We live in a society where if a man sacrifices a promotion or his hometown in order for his partner to keep working, we automatically blame the woman for being selfish. Everybody wants to talk about how controlling she is, how she's got the man wrapped around her fingers, he's her puppet, *"poor him"*… My partner moved countries to be with me; trust me, I have heard it all.

However, *"should a woman sacrifice her hometown or a promotion for a man?"* is not a question; it's the norm. If she doesn't want to, then we will judge her, insult her, and dissect her character—and this is on top of all the judgement and character breakdown we do *anyway*.

You and I, as independent as possible, will still live in a world where the *norm* is very different for men and women, and it's difficult to tell when you're in an abusive relationship because we're raised to think a lot of this abuse is a part of love, and some forms of abuse should be *forgiven or forgotten* for a longer-lasting, *healthy* relationship. When conditioning isolates and compromises on a woman's identity, well, sometimes by the time you are old enough to be aware of the abuse you're putting up with, it's already a little too late.

No one told me that many of my relationships were toxic and abusive. I didn't realise it even with the obvious mental and physical abuse. I *still* thought it was *my fault*.

Being in a relationship with someone that constantly told me that I wasn't allowed to visit him at his house because his family thought I was damaged goods and *"how could a girl with divorced parents ever have a family of her own"*... was toxic. My single mother, my shorts, my childhood in Australia—everything was a problem for him and his family. *Bad upbringing*, they called it... because, you know, after all, any upbringing that isn't Indian must be bad. I was perpetually embarrassed of myself and where I came from because I let a bunch of random people tell me what was/wasn't okay with me.

One of my somewhat serious boyfriends was so extremely insecure and jealous of my career growth that he would constantly tell me how I didn't deserve what I had because I never worked for it as hard as he had been working. He said, *"You wake up late and you only give the auditions you want to give, you don't deserve being signed on for a TV show."* I didn't say anything. When my billboard finally went up all over India, I really wanted to go see one that was near my house. He said we'd go see it together after I pack up, but then got drunk the night we were supposed to go and said he didn't want to see it anymore. It was obvious that he was bitter about me working, and I hate to say it, but *I felt so guilty for it too*. So, I never really saw my own hoarding, until weeks later when I just happened to be crossing the highway and I looked up to see myself. I was always so sorry for the things I had going well for me. For his sake, I would come home and lie about what a bad day I had on set. I would never talk about the things I enjoyed, or how lucky I felt, instead I made everything look tiresome and terrible, just so I wouldn't hurt his feelings. Despite all that, whenever I cried in our fights, he'd yell at me and say, *"Yeh randi rona (prostitute tears) band karo."* To my surprise, I would howl even more at hearing those words. Eventually, I'd stop crying and focus on what he was saying, on what he needed from me. *Why was he so upset? Why was he feeling unwanted? What had I done wrong? Why is he saying I'm frustrating him? There must be something I can do differently to stop this. To make this go away.*

I was always made to feel like *he* needed *me* to fix this. Regardless of how controlling, jealous, selfish, and narcissistic he was, *he needed me.* It's a toxic, gender-based, patterned behaviour where men feel like the only way they can express themselves is by screaming, yelling, shouting, abusing, or controlling. While women tend to cry, howl, scream, be submissive, apologise, or *change what they're doing.*

Don't get me wrong, all these years later, when I think back to those memories, I'm well aware that maybe he was *also* struggling with self-confidence and work rejection back then. I still do stand by the fact that he needed help, but the thing is… *so did I.* I'd just come out of an extremely damaging, physically abusive relationship, and I hadn't even realised it or told anybody about it, and before I could come to terms with that, I was now with someone who was verbally abusive. After every toxic fight, I'd say to myself, *"At least he doesn't hit me"*… like he needed to be rewarded for stopping at *randi rona.* If enough people yell at you, regardless of whether you're at fault or not, eventually *you will learn to apologise, which is exactly what I did.* Even when *I needed me,* instead of being there for myself and standing up for myself, I chose to be there for him, and if I can convince even one of you to let go, then that's all this is for.

Today, I know where to draw that line because it isn't my job to be there for somebody that is verbally abusive towards me every day.

Someone else's personal, internal issues aren't a good enough reason for *you* to suffer. Encourage them to get help, and if they don't want to, then that is *their* journey. Today, I can look beyond the conditioning and social expectation that *as a woman, I'm supposed to fix my partner* regardless of how disrespectful he is.

Thinking back to these memories still makes me cringe. Today's Saloni would've shown him the door. I wouldn't be caught dead dating a man that didn't respect me as a person and thought it would be okay to insult everything I stand for. Today, I know better… better than to fall for the *"women shouldn't be opinionated"* bullshit because I have been there, I have been controlled, I have been told what to do, and I have quietly done it. And I've finally learnt to say no. Maybe the learnings are an outcome of the strong safe space I have created for myself, maybe I still blame myself sometimes when I don't need to, as I am conditioned to, but every single day, I am learning to respect myself more than the day before.

I see so many women that are in extremely harmful relationships with mentally abusive, gaslighting, manipulative, controlling, aggressive partners. Some of whom are verbally abusive, others inflict physical pain in the name of love. Even though these women cry out for help, *a lot of them don't actually want to leave.* I've been the girl that was being physically abused but refused to ask for help or leave because *I genuinely believed it was my fault* that he was hitting me. Some of the biggest reasons women don't want to leave toxic relationships are: 1. They *believe* their partner *loves* them, and that's why he's so angry and hence abusive, and 2. They think it is their job to fix him.

"He doesn't mean to hit me... it's just that he's so protective of me, and he's very angry, you know, as a person... his father was an alcoholic, you see, he's got so much childhood trauma, but he's trying to be a better person. In fact, he doesn't hit me that often anymore, only when I make mistakes. He's changing... just for me."

I have lost count of how many times I've heard women say *that*. Bruised and bleeding, yet making excuses for their partner's abusive behaviour, convinced that he still loves and needs them. We are so busy trying to be the perfect girlfriends/wives that we forget we ever had an identity outside of our relationship. We think we have to fix men that are abusive, because *we* grew up in families where our mothers didn't leave, instead they kept everything glued together. Even if *you* personally didn't have that family dynamic, you know growing up it's exactly what we as women are conditioned to do. *Keep the family together. Stop complaining. Know what needs to be done. Help everyone. Know everyone. Adjust. Fix things.* And so what if he hit you once? It doesn't happen every day, does it? After all, our teachers and parents always hit us because they knew what was right for us… how is our partner any different? *"He's doing it for my own good,"* we tell ourselves. Women don't just *leave* men—that would be so fucking selfish, wouldn't it? It would be selfish for a woman to realise her own worth, to admit that she has her own desires outside of doing what's allegedly best for her children, her husband, and his family's reputation. Only *selfish women (and pretty much all men) would put themselves first in an acceptable society where family comes first.*

"These are terrible Western influences, ghar aise toh nahi chalte (this isn't how families are made). What values did her mother even teach her?!"

In the process of trying to fix our partners and continuously telling ourselves that the abuse has nothing to do with love, we allow ourselves to stay. And our families and friends normalise our sacrifices, and eventually, our children glorify our compromises every Mother's Day and birthdays, until finally one day when society looks at you and says, *"This… this is what a great womxn is supposed to behave like. This is a real wonder womxn."* By this point, we've been selling this lie ourselves too, preparing our daughters and demanding a daughter-in-law that's ready to make all the compromises we've made—*"she better know her family values."*

I'm here to try and tell you before it's too late—*putting up with abuse in the name of love and compromising your own needs just to keep your relationship/ family together doesn't make you "great" at all.* I'm sorry if you think the way your mother has lived her life is commendable because, against all odds, she kept your family together. I'm sorry because what *you* think is *commendable* is actually you just saying that she's *wonderful* because *she put others first and gave up her own dreams instead.* If it is anything, it is painful, it is sad, it is depressing, and it needs to be stopped in future generations. We don't need to keep making womxn sacrifice their own identity and needs in order for families to stay together. If you keep glorifying those sacrifices, then it may never end. *You don't need to glorify people's sacrifices in order to show respect to them.*

Perfect example? Think about why we respect the hierarchical men in our families.

If you want your daughter to one day grow up and stand up for herself, then *become that daughter.* Raise that daughter. Raise a son that admires an independent womxn. *Acknowledge the sacrifices womxn that came before us made just so we could own our own bank accounts and have a voice today, instead of glorifying the oppressed sacrifices of our mothers.* Be the womxn that says no to the abuse and does not try to fix a man that is harmful. *End the cycle.*

If this womxn is not you but you have a friend that's living this life, talk to her. Remind her why she is enough just the way she is and she doesn't need to punish herself in order to be loved or appreciated.

We do not need to marry our fathers.

We do not need to compromise all the time.

You and I are the only ones that can change this world for a future generation by raising men that are less entitled and womxn that have more self-respect. Maybe, starting right here, with ourselves.

Have you had a bad relationship and not known it was toxic till much later? If you could tell the old you anything that would have helped, what would it be?

My Notes

My Notes

CHAPTER 9

BEAUTOCRACY

One night, at a bar in Cambodia, I told the bartender that I thought she was *so pretty*. She smiled back politely. This was maybe the third time I'd given a woman a compliment on the *two-week-international-date* trip Rahul and I were on, after having known each other as adults for just a month. As we sipped on our drinks, he asked me why I felt the need to compliment a woman on her looks. Did I not think that maybe, in some ways, it was a sexist thing to do?

I was very offended at first. Why would a compliment be sexist? *What?* I meant no harm. I definitely wasn't being *sexist...* I just thought some women were *so pretty*, and there was nothing wrong with a woman telling another woman that she's pretty. We did it to each other *all* the time. What was wrong with *him?* Ugh. He was getting minus marks at this point.

I was so worked up by the mention, and I wasn't sure *what* I meant, so he let it go. And so did I... until recently, when one of my girlfriends casually pointed out that she thought a girl in a TV show was very ugly, and I quote *"even make up doesn't do anything for her, she's that ugly,"* and the statement irked me. I flinched as she said the words because

I'd stopped seeing people as *ugly*. I didn't say anything because I was in the middle of something really important, and well, I chose my battles, but after I hung up, I exhaled and sighed, asking my partner, *"Why do we feel the need to insult women like that? Based on their physical appeal? What is ugly, exactly? How is a woman ugly or beautiful? Isn't it all just subjective…? I find her pretty, to be honest, because she's such a great actor and her eyes are so intense, and she really has a beautiful smile. What do people, in general, mean when they say things like 'that girl is so ugly'? Why do we as women do this to each other when the standard of beauty is simply based on what men find attractive, and hence, we're doing nothing but catering to it?"*

I said all that in one rant—I swear I did—and as I said it out loud to a somewhat attentive, working-from-home Rahul (he knows I have these rants every few days where I just need to release my frustration so I don't go in a negative space), I suddenly realised what he had meant two years ago in Cambodia. *I had felt the need to confirm to women that were conventionally pretty, that they're really pretty, as though their beauty was their merit in this world.*

I didn't say specific things like *"I love your hair, you have a nice smile, or I love the colour of your eyes."* Nope, it was just a *"you're so beautiful,"* like that really counts for something. Like she's made some sort of achievement by just being attractive as per the standards set by men.

I see women do it all around me. Up until my early/mid-twenties, I did it too, *a lot.* I am not proud. The constant judging and picking on other girls based on how they look. I've gossiped with my girlfriends, dissected another girl's physical appearance, and now when I think about it, I'm not even sure why. I have no idea what we get from claiming that a woman is ugly—*does it make us feel better? Does it help in any way? Do we feel less insecure? Less sad? Do we believe it to be the absolute truth?*

Maybe we have succumbed so far into believing that a certain kind of beauty is the only beauty. Maybe we spend so long hating the things we don't think are *beautiful* about *ourselves* that we feel it's necessary to spew the same toxic hate onto other womxn because *why should they be treated any differently to how we treat ourselves?* If we can regularly hate ourselves, then *why would they be an exception?*

I don't know what is worse, the fact that we hate ourselves so much that we constantly need to put ourselves down, or that we hold other womxn to the same standards through no fault of theirs? We let little girls grow up in a society that is toxic, a lot of it thanks to our own contribution.

So, I admit that I was once the womxn that looked at other womxn and thought, *jeez, what's up with her,* and I was also the womxn that looked at other womxn and thought, *oh my God, she's just so gorgeous,* because it's how we've been conditioned to evaluate womxn. It's never *is she smart, do her eyes light up when she talks about her passion, is she kind, maybe she's funny...?* No, it's either she's beautiful, or she's just not; sometimes, she has potential. And all the *beauty* is solely defined by *what men want to fuck/take home* (unlike womxn, men don't necessarily want to take home doctors and lawyers), and I think it's about time that we become more conscious about what we say out loud.

We cannot often help the self-loathing we do because that consists of systematic oppression in huge parts, but how we speak of others, how much we choose to hate/judge other people are very much in our control. You won't go from believing in these standards of beauty to believing that everybody is beautiful overnight... but if you are more careful of what you say, and you're consciously aware of not always voicing your ugly thoughts and/or immediately apologising for them after, then you're one step closer to changing your mindset every day. There is a reason why most of us won't say such awful things to other womxn's faces—that reason is the same reason you shouldn't be saying it *at all.*

I don't think anybody is *"ugly"* by appearance; it's their actions that might make them ugly. Everybody is beautiful because beauty is, in reality, subjective.

I used to think that self-love made me more accepting of other people. I used to think that because I fell in love with my body, I started to find other womxn of all kinds more attractive and beautiful, but the truth is that this journey was quite the opposite. *It was when I started finding all womxn beautiful that I started to love myself a little more.* It is when my definition of *"pretty"* and *"beautiful"* changed, and there was no such thing as *"ugly"* when I looked at other womxn, that I stopped finding so many flaws in myself. When I started looking at womxn as human beings (and the way I see men) that are beautiful in their own unique ways and often do good and bad things, I started having *real conversations* in bars with womxn about their lives and their interests, instead of telling them that they are *beautiful.* Because of course, they were beautiful, so were the other 20 womxn in the same room—that just wasn't something out of the ordinary to point out. Their attractiveness wasn't an achievement or something to be extremely proud of. Their physical beauty and the fact that men may desire them wasn't their *merit.* Instead, I wanted to know what made them excited, what moved them… what was it like to leave their country and get a job in another part of the world?

I still tell womxn they are beautiful, but I tell them that after I've talked to them because I genuinely find womxn so beautiful and interesting to talk to. Maybe it's because of the years of judging and hating that I am now well aware of the individual uniqueness each womxn holds when I'm talking to her, and I can't help but wonder how they glow in their imperfections… Despite the way our world treats womxn, do you ever see just how they shine through it all?

We obsess so much on a womxn's physical appearance that we often forget to treat them like real people with real lives. We're either putting them on pedestals or treating them like they're not worthy enough. And as a womxn myself, *I refuse to continue that pattern through me.* This subtle conditioning of men holding so much power in society to decide the definition of appeal for all of us, including themselves, *can stop. It can be ended.* The power *is* in your hands. *For me, this is where it ends.*

Also, if you're reading this, you are beautiful:)

Tell me what are the things you don't like about yourself, and why?

Then, tell me what you absolutely love about yourself, and why?

Does it reflect on how we, as a society, view beauty?

My Notes

My Notes

CHAPTER 10

IS IT A GENDER THING?

People fight all the time, and often in these fights and disagreements, I sometimes hear womxn say, *"As a womxn, I'm feeling suffocated,"* and then men say, *"This really isn't a gender thing, don't make this about the gender,"* and I wonder *what is it about?*

I think the problem often arises when we fail to acknowledge the world we live in and the privileges we have as individual human beings are based on our gender, class, status, origin, caste, country, age, race, sexuality, abilities, and so on.

Human beings collectively do good and bad things. Nowhere does it say that a man is without doubt abusive while a womxn is always a victim; that's not true at all. There's plenty of womxn out there that abuse their power and their rights. Many that manipulate, seek revenge, commit crimes... *as do men.* That applies to all human beings, I'd assume. The only difference is that when womxn do wrong, the fight towards equality goes back a decade because womxn are held up to a much higher standard than men. When men *do wrong,* well, we say *not all men.* But yes, men and womxn *both* do bad things.

However, what I *am* saying is that the problem lies outside these individual cases. The problem lies in society collectively oppressing one gender.

When a big cosmetic brand underpays a transgender model of colour for an ad campaign, that is part of larger systematic oppression. Choosing to underpay a white male model, well, that can be a *choice,* an unfair one, but still a choice. But it isn't the same when you oppress the already oppressed because you are validating and reinforcing the inequality, contributing to the injustice certain people face on a daily basis.

When you underpay your house help and other people who work for you that are from a lower class than you, your one simple *"choice"* is a social and political problem. It is no longer just a tiny, harmless decision you made, but a way in which people are oppressed through our entire country, often even globally.

When men in a society are expected to lack sensitivity, be masculine, strong, breadwinners—that is a *problem.* It is *not okay* for society to expect any and all men to undermine their own feelings and then take up the burden of an entire household, and in order to change that, one would have to *listen to and partake in* conversations about feminism because it isn't possible to empower men without uplifting womxn, and the people of trans, queer, and non-binary communities, to the *same standards of freedom, education, and opportunities.* Why, you ask? Because we *all* occupy a space that needs to be shared, to be balanced, to be without borders, and in order for one to have what the other already does, all of us will have to stop feeling so threatened by the other's presence in *our space.*

When you *choose* to hire a man over a womxn because you want someone that's dedicated and not looking to take time off to start a family, that's systematic sexism because *men are already treated like they're superior.* Men that plan to have families don't need to take time off of work and that's only possible because the womxn they're with give up their jobs instead. However, even if these womxn chose to work, the same opportunities that men are offered aren't even possible outcomes for womxn who are child bearers, but we don't consider these factors. *The core foundation of how we run workspaces, therefore, are more man-friendly and simply less accessible for womxn.*

You could also *choose* to hire a womxn instead of a man because you want to contribute towards closing the gender gap and give an opportunity to those that don't usually get them.

When you build a public place with stairs but *choose* not to have ramps for wheelchair access, your choice has a direct impact on those that cannot get past these barriers. In many places, it's not mandatory and you can *choose* to do nothing about the lack of accessibility for people with less or no mobility and say, "*It's nothing personal towards people who use wheelchairs, right? It's just a choice.*" Except, a choice made by *you* can then definitely *limit the lives* of many other people.

If the choices you make are actively contributing towards the oppression of groups of people, then it isn't just a simple *choice* anymore; it's a choice you must be more aware of while making it because you're part of a bigger problem and will eventually be held accountable for it.

I think in discussions and arguments, a lot of the times the people saying *"this isn't about the gender"* are the ones that are superior and privileged, while those feeling attacked based on their gender are coming from a place of oppression. Now, remember, *"a lot of the times"* are all keywords.

I have heard womxn say they're feeling attacked and oppressed *as womxn,* and I have quite often felt it myself too. In workplaces, in relationships, and in families. While the person in power tends to think what they're doing has nothing to do with sexism, if the way you're treating a womxn falls hand in hand with why womxn are collectively oppressed all over the world, then, unfortunately, the choice you've made is not in isolation—it's a part of the problem.

I once said to a man that I cannot be with him anymore, "*because I couldn't be in a relationship where his family didn't respect me, and we weren't having sex either, and I felt unwanted, and in order to be kind to myself, I needed to leave him.*" To which he responded, "*Yes, we're not having sex, and you're not validated by my family, and you've just had enough because you're selfish and you think the world revolves around you."*

I ignored the privilege he was stinking of and instead told him I didn't want to pick up after him anymore. I wasn't his mother and I was not obliged to rectify all the mistakes he made just because he expected me to do so. So, yes, maybe I am selfish... and he then frustratedly said, *"Why are you making this a gender battle? It's not about man or womxn."*

Oh, but it was, and it still is.

Womxn are *conditioned* to take up less space in this world, to let men lead, to always tiptoe around them. So, when you tell a womxn that her choosing *herself* in order to be happy and healthy is her thinking the world revolves around her, when she tells you she wants to be more sexually active and you tell her she's being selfish, in a country where womxn end up married, with multiple children and yet never know what an orgasm feels like, you tell her that she thinks the world revolves around her, when you tell her that *her choice to walk out because she doesn't feel like she has the respect she needs is because she thinks the world revolves around her*—as a man, you are only reinforcing the age-old patriarchal narrative *that she needs to stop; she is taking up too much space.*

We don't raise men like that. We don't raise men to stay in relationships where they are constantly abused, judged, insulted, or questioned. To keep their thoughts to themselves unless they're asked. We don't raise men to sustain relationships where they feel unwanted, we don't raise men to pick up after every mistake their womxn make, we don't teach them that the womxn they marry will, *of course, get frustrated if they don't know how to do things around the house,* and *we sure as hell don't tell men they're being selfish and they think the world revolves around them when they choose to leave for inner peace, self-respect, and happiness.*

It took me 28 years, uncountable heartbreaks, toxic and abusive relationships—some encountered by my friends and others my own—to finally *sometimes* be able to pick up on misogynist and sexist behaviour. On most days, I still blame myself when a man is angry with me. My natural instinct is to apologise, as I have been conditioned to think *it must've been my fault.* But when history repeats itself, when I see things that I've seen before and they happen over and over again and *they just don't fit right,* when I see a man behave like a womxn's desire for sex in a relationship is petty and unimportant in a time when families still get their daughters' hymens replaced before marriage, when I see a man indirectly tell a womxn that she's taking up too much space for demanding respect, when I see men make mistakes and then lose their temper at womxn that refuse to help them rectify these mistakes, as though it's the man's birthright to *demand* her support instead of politely asking for it—that is when I am aware. I am very aware… and it hurts me to think about all the times that I was/am unaware.

I wrote this chapter because I needed you to know that it often *is* about the gender, about the race, the caste, the colour, the mobility. The fact that you think it isn't is because you come from a place of privilege, but for those that are at the bottom and are systematically oppressed, it is a problem that needs to be addressed and considered in every step we take. You are only able to misuse/abuse your power over people or be superior *because* of the privilege you hold in those equations. *Everything* we do, we do within the way our societies are built, and societies are not built with equal distribution of wealth and power. While you are powerful in front of some, you may be oppressed by others, and if we don't start to empathise with those beneath us, then how can we expect those above us to do the same?

Be aware of your gender, of your choices, your words, your privilege, and the decisions you make—every day.

My Notes

My Notes

CHAPTER 11

WHORE

One day, I'm going to print myself a t-shirt that says randi, and I'll get another one that says slut, another one saying whore, one saying bitch, kutti, hijra, laudi, kulta, chakka… Feel free to add to the list, I'll even leave some space for you below.

Many of these terms are homophobic, transphobic, misogynistic, and I'm sure they're also triggers for some of us. You might not want to wander across the word "Randi" while reading a book because it's too confronting for you, or it's too much, but here's the thing—not wanting to read it here does not *change the fact that womxn are being called one every day, and not just due to their profession, but to put them down.* Where do these words come from? What do they mean? Many of these terms come from the jobs womxn catered to, to their personalities, rebelliousness, actions, to the way that many of us are just born.

If you really think about it, a randi wouldn't have been a bad word. It became an *insult* because being *a prostitute was insulting.* The term hijra sure as hell wouldn't exist today either, but an entire community of transgender people were excluded, abused, and looked down upon. To *be considered one* was derogatory. People thought, *what is the worst thing you could call a man or a woman? Tell them they're neither.* Well, thank you, because we then came up with different ways to be *inclusive.*

Unfortunately, we think telling a man that he is a womxn or telling a man he's queer is as insulting as one could be, disturbingly far more insulting than telling him he has sex with his own mother. Isn't that so strange?

All the insults we have for men are terms that demasculate them into being feminine, i.e., *"wear some bangles."* However, all the praises and words of motivation and appreciation *add* masculinity, like *"you have some balls/grow a pair of balls."*

When it comes to womxn, it's as simple as destroying their character—*character being defined by what men would like womxn to behave like.* A womxn that isn't feminine by male standards becomes a hijra, one that likes to have sex becomes a slut or a whore. Often, if they want it but she won't give it to them, she's still considered one because *how dare she make you want her* and then not say yes? *"Why was she smiling? Why was she so full of life? Why was she wearing a colour that bought out her eyes, or a top so tight that you could see the shape of her breasts? Why was she wearing a skirt, or talking to boys? Why was she out at night? Well, if she has a boyfriend, then she's a slut and she must sleep with the rest of us too."*

What a slut, a whore, randi... kutti... saali... *that bitch.*

As a society, *we allow* rape. We allow rape when we allow men and womxn to talk about womxn so disrespectfully. And I am not biased here. If your fight for womxn's rights became allowing womxn to say things like *"he won't sleep with her, his balls should be chopped off, what a piece of shit,"* then I wouldn't fight that fight with you. I'd tell you that it's wrong. Today, as a society, we *allow* men to not only speak to womxn like that but also act upon it. On the internet, in families, in public spaces, in marriages. *We allow rape by attaching a womxn's character to her clothes. We allow rape by letting womxn's characters be exploited in our homes and our newspapers. We allow rape when we put a womxn's honour in her vagina and claim that marriage means "yes." We allow rape when we slut-shame.*

I had a message from a young girl a few days ago, telling me that she put up a mirror selfie of herself on Instagram after working out in a sports bra and track pants, to which her mother sent her a text saying *"there was no place for a whore in this house, they're open-minded but if she wanted to behave like a slut, she should leave,"* and her sister reached out to her right afterwards as well, texting that she was *sick and tired* of her rebelliousness— *"When did she turn into such a slut? Why was she embarrassing their mother? She should leave the house if she just wants to encourage rape and can't have any decency."*

My hands were shaking after reading those screenshots. I couldn't stop crying, and I didn't know what to do. I was so confronted. Every time I reach this junction, I just feel like I have lost, like it's all been worth *nothing.*

Do you realise what we're doing to young womxn in this society?
Do you have any idea how damaging this is?
Do you then expect these young womxn to come and talk to you when they've been molested?
Because they were probably asking for it, weren't they?

Every 15 minutes, and maybe even more often, there is a womxn in this country being abused, raped, beaten, murdered—simply for *being a womxn*.

Every day, I get a comment calling me a hijra, a randi, a slut, a whore, and I'm *so fucking tired of it*.

I'm tired of being attacked, I'm tired of being hurt, I'm tired of feeling ashamed of having sexual desires, of wanting to wear makeup, or not wanting to wear any makeup, of having a boyfriend. I'm so tired of being embarrassed of my facial hair, and I'm tired of feeling so miserable every single time I find out that some guy I once knew said that I was a whore to someone else. I'm tired of being called fat, like it's an insult.

And so, I'm reclaiming it. I'm reclaiming the words that have been used to hurt me, insult me, abuse me, and put me down while simultaneously putting other communities and professions and body types down too. I'm reclaiming the words that were altered and used to make me feel small, or to compare me to someone that I don't think should be considered an insult to begin with.

So, call me a queen or call me a hijra, call me a boss or call me a randi, call me a slut or call me lady—if I'm not offended by your tiny thought process, then your insults don't wear me down.

The fact that so many people in society feel that the best way to insult you is to call you a womxn that sells her body *to men* in order to earn an income, or call you a term used to describe *sexually active, independent womxn who enjoy sex*, or tell you that you're part of the trans community *speaks more about their small minds than it could ever say anything at all about you.*

They hold the power because they think they're *insulting us*. Maybe they wouldn't hold that power… if we could find different ways to try and *take back ours.*

Lizzo said she's a 100% that bad bitch, and I'm going to slut-shame myself to an extent that reminds you that it isn't *shame if you're fucking proud of it.* Yes, sometimes I look a little like a man, and I don't see what's wrong with that—unless *man* is the insulting part? Or am I supposed to be insulted by anything and everything that a heterosexual man isn't attracted to? You know what *is* an embarrassment? How we treat the trans and LGBTQ communities and other minorities that exist *within our own society.* Now that should bring you shame.

You know what else is embarrassing? That prostitution isn't legalised in our country, and so we turn a blind eye to the fact that there is a *supply for demand by men, which isn't reducing or going anywhere,* but do you give these womxn any legal rights? No. Can they report abuse? No. Can they seek help? No, *because we criminalised their only source of income.*

So, is society's issue prostitution? Because then the *men* in our society have a *lot* to answer for. Or is our issue a moral one where we judge the *womxn (many of which are trafficked, sold, oppressed) that are in the business?*

If your issue is actually the unfair treatment towards womxn, here are some solutions:

Let there be brothels, and every time a man visits one, jail him instead? Let there be womxn standing on the side of the streets trying to earn their bread and butter, and every time you see men roaming the streets in the middle of the night, fine them instead?

Let there be porn, but instead of judging the womxn that are in it (many of those trafficked and oppressed as well, but many are there by choice), judge the men watching it?

For some reason, we said Sunny Leone wasn't welcome in our society when she first entered the industry, even though every single person in a household knew who Sunny Leone was?

How do we go around the world wanking off to womxn, womxn that we then outcast for helping all your sons cum for a decade?

When a sex tape is leaked, it's not usually of a womxn masturbating. There are two people in it, yet we destroy the life of one.

We punish womxn at every step, for a crime they have not committed, and if we turn around and ask them to restrict our men instead, they'll call us feminazis, they'll call us crazy... "crazy," for calling them out.

Yes, I often act like a whore on weekends, sometimes even on Mondays. I'll wear a t-shirt that tells you so without you having to directly talk to me and that'll begin to threaten our society *enough* for people to be outraged and say *"you're degrading womxn's rights to as little as a vagina,"* even though *you're taking away our rights, simply for having one.*

My Notes

My Notes

CHAPTER 12

PRIVILEGE

Even inequality comes in layers, measured disproportionately for everybody. White men are usually on top of this privileged chain of equality. Underneath them are heterosexual men of colour and race, poor men, poor men of colour, queer men, men with disabilities—not necessarily in any specific order. But now imagine being *all* of the above—a queer, poor man of colour, with disabilities—that would mean inequality affects *you* in multiple different ways than it does to just a heterosexual man of colour.

Or, imagine you are a womxn (maybe you even are).

I often read opinion pieces and arguments against *white feminism*. Many people that identify as *feminists* are so angry with white womxn and their priorities. This *"first world, privileged white feminism is ignorant and entitled,"* I often hear people say. They're not wrong about the privilege part. White womxn are definitely privileged. While in India we are fighting issues like child marriage, female foeticide, and marital rape not being criminalised, they're focusing on the gender pay gap and statues of womxn in parliament, more jobs being occupied by womxn in arts and films so that more womxn are writing and telling the stories of womxn.

Here, back home in India, you're extremely lucky if you even make it to the film industry. Most of our A-list female actors still play the *Hero's* love interest in movies before often being written off at 30 years of age to make way for the younger lot of womxn that then continue to romance the same male actors, twice their age, that haven't been replaced for the last two generations. The men get older, and they are repeatedly paired with womxn who replace each other, each one younger than the last. *That female protagonist film with a female writer and a female director* is extremely rare, and rarely a blockbuster. They're *Indie films*. So, yes, it's safe to say that our battles, even as womxn, are different depending on where we are from.

We tend to think that womxn in the West are extremely privileged and ignorant towards our problems, and as I agreed, many of them are. But amidst the fights we are fighting individually, adamant that womxn in other parts of the world don't *truly* understand our struggles because they have better opportunities or live in different cultures, every once in a while (2016) you hear about a gang rape somewhere in the world (Spain) where five men raped an 18-year-old girl and the public's outrage at the young woman being judged and questioned... sends chills down your spine. Or the statistics of white womxn that are petrified of walking home alone at night somewhere in the US because they're scared of being raped and abused, often by men they know, or the viral video of a woman walking down the streets of NYC being catcalled, groped, followed, and harassed. Or the studies that clearly indicate that womxn still, *absolutely everywhere in this world,* do more unpaid labour than men, or the widespread abuse outside abortion clinics, or the excess amount of increase in domestic violence cases during the lockdown, or the #metoo movement and how it brought together womxn from all over the world, privileged or not. It is in these moments that you realise that even though so many of them are ahead of us in this war, they are still *at war,* and on most days, they are fighting for the same rights that we might want to fight for in the coming years—*freedom of choice.*

I am not justifying or denying that white womxn are born more privileged, and many of them can be extremely ignorant of our journeys.

In fact, I'd say that applies to *all womxn and men*. I'm well aware that a lot of womxn lack sympathy, are racist, enable patriarchy, misuse their privilege… *as do men*. I don't think we should assume that all womxn are messiahs of feminism or any sort of movement towards equality and equity. That applies to all womxn that support a cause, including me… as a side-note, let's maybe not put *any* human being on such a high pedestal, where that person overpowers the actual cause to the extent that when they make mistakes and/or fall from grace, *the cause falls with them*.

So, no, I'm not denying that some womxn abuse their privilege. Let's establish we are on the same page with that before we move ahead.

Privileged womxn from Western countries are still scared of the same things that womxn in India are scared of: rape, abusive relationships, catcalling, pay gap, inequality, unpaid labour, domestic violence, sexual harassment, rape and/or death threats in person and on the internet, abortion rights, being disrespected for simply *being a womxn,* unfair gender roles, lack of control over their own bodies. These issues exist *everywhere.* So, while you hate them for being so ignorant towards your problems, here's an awfully saddening reality check: *just because they're more privileged than us doesn't mean they aren't fighting the same fight.* White womxn *also* have their drinks spiked before they're brutally raped. White womxn are also shamed for getting an abortion. And very often, when I look at the womxn in the West fighting for things we are collectively still so far from desiring, more than envy, I am filled with hope that one day, we too can get there. Simultaneously, I'm also filled with sadness at the reminder that we have such a long way to go, even just to get to the battles that they're fighting.

I give the example of white womxn and privilege because I see a very similar sort of *blame game* that we largely play back at home, within our own country. Womxn often tend to be extremely bitter and angry at other womxn of privilege. One of the most common things I'm told when I write about women's rights is *"why don't you talk to the women in villages? You write on the internet and the only women that read your words are womxn with phones and degrees and money. They don't need to be empowered; they are already empowered. Why don't you empower poor women because only they need it?"*

First things first, I don't know if I am the right person for *that* job, even if I did in some way resonate with their struggles. I could talk to religious womxn, I could talk to Hindu/Muslim womxn, I could talk to womxn in villages, I could talk to stay-at-home mothers, but I don't go out of my way and reach out to most of these womxn—not because I don't think they need it, but because 1. I don't think defining *freedom* for other womxn is feminism, and 2. I've never told womxn *what* they should want, but I'm here for those that find me and resonate with me. I would never knock doors with my idea of feminism.

I care about a lot of things, but I don't think I'm necessarily okay with advocating on behalf of womxn that actually may not want me to be a part of their journey. They may want someone they resonate with more. I fight for what I believe in, when I am physically and mentally capable of doing it. When I am drained, I carefully step back and allow myself to heal. I also don't go out of my way to tell womxn who they should be, what they should believe in, what they should/shouldn't wear. I simply share my thoughts, my experiences, and my opinions on a platform large enough for people who want to be reassured that they're not alone. But who the hell am I to tell other womxn what to do? Who is anybody, to tell a womxn (or man, or person) what to do with their lives? The day we start trying to tell womxn what they can and cannot do in order to be *free,* we're giving them the opposite of freedom; we are clipping their wings.

I don't tell womxn to be topless, as much as I don't tell womxn to cover themselves. I don't tell them to go out there and have casual sex, as much as I don't tell them not to. I talk about my own desires and rights that *I wish I had.* I talk about how women should have *the freedom to choose for themselves,* whether or not another woman would do the same things or not. Our definition of freedom does not need to be aligned in order for us all to have it. It's not like there is only a certain amount of freedom left to be allocated, and womxn must all choose the same kind. No, that's not what *freedom* is; that is *control.*

I also strongly disagree that womxn with education, money, or privilege don't need guidance and support. *"Women in villages need to be saved, the women in big cities are already saved"* is a school of thought that comes purely out of bitterness, resentment, and extreme ignorance. If anything, it is misogynistic. It blows my mind that there are people in this world *that truly don't understand how inequality works.* Womxn almost everywhere need to be empowered in one way or another. Some more than others, but that doesn't change the fact that they all need it. White womxn, queer womxn, womxn of colour, Muslim womxn, Hindu womxn, Christian womxn, non-binary womxn, womxn from "lower castes," womxn from "upper castes," womxn from big urban cities, womxn in villages, working womxn, womxn that are homemakers, womxn who are oppressed, womxn who are oppressing other womxn in the name of tradition—*there is nothing wrong in resonating with some women's struggles more than others, as long as you don't put down the ones you do not resonate with.*

I resonate more often with womxn who have similar backgrounds to me or have had similar lives/faced similar battles. Acknowledging my own battles doesn't mean that I don't think other people in the world have bigger ones. I am well aware of the fact that they do. I don't always resonate with white womxn, and I don't always resonate with womxn from villages either. We fight different fights every day of our lives, and in my head, if I cannot even educate and empower the women that *resonate with me* every day, then how the hell am I to reach out to women that wouldn't even see me as one of them?

In many villages, womxn don't wear a bra. Bras are an unnecessary luxury a lot of them can't afford/don't care for. Think about it, some womxn are in awe of lingerie, some are fighting to remove it, some want to normalise it, others want to erase the taboo around it, and some just don't understand what all the fucking fuss is about. One woman's battlefield is another womxn's love boat, and it's not my job to decide what's what for any of them.

I once saw a womxn selling vegetables in a village in the outskirts of Maharashtra, and she was breastfeeding as she sat there, selling her vegetables. It blew my mind because you know what a lot of womxn in urban cities cannot do? Breastfeed at work and in office/public spaces. You know what else they cannot do? Wear a saree and a thin cotton blouse, without a bra inside. Yet, we have magazines with cover pages of womxn breastfeeding that go viral, because *the point* isn't that *"when womxn in villages can do it, then why are you crying?"* Evidently, a lot of womxn can, while other womxn can't, and while some do it nonchalantly without a care in the world, others would feel extremely empowered if they didn't have to hide away at every point. To be clear, I'm not saying that womxn of the lower class have it better off. *Of course not.* Human beings in general with money and education have better opportunities and more rights—the same applies to womxn. But what I *am saying* is that we as womxn are all fighting different battles and that *is a point worth focusing on.*

Womxn that live in villages actually work because they *have to work.* From the daughter to the mother, to the grandmother, womxn work and not out of *desire* or *passion*, not because they are educated, but purely so they can survive. Sometimes men and womxn work on the same construction sites. They don't have the means to go to school or graduate and get a well-paid job, but they still *work.* And in certain ways, they are *financially* more independent than homemakers in cities and urban areas. But what good is that independence, without the knowledge of what to do with it? There is systematic oppression in our culture that makes womxn dependent on men. My mother's house help, for example, works four houses while her husband sits at home, gets drunk, and occasionally hits her. She brings the money home, she's the breadwinner, but she isn't *independent* because, within her society, she is expected to live with this abuse every day. He holds the power because being a divorced womxn with two children is worse than being beaten up by your husband. She would not only be judged but also be more vulnerable to being teased, raped, harassed, or worse, seen as a threat to the neighbourhood and therefore unwelcomed in her own community. She once said to me that having a man in the house meant that *at least her daughters weren't being touched by men in the neighbourhood.* I went numb.

She stays in that abusive marriage because without education, freedom, and the right environment, is financial independence on paper even enough? The answer is no.

Womxn of privilege, who are raised in expensive houses and with fancy degrees, are also often married off after they complete their studies and aren't *allowed* to work because *"we have a family business, there's no shortage of money, why do you need to work? The women of our house give birth, raise their children, look after their husbands, shop, and live like queens."* Womxn that have chauffeur driven cars and expensive bags are often restricted in completely different ways where they're told they can maybe have *hobbies* but not careers because, in their society, *a wife with a job is often looked down upon.*

Womxn of the family working is considered a sign of struggle—*"Your daughter-in-law is working? Is the financial situation okay?"* Because why else would a family in their right mind allow her to distract herself from her real purpose in life, right? What womxn would actually *want* to work, after all? According to society, all we should want to do is breed and cook for our families.

And God forbid she does work, then *"she is probably bored at home all day, so she's started her own chain of jewellery; it's just a hobby until they start a family."*

I meet so many womxn that have to give up their jobs just because they are getting married. They often tell me that they're not given enough time to go to work amidst the marriage preparations. Parents from both families have too many things planned for *her*, as though it's some sort of a life event that is a stepping stone in *her* life, while her husband must continue to earn for their future. Notice how no one is asking the man if he actually wants to work this hard? Maybe *he'd* like to sit at home and choose sherwanis instead?

I meet womxn whose mothers-in-law don't like them working because it's now time for her to focus on her family… if she needs anything, they are there to help. Womxn that actually loved studying and topped their class just to study further and then get a great job in their chosen field but were later discouraged because of their biological clock… and if both the partners focus solely on their careers, then who will look after the children? Even if they're not ready for children, but if the *husband* is working towards a promotion, then the wife being equally ambitious comes in the way of a peaceful home. This may not be happening to you, but it's happening alright. *It's happening in our world, it's happening in our country, it's happening to our womxn.*

Privileged womxn are often told that they don't need to work because we, as a society, don't see the need for women to be *working* in order to feel important or ambitious. We don't consider having a job as a sign of independence and identity for womxn. Instead, we see it as a distraction of The West to ruin our culture.

The one thing we forget when we are talking about women, privileged or not, is the lack of freedom of choice. Womxn, regardless of class, caste, sex, status, sexual preference, and colour, are fighting for their right to *choose for themselves*. What they fight for may be different from *your* needs, you may not even agree with them, and sometimes you don't need to either. It's not your place to agree or disagree—all you *need to agree with* is that they deserve a *choice*. Privileged womxn in urban cities demanding the right to sexual liberation and equal pay does not in any way *demean* the fight for sanitary napkins and education in villages. We are stronger together, and we *can* coexist, you know?

Here's a situation: A rich family with their own family business has a daughter, let's call the daughter Ananya. She falls in love with a man, not as rich as herself but he fits into the parents' other criteria; let's call him… Dhruv. Ananya and Dhruv love each other. Ananya has graduated with top marks but has never been allowed to work because her father's business is successful enough to sustain them all. Dhruv doesn't have a job at the moment. He's looking for one, but he doesn't *have one*. He doesn't have any savings either. Ananya's parents aren't exactly thrilled that Dhruv doesn't have a job or any money, but they know their daughter is madly in love, and she's the most pampered child in the family—

she's going to get her way. They lecture Dhruv, *"How are you ever going to look after our daughter if you have no ambition, no money, no job?"* But eventually, when he cannot get the sort of job that's good enough for their family's standards, they welcome him into the family for the sake of their daughter and simultaneously welcome him into the family business too.

Now, let's reverse this. Dhruv comes from a rich family. Ananya doesn't have the kind of money that they do. Dhruv's parents aren't thrilled about it, but they're progressive and they like her. She's a *nice girl with good cultural upbringing*, so they welcome her into the family and tell her that the women in their family don't work anyway, because they have so much money that women don't need to earn any. Ananya doesn't get offered the family business. Ananya doesn't get asked who will earn for the whole family. Ananya doesn't get the option to focus on her ambition instead of having children.

In both scenarios, if the family is rich, then there is no need for a *womxn* to be working. The important lesson of this story is that *patriarchy and unequal treatment impact people in different ways*. When you excessively oppress one gender, you are automatically giving more privilege and power to the other gender. When one holds more *power* than the other, they then also have the pressure of being *more (more successful, more strong, more educated, more dominant, more controlling, and so on)*. But we forget that we're being unfair to *both* Dhruv and Ananya. Dhruv shouldn't have to earn for an entire family and Ananya shouldn't be restricted from working altogether. Let people *choose* what they want to do with their lives, let them live out their desires. *But for starters, raise human beings equally, with the ability to be independent on their own.*

The other argument people often make while I'm talking to them is *"let womxn be homemakers and housewives if that's what they want to be, the biggest job in this world is of a mother."* I have three major issues with that sort of statement. 1. Not all womxn want to/can become mothers. 2. That job isn't paid labour, and to survive independently in this world, one needs to not only be *acknowledged* for their work but also be *paid* for it. My third issue with that statement: every single day, we are writing our own history, a history that will one day be told to the future generations. And if womxn just contributed to *solely* being mothers, then everything ever invented, created, changed, discovered, rebelled against, and every single revolution *will be credited to men.* Writers, poets, freedom fighters, artists, doctors, teachers, scientists, and sports*men* will all be *men.* When you encourage women to only be homemakers and mothers, then history repeats itself. And one day, when a young girl somewhere wants to grow up to be independent, despite the norm, when she fights for her rights, she will be shut down by the same people that made the earlier argument, except they'll now say *"if men and womxn are equal, then tell me why is everything invented by a man?"*

Because while men were getting jobs, fighting wars, and *changing the world,* some womxn… were giving birth to them, and raising them, because someone somewhere once believed that the most important job in this world was of a mother—except being a mother doesn't make it to history books, does it?

> *"You're a privileged womxn, you won't even get it."*
> *"You're a man, you'll never get it."*
> *"You're heterosexual, you won't ever get it."*
> *"You're rich, what do you know about being poor? You'll never get it."*
> *"You've never been assaulted, so you won't get it."*
> *"You have everything you ever wanted. You'll never get it."*

After having used them myself, as well as having witnessed people around me use the aforementioned statements, I've decided to ask myself—what exactly is it that we *want* from people? Do we want them to *get it,* or do we want *change?* If *change* is what we want, then maybe we should be welcoming the people we think are more privileged than us in these conversations instead of telling them *they're not one of us, so they'll never understand.* Telling men or womxn of privilege who *want* to join the conversation, that *want* to help and listen, that they *just won't get it* isn't going to make them more receptive, nor is it going to make them empathise. Maybe they can't and won't truly, entirely, wholly ever *get it* because they haven't lived our individual experiences. That applies to *everyone* around you, *privileged or not*. But if they get it *enough* to want to be part of a changing, better world, if they get it *enough* to want to join us in spreading awareness and raising our voices, then isn't *that* what matters? One doesn't have to be a womxn to resonate with the fact that womxn deserve equal rights (you'd be surprised by how many womxn from the same paths of life don't *get it either*). You don't have to live through rape to know it's gruesome, and you certainly don't have to want the same things in life to fight for other people's right to choose what they want.

Maybe it's time we come on board together instead of constantly throwing shade at each other for having more than others or fighting for things we don't resonate with. If every time a man wanted to be part of a womxn's rights movement, we chose to shut him up and say, *"You are not a womxn, so you'll never get it,"* then maybe we need to stop and ask ourselves *what* is the change we are hoping for? Because for a future where we all coexist, you'll need to want him to try and *get it to the best of his abilities* in order for him and others like him to step down from their privilege and share the space they occupy. For that, *they need to come as close to getting "it" as possible.*

Not all people of privilege are against you—some of them are just fighting their own battles, the same way that you are fighting yours. You too may be unaware of your own privilege. That doesn't make you a bad person, and you're not going to be any closer to empathising with other people's problems if they started throwing shade at you every day, are you? We as people aren't perfect. We will always be lacking, and we *will* make mistakes… but we will also learn from them. Allyship is complicated, and it's an ongoing process. The only way we can learn is by listening to people when they speak, by acknowledging that yes, in many ways, we too are more privileged than others, and there is always someone who is more oppressed than us, and then *listen to people again.* A lot of people around the world are speaking, and they're asking for us to join their fight, give them the opportunities they deserve to fight for a better world. A world *they* want to be a part of, instead of one we want to create *for them.* Ask more questions, stop being offended, and try to be kinder.

Treat others the way you want to be treated.

Make me a list of things that make you privileged and also the areas where you lack privilege.

My Notes

My Notes

CHAPTER 13

HELP

My husband helps me clean the house. My husband is amazing, he actually helps raise our son. Sometimes, he helps by picking her up from school. He's helping me by staying home this Friday, so I can step out. In fact, he helps a lot on weekends.

My boyfriend helps me a few times a week.

My dad helps mum in taking care of my brother when he's not at work.

My husband is such a great father, he really helps a lot.

My son helps his wife.

My brother, he's so great, when mum and dad are away, he helps me with the chores.

You're so lucky your boyfriend helps you cook when you have friends coming over, mine just eats!

How often have you genuinely heard womxn say that/said it yourself? Because I hear it every day—I've even said it myself. It seems so normal that you don't stop to think twice... and that is precisely what makes it so damaging.

My wife helps me clean up the house when people leave. My wife helps me raise our son. Sometimes, she even helps by picking our son up from school. In fact, she's helping me this Friday, so I can go out.
This week, my wife is helping me by staying home, so I can work.
My girlfriend helps me a few times a week when she's not busy. She helps with the dishes and washing the clothes.
My mom helps dad take care of my brother.
My wife is such a great mother, she helps a lot with raising the kids.
My daughter actually helps her husband at home.
My sister is pretty considerate, she helps me with chores when our parents aren't home.
You're so lucky your girlfriend helps you with house chores before friends come over, mine just eats!

Sound a little odd to you this time? Why do you think that is?

The first time I realised this was while reading the book *We Should All Be Feminists* by Chimamanda Ngozi Adichie. We naturally tend to refer to anything a man does as *help*, but anything a womxn does as her responsibility, which is why when a man does something that you subconsciously believe in your head to be a womxn's job, the man is clearly *helping* and deserves appreciation. Seldom would you hear a man say that his wife/girlfriend/mother *helps* him if the things they're doing are considered to be his responsibility to begin with.

Things men do, such as parenting, cooking, raising kids, washing clothes, dusting, cleaning, or other chores around the house, in our head, are seen as *their help*. Therefore, we have so much gratitude... for their *help*.

Help implies that the job is to be done by you, and the other person is kind enough to provide you assistance. You can help someone with their homework, you can help them lift heavy things (that they were already going to lift), you can help someone cross the road, or help a person complete something that is originally *their job to do*—not yours. For example, your mother can *help* you raise *your* child when you are working long hours, but a husband? *That's their child too.*

The words we use really matter because language makes up for a lot of how we see people and their roles in our lives. Language is important because it communicates what we are *thinking*. Gender, for example. That's why when someone says doctor or lawyer, lots of people might automatically think *male* (I'm guilty of having done it in the past) but for a nurse—we automatically think *female*. Even for most jobs that *should* be gender-neutral, people assume a *male*. From driver to chef to lecturer; in fact, even when someone says, *"Imagine there's a child crossing the road,"* I am ashamed to admit that I usually think of a *boy*. Slangs like "bro/guys"— dude, don't even get me started... see what I did there?

Humankind, *mankind* – the default human, presumed to be a man.

Language, and how we use it based on how much privilege or lack of it we hold, is important and says a lot about our social conditioning. Even though at first it seems so silly, the constant use of *gender-based terms* eventually shapes how we behave, what we think we can achieve, the possibilities around us, and how we imagine this world of ours. If that wasn't true, we'd be saying *"oh, womxn! I missed the bus"* as casually as we use "man" in sentences. *Words matter and I cannot stress on that enough.*

So, when you say someone helps you, you are taking full responsibility for the job to be done and also letting the other person think that they've done something wonderful—*they've gone out of their way to contribute*, even though they haven't actually done *enough* because maybe a lot of it wasn't supposed to be *help, maybe it was their equal responsibility.*

(Mid-chapter disclaimer: This thought isn't my own, but then again, most of the things I talk about to you are lessons I've learnt, through books I've read and conversations I've had that have shaped my mind. Words, often used by womxn I look up to, that have left me with so many questions. These womxn have "helped" me realise what's wrong with our society and its gender stereotypes.)

The book *We Should All Be Feminists* makes me so angry and yet so helpless, because even though Chimamanda is talking about life in Nigeria, I, having been raised in Australia and now living all the way in India, realise how shockingly similar the lives of womxn all over the world are. How, no matter where you go, patriarchy is just not a trend that goes out of fashion. It's the goddamn cheetah print that keeps coming back, year after year, no matter how hard you fought for it to be gone the last time.

For three years, I've tried really hard to make it a point *not* to use the word *"help"* when what I really need is for my partner to be equally responsible. But it's just so much more complicated than an overnight change we make in our lives after reading a book. Patriarchy and systematic oppression don't end when you flip through the last pages and put the book down. No, in many ways, it is harder to live life being fully aware of the injustices you face every day. That's when you become *difficult* to people. *Constantly complaining. "Relax," they'll say, exhausted, like they're the ones having to put up with unfair norms.*

Womxn are so conditioned to overburden themselves with things they firmly believe to be their responsibility that even though I had never lifted a finger at home as a child, suddenly, when left on my own, I became this strange, unknown person that now puts *coasters* under cups and *knows* when shelves are dirty and need to be cleaned, and which clothes can't be washed together because colours *bleed*, when and *why* the net fabric under the tv needs to be washed every few months, how often the toothbrush holder has to be rinsed, and where things need to go when arranging a drawer... none of this was taught to me. It was as though I thought homes just maintained themselves because as a young teenager, I sure as hell didn't do *a thing* in my mother's house... and yet, now I check expiry dates of canned food and I put plastic sheets on the shelves of the fridge, *and I wash curtains*. I don't even know who I am anymore. Was there a switch installed inside me, somewhere?

You won't be surprised to learn that my partner, however, doesn't feel the natural urge to do any of these things because he just hasn't even *thought* about them. In his head, curtains don't need to be washed, and to be honest, it's not entirely his fault; it's his conditioning. We had a conversation about this two years into our relationship. Until then, his routine consisted of treating the chair in our bedroom like a wardrobe (chairdrobe). And as I write this, I realise that so does my brother, and *most* of my male friends, *because why put washed clothes in the cupboard when you can just wear them as you go and put them back in the wash?* I then asked Rahul one day if he still needed a wardrobe, given that he wasn't stacking his clothes inside it? I was passive-aggressive, and that wasn't the right approach because, evidently, it didn't solve anything.

He did *wash* clothes very often, but it felt like he was only doing so because *he* needed fresh clothes. Which then made me realise that he's obviously not incapable of the things I am capable of. It's just that anything that doesn't come in his way every day didn't need to be washed/cleaned, according to him—like that cloth under the TV.

Once I learnt that it wasn't entirely his fault, my approach began to change. A less condescending, more vulnerable approach to this issue made things much easier to deal with. You must know the problem first in order to try and fix it, and *men* are not the problem; *how men are raised is the problem.*

I tried again. This time, I asked him to please start putting his clothes inside the wardrobe because the mess on the chair made me feel like I had far more to do around the house than I should have to, and with that reasoning, he did. The less toxic, more honest approach was a much more successful one. It became my go-to approach in our relationship.

When I started to think about his input around the house, I realised that he's actually very clean as a person, very aware of hygiene and bacteria. He likes to separate wet and dry waste. He's aware that even water tanks need to be cleaned often because bacteria grows inside them—*that's something I didn't even think of.* He puts our taps and hand jets into vinegar and boiling water every month to clean them. He is less like the *stereotypical Indian man,* but having said that, he is not the *stereotypical Indian womxn* either. He's not someone who dusts photo frames, or cleans the study table, or checks for expired veggies in the fridge regularly (unless something is stinking), or opens drawers and reorganises them once in six months, checks if the bookshelf is dusty and if the cloth we dust with needs to be changed, and do the shelves in our room have empty bottles or things that can be thrown away, and should we put all the coins in one box? Is the maid keeping all the plastic containers together, and do the lids all still fit? Did she clean the fans this month, and should we maybe now throw out the empty shampoo bottle that's been sitting in our bathroom for two months?

No. He doesn't think of those things. He goes to work, comes home, and interacts with as many things as he needs to interact with and then relaxes, has dinner, spends time with me, and goes to bed. The things he cares about are hygiene-related because that's what he relates *cleaning* to. So, from clean hand towels to the toilet seats to showerheads—*that's his concern.* Maybe bacteria is still more of a *man thing,* or maybe I am talking out of my ass, and he's just an exception to the rule and hence he's extremely cautious about bacteria. I don't know. All I know is that it never even crossed my mind, and *he is always on top of it.*

When it comes to looking after the rest of the house, it seems as though it just doesn't cross his mind. When we moved in together, he lived the way I used to live in my mother's house at the age of 14. The me that didn't lift a finger because *"what the hell do I know about cleaning and looking after homes… and is it even necessary? Why are mothers always cleaning anyway? Why can't they just chill out?"*

We tend to learn that girls are conditioned to clean and look after the house, but I just wasn't. My mother did *try* her best, but I was a stubborn kid that refused to do things around the house. Rahul, however, used to actually *help* his mother growing up. He would have daily chores he needed to do before he went to bed, and so I always wonder, *what happened to the two of us that even though he did a lot more cleaning around the house than I did as a child, upon moving in together as adults, how did I still turn out like this? How did we end up falling into our gender roles?*

This is why language is so important:

I believe that the whole time when Rahul was doing chores, he thought he was *helping* his mother, and I thought I was *rebelling* from what womxn were supposed to do. Even though I wasn't doing any work at home, eventually, when left alone, I subconsciously considered it to be *my job*. Conditioning isn't just about what you are directly *taught*, it is also what you see when you're growing up, and it's what you're surrounded by. You may think you're this person whom you've labelled with the labels you've chosen for yourself. Mine were "rebellious, lazy, scattered, messy, bold, vocal, careless, strong," but when push comes to shove, when it's about *survival*, we become what we know best. And what we know best is where we come from, what we have grown up to see, consciously and subconsciously. While you were busy making plans for your life to not follow the path laid out by your family and your society, *conditioning was still happening to you*.

When we finally moved into a house that I called *my home*, even though I may have never lifted a finger in my mother's house and been as pampered as him (arguably more), I still moulded myself into what a woman is expected to do, because it is *what I knew best*. From my mother to my grandmother, from our house help to my neighbours (and their house help), from my mother-in-law to my mom's friends (and her friends), from movies to teachers and friends' mothers—*each and every womxn I was raised around knew what to do in the house, or at least pretended to*. The humans that were in charge of all the house chores around me were womxn. When I pictured a house being cleaned with a mop or a duster in my head, *I saw a womxn*. I saw a womxn dusting, cooking, mopping, cleaning, bathing the kids, and even folding the clothes. I also saw men, but I saw them fixing toilets, plumbing, spending time in the garage with the car, gardening maybe, lifting things, barbequing, kicking a ball...

I didn't see womxn kicking balls in my imagination growing up, even though I did watch *Bend It Like Beckham*. Womxn were the ones that knew where everything was *kept*, and they knew where everything *goes*. From his chai to his tie to his wallet. Almost as though it was *"natural"* for it to happen, I unknowingly found my place in the same places as the womxn that have come before me. The same place where I let womxn belong for decades, in my own head.

When you think about it, the same thing must have happened to Rahul too. Though he was raised to do chores daily and *help* at home, he fell into a pattern justified by his own conditioning of what his own father and every other man around him would've done. He too would have knowingly or unknowingly been conditioned to see women as the home*makers,* and so taking up equal *responsibility* for that goddamn TV tablecloth didn't occur to him. In his house, womxn must have done most of the housework, and so he automatically felt like doing one odd thing here and there more often than what other men would do was him probably doing *a lot.* In his head, he probably wanted gratitude, or at least he wanted to be *recognised* for his help. And so, when not praised or thanked, he would've easily gotten tired because it's more than what he is used to doing, with little to no gratitude. He wouldn't, however, feel like this when he was doing things that *he thought* were *his* job to do—the ones I didn't allocate as *his* but he thought of them himself because guess what? That isn't him *helping me* anymore.

Gender roles not only affect womxn but men too. If Rahul wanted to grow up to be a stay-at-home dad, or cook meals while I go to work, he would've had to deal with a lot of criticism from our families for it. Society would tell him to *"stop being the daughter of the house"* and work a job that *pays.* Without meaning to, or wanting to, he and I would often fall straight into an extremely limiting stereotype of what we were conditioned to believe our gender roles are, and this is when history would often repeat itself—when I would crib and cry, frustrated, fighting about inequality, and wishing he'd do more around the house. Asking him to just *help me* more often because *"I don't want to play the role of the stereotypical womxn while he plays the role of the stereotypical man"* and that I was so *"sick and tired of the patriarchy"* while he, frustrated, didn't *"understand what he was doing wrong"* when he thought he's *"helping all the goddamn time"* and he's *"trying so hard but it's never good enough"...* and there it is, the most popular lovers' quarrel of every household.

But take a few steps back, history doesn't *have to* repeat itself if you don't want it to. Yes, it's extremely normal and easy to fall back into your conditioning. It's easy for women to take the role of a *woman* and for men to be comfortable taking the role of the *man*... but you don't *have to* do it. We are gifted with the ability of awareness. We can ask questions, adapt, change, evolve, empathise. We do not have to fall into the stereotypes that have been laid out for us by an orthodox, conservative society.

When Rahul and I noticed we were being sucked into this vicious cycle, we sat down and talked about it. I told him it wasn't working for me because I couldn't be the womxn that looks after the house and also works and writes while he just takes care of his own belongings. I expressed my helplessness and that I actively needed him to do more than just *help* me. I needed him to be equally responsible for this house—from ordering vegetables to tucking the bedsheets in when he notices it's untucked, to making sure the fridge is clean every few weeks and the bin under the bin bag isn't filthy and the cloth, yes, the cloth under that damn TV, that I have spent hours of my writer's block staring at, *gets washed*.

It wasn't any sort of a miracle. Things didn't just suddenly change. It took weeks, months, constant communication, and pointing out when one of us was falling back into our habits. In fact, I think it's safe to say that we are still learning every single day. If he slacks according to what I need, then I remind him. If I am silently doing all the work in the house and taking too much burden because I've forgotten to share our responsibilities, he tells me to slow down. I have to consciously ignore a mess when I see it, and he has to consciously look for things he wouldn't otherwise look for himself. When one of us falls too far back into our conditioning, we have a fight, and then once we calm down, we talk about finding a better way to handle it next time.

Breaking generations of pattern and habits isn't an overnight process. It is a change that may be something we have to work on for the rest of our lives, to keep reminding each other not to cater to gender roles, and learn to work together.

This is not the sort of task that we will eventually be *done with* within our lifetime. Five years from now, you're not going to find a world where couples no longer cater to any gender roles. That's not possible because we still live in a society where every day, unknowingly, we watch things, meet people, see stories where womxn and men have a role to play. We try to break the stereotypes, but *breaking* isn't the same as *erasing*. You can wake up every day and be adamant about wanting to make your own habits. Today, we've been in quarantine for over a month and we have a routine that works so amazingly for both of us. We have our own chores that we've taken up based on what we like doing. The things we mutually hate, we take turns to do. Neither of us *forgets* to do our part every day, and even if once in a while we do, it doesn't matter anymore because neither of us is catering to a stereotype. Hence, neither of us feels attacked or frustrated. We laugh and laze and often try to bribe or shotgun each other into doing tasks, and for the first time, it feels as equal as it's ever been; it doesn't feel *unfair*.

You have to work towards the kind of world you want to live in every day and hope that there are others out there like you, who are doing the same thing so that one day, when our generation has children, they grow up to parents that share the work, and daddy doesn't just *help* mom, but they are both *equally responsible*. They share chores not to "unburden mum" but because that's just how normal people live. Your children will probably still be raised in a society that goes by patriarchal stereotypes because societies don't just change over one generation, but maybe what they're learning at home, from their own parents, will be far more impactful than the things they pick up outside. Maybe they'll also have other exceptional examples around them—one can only hope, which you must do because what even *are* we without hope?

And when the time comes for your children to fall into their own conditioned gender stereotypes, they'll be one step closer to being more *equal* than before, and the only way to do that is to understand the problem, where it comes from, and how we can fix it at a foundation level. Falling into a trap where we hate and blame people who are *trying to change and be a part of our fight* is toxic and only makes the problem bigger, instead of minimising it. Don't punish the people who want to walk down this path with you; you're going to need them too.

It's never too late to start talking to your partner about sharing responsibilities and breaking these sexist learnings. It's never too late to stop using the word *help* so casually. It's never too late to express that you want to do equal work and you want equal time off. Just because you've been conditioned not to do it until today, doesn't mean you can't change that. Your safe space is a place where you should feel like you belong, where you can communicate. If the people you love don't want to help make this a better and safer space for you, then ask yourself—*do they really love you?*

It's never too late to start a dialogue and keep reminding your loved ones when they slip back into toxic patterns.

It's time to create our own society and be accountable for our actions. You and I aren't children anymore; we are the ones *setting examples* that the next generation will grow up to. What is it that you want them to see you for? It is time to be the change you wish to see in this world.

What are some of the gender roles and stereotypes that you would like to break in your lifetime? One day, you're going to meet someone (maybe you already have) that will help you change the world… but that isn't possible until you know exactly what you wish to change.

My Notes

My Notes

CHAPTER 14

———

TAKE IT WITH A PINCH OF SALT

I once dated a man that told me I lived in my own little bubble, where everything was a movie and things happened the way I wanted them to. He yelled in a fight, *"Your life is not some fucking book, Saloni!"* What? Someone send him a copy of this book, please. His biggest problem with me usually was that I had dreams... sorry, *"unrealistic dreams,"* according to him. He seemed so bothered by this *bubble* of mine.

He wasn't the first man to have raised this, you know, and he wasn't the last either. Most men made it a point to tell me I lived in a bubble. In fact, it's not just men, even womxn would tell me this, but I routinely heard it from the men I dated. Do you wonder why they thought I lived in a bubble? What was it that made my expectations in life... so unrealistic?

The unrealistic notion in my head: that I had a voice.

"You're being casually sexist," I would say at something that was usually very sexist, but I'm obviously conditioned to tiptoe around a man's feelings, so I don't hurt him but still find a way to get my point across. I would act like his statement is *a little sexist* and he would very often turn around and say, *"Oh, my God, not everything is sexist. You live in a bubble where womxn are the victim."*

Umm… if by bubble you mean Earth, then yes, sure, because womxn *are*, in the battle of sexes, *usually* the victim.

Once, an ex-boyfriend's brother (let's call him… Dee) actually tore apart my whole identity to the extent that for the many months to come, I wasn't entirely sure of who I was anymore. *What did I want from life? Where was I headed? Where did I want to go? Was I capable enough? What was the fucking point?* These were just some of the thoughts I had every day. It was the first time I started actively lying about my professional growth at dinner parties, talking to strangers on autopilot, numb, unaffected by my blatant lies. I felt more *little* than I ever had before.

What had Dee done to have this effect on me? Well, somewhere on the other side of the world, Dee turned to me and said, *"You're a naive girl. You are not even a real writer. To be honest, your writing is pathetic and banal. You're nothing but a floozy. You're not an actor either. You're just… some influencer that my brother is blinded by. Who even are you? My brother just can't see that he's wasting his time on a woman that isn't good enough for him and is breaking our family,"* not just once, not twice, but repeatedly, over six hours.

These are *not* things that would usually affect me because I don't let what the world says get to me. I used to, before I learnt to filter it out. This time, however, I was vulnerable because I had let down my guard. I had opened up… to get to know this man's family. I was looking to be *validated.*

When Dee said these awful things, I let him speak…

1. Because he seemed so angry that I thought he needed to let it all out of his system.

2. I wanted very much for his family to love me. There's always a power imbalance when you're the *girlfriend* meeting his family (as we've established in Chapter 6) because you have to *prove yourself* and *win them over.* And in that process, they *usually* have the power to treat you like absolute shit and get away with it. You

cannot, of course, do the same back because then you'd be an absolute *bitch*, wouldn't you?

My boyfriend at the time stood up for me the best he could... but the problem wasn't that at all; the problem was that I had opened myself up to a group of people (his family) that thought it was okay to insult me, my identity, my dignity, my self-worth in the name of *"casual debate."* When he was asked to apologise, he refused to because he said he's *"learning to bite his tongue"* and *"not speak the truth as often because evidently, people cannot handle the truth."* He said that if he's poked too hard, then he's not going to lie about what he thinks. He's going to tell the truth, as he did that night, and maybe *"she (that's me) should learn to take it with a pinch of salt."*

Take it with a pinch of salt.

The man I was dating accidentally repeated those words to me in a fight once. Frustrated, he said, *"Why can't you just take it with a pinch of salt?"* He was immediately sorry. He was also sorry the next day, but that's still not the point. I wasn't even offended because I suddenly realised that *conditioning* is such a powerful tool. If enough people repeat something often enough to you, you will begin to *think* it. Which is why it's so important *who* you surround yourself with. Which is why when his brother insulted me, I absolutely broke. I broke because I knew... that at some point in my life, I'm going to have to make a choice.

A few months later, Dee said, *"Why does it matter to her what I say about her? Why does it matter what anybody is saying? If she loved you, it wouldn't matter to her. My wife doesn't care when the family speaks shit about her, so what's her problem? Maybe you should ask yourself if she even loves you enough?"*

This would be a good point to acknowledge that people aren't always aware of what they're *really* saying underneath all the pretence bullshit. His words were drowning in his misogyny, and thanks to all the years of struggling to catch a breath in this ocean of sexism, I knew I wasn't going to let it drown me. What he was *really* saying was, *"If she loved you... she would put you above her self-worth. She would put the relationship above her own identity, just like my wife has."* Because what is a womxn that doesn't compromise? What is a womxn that doesn't let go of her own dignity to avoid conflict? I'll tell you what she is, she's a *homewrecker.* She breaks homes and makes families fight with each other. Because how dare she demand any more respect than she is voluntarily given? How dare she object and take you away from us... for the sake of her own self-respect?

After months of abuse from my ex-boyfriend's brother, his mother questioning my character, his father questioning my career choices and why couldn't I find another *hobby* that complemented his son's life goals, I finally told my ex-boyfriend that I no longer had the strength to continue the relationship anymore, that I couldn't hold onto this much longer, knowing I am not respected, that I had to let go because I was tired. *That's* when his family turned around again and said, *"Why is she so insecure that she needs to be validated by everybody?"* By the way, it wasn't one of those *"tell her not to care about people that don't respect her, why does she need our validation, tell her to ignore us."* No, not at all. It was more of a *"keep talking to us when we want to talk, act polite, drink with us, sit with us, come across the world to meet us, reply to our messages and be the good girl that checks up on our family and talks to the parents now and then and keeps the family together, but isn't insecure in a way that she needs some sort of appreciation, respect, or validation from us."*

We will disrespect you. We will then deny it. When asked to apologise, we will refuse to. We will insult our son's choice, but if he *dares to fight with us because of you,* be sure that we will hate you. But *you* ignore it all and be nice to *us—because if you loved him, that is what you would do.* You would forget your own identity and cater to our existence.

Basically, don't be a fucking hindrance. Whatever you're going through, whatever you are feeling, fix it. Why can't you just stop feeling that way for the convenience of everybody else? Why can't you... just behave the way a woman should?

"This is just life, my friend. You live in a naive bubble if you think it's any different" were the words that made me break, now that I think back. I couldn't take it anymore. My first thought indeed was the filmiest of thoughts. I thought to myself that if only my mother hadn't raised me with so much self-worth and dignity, I would've handled this better. Compared to a lot of the womxn I grew up around, I was too privileged. I wasn't *taught* directly to be as accommodating as this just to make men feel better about themselves. I wasn't taught too well to bow down and take up less space. I was underprepared... for a man's world.

When someone says to you, particularly to *you* as a woman, that *"life is simply like this, it is unfair,"* they're not *usually* talking to you as a *human*. They're talking to you as a *womxn* because life *is* unfair to a whole other degree for women. Your character will be assassinated, your past will be used against you, your story of assault will be spoken of as though you could've done something differently, your clothes judged and your intentions questioned. You will have to pass a hundred tests before you are accepted, and even then, you'll constantly have to tiptoe around people's feelings for the rest of your life—because, remember, *life is unfair.*

What happens when men meet a woman's family in our culture? Quite the opposite. The parents are warm, loving, accepting, and welcoming. Especially if the man in question has a good stable career, like a lawyer, doctor, engineer, then the woman's family tiptoes around the boy, his feelings, and his family's feelings because they don't want to upset or hurt them. They don't want to ruin their *daughter's one chance at happiness.*

It turns out that life throws different types of lemons at you, depending on whether you're a man or a woman. We seem to get the old, rock-hard lemons that bruise when hit with, and there's no "make a lemonade."

A quick example of these lemons is *the family dynamic.* In most Indian families, womxn leave everything behind and live with their husband and their in-laws. Men don't live with their in-laws. Maybe there are exceptions for some single mothers, but *usually*, the womxn's parents *themselves* aren't comfortable with that atmosphere after they've *given their daughter away.*

Can't say the same about the man's parents. Why is it that a woman's parents after marriage automatically consider themselves a liability for the couple, while a man's parents consider themselves to be a *responsibility*?

How often have you heard stories or seen movies about the man and his evil mother-in-law? Stories of a mother torturing her daughter's husband in the kitchen or giving him grief about his shorts in the house or what time he came home from work, why he has never bothered to make chai for her, *did his mother teach him nothing?* In fact, the womxn's mother is *usually* the kindest to the man because, in the end, she wants her daughter to be happy. However, if the same womxn has a son, then she's likely to turn into this irrational, privileged, demanding, and abusive mother that thinks she's deserving of all the respect in the world from her son's wife, without having to bring anything to the table herself. This is how little respect we—the men, womxn, and society—think womxn are deserving of.

How crazy is that? We want our daughters to be loved, adored, and pampered in the family they marry into, but we do not welcome the daughters our sons bring home in the same way.

My fault, in all of this, is that *I expected to be treated like a man* because I didn't realise that being treated like a womxn was even a thing. I forgot that the rules were so different. My bubble was that in my head, I lived in a fairer world, where if men could get respect and opportunities in life, then so could I. I forgot that they were entitled in ways that I wasn't, simply because I was born a womxn. I forgot that *"this is the way of life, my friend"* was just a fucked-up excuse for treating womxn terribly. *Naive little me.*

I lived in a *bubble* where I demanded the same respect that men were given for simply existing, for doing nothing particularly special at all. In my bubble, people didn't just get away with saying terrible and awful things just because they were men, and women weren't expected to be more compassionate about saving their relationships than they were about their dignity. In my world, when you hurt somebody, you apologise. And if my mother had to be nice to a man and his family, then *I demand the same politeness back from his family too.* Neither of us is doing a favour by being with the other person. Let's not fool ourselves, eliminating dowry isn't good enough if you don't start treating the womxn's family as *equals.*

In my *bubble,* it wasn't okay for me to lower my self-worth just to cater to his family's ego. My mother didn't raise me like that. She raised me to be strong and independent and value my identity. Because *who even are we, in the absence of what we think of ourselves?* It is important to be humble, kind, and grounded, but don't you ever, ever let anyone make you feel like you're too little for this world and all of its conveniently laid out opportunities for a man.

It doesn't matter how short your shorts are, or how much money you make, or how much cleavage your last display picture showed. It doesn't matter if you're naive and you believe in the goodness of this world. It doesn't matter if you live in a bubble where you think people should be kind-hearted, and it doesn't matter if you're hurt every single time, even when they aren't. It doesn't matter if you like to write poetry or movie reviews on Google. Or maybe you're 30 and you still write in your diary. Maybe you write to make other people feel good about themselves. Maybe you love with all your heart and hurt with all of it too. Maybe you're too forgiving, and you're trying really hard to save money so you can travel, or help your family, or maybe do both. Maybe you have some really bad days when you look like shit and your hair is a mess, and on other days you don't even want to get out of bed at all. Maybe in summers, you like lying down in your shorts and tank top so you can think better. Maybe you do it in winters too. Maybe you want to stay out with your girlfriends until 2 am on Saturday, and you know what, *maybe you just don't like making chai*—not for your own mother and never for his either.

Maybe you are all of the above, but maybe you are none…

It doesn't matter. It doesn't matter how you identify with yourself—for whoever you are, however big or small, *you are fucking amazing.* You are beautiful and flawed and sexy to someone else, *yes,* but first, you are the most amazing thing that's ever happened to… *you.*

Don't you ever dare let them make you feel so small about yourself that you prove them right.

I wish someone had told me that, and I need to make sure you have that someone in me. I let myself feel too fucking little. I let myself feel pathetic and unwanted. I let myself feel like there was something wrong with me for far too long. I felt like *I* was the problem, like *I* was too demanding. I told myself that *maybe I was just as selfish and insecure as they told me I was.* Maybe I was an *"attention-seeking slut"* and he deserved better. Maybe my words were banal and my writing too ordinary and who did I think I was anyway, trying to *"write to womxn"* like I even knew anything about womxn... Who did I think I was, other than *just some girl somewhere who was wasting her time along with everybody else's,* and *he* deserved better than *me.* *"I should stop being such a hindrance in people's lives,"* I began to tell myself. *"Maybe they were right when they called me a drama queen and a bully, for standing up for myself."* My desire to be respected was too demanding. It was causing people trouble, so *why couldn't I just stop being so difficult? Why did I need to be respected by people that demanded a lot more than just formality in return? How selfish could I be...? I... should be ashamed of myself for breaking a perfectly happy family. I am a bad womxn.*

I have let myself feel all these awful things about myself in the past. I felt pathetic and small, and there's very little left of you when you're constantly told not to take up too much space in this world. You're told to shut up and not express yourself, not demand anything, and not to be so difficult. I went through an extremely dark place, and I dug myself a deep hole. I was so depressed for a year that I stopped writing. I stopped wearing what I wanted. I stopped doing the things that made me happy. I stopped looking for work. I stopped telling people what I was thinking. All I knew was that *I wasn't good enough. I just wasn't enough.* Something was wrong with *me.*

Eventually, it took the elimination of constant toxic behaviours, elimination of toxic people, addition of therapy, and a lot of help from the people that love me (hence, I always say a safe space is so important) to remind me *why I mattered. Why it was important for me to not give up.* I was reminded that for every young womxn that resonates with my words every day, *if I gave up now, then I wouldn't just be giving up on myself, I'd be giving up on my womxn too.*

Now I couldn't let that happen, could I?

I need you to know that often, *it is not your fault.* Even when they tell you it's your fault, usually your only fault is that as a womxn, you dream of a world where you're treated with equality.

You have to stop blaming yourself.

Stop surrounding yourself with toxic people that make you feel small.

You are important.

You are beautiful.

You are talented.

You are strong.

You deserve to be respected.

You deserve in-laws that bloody well *respect* you as a person and acknowledge that their child has done you no favours by being with you.

You deserve a family that respects you and treats you with the same amount of dignity that they expect in return.

Your clothes are not too short.

And the length of your clothes is none of their business.

Your breasts and your legs are not theirs to control or hide.

Don't let anyone else decide if you're going to work or not, or what sort of work you're going to do.

Don't let other people *decide* when it's time for you to have a child, including your partner. They don't have the right to *force* you to have a child. Having a family is a huge decision to make, and while it's the decision of two people (communicate if you are ready or not before you go ahead with it), it is *your body* that goes through the hormonal changes. It is your routine and life that will halt/change forever more than anyone else's, so don't you ever let anyone tell you when it's time for you to compromise on your future to get pregnant. *It is time when you feel it's time,* and if you're ready today, then you should speak to your partner about their plans. *But if you never feel it, then I guess you just never feel it.*

You are enough.

You are more than enough.

You are not taking up too much space.

If you're feeling difficult, then *be difficult.*

If you're feeling angry, *be angry.*

If you're feeling unwanted, *leave.*

Don't stay just because you have to prove your love to others. If anyone should be proving their love for you, it should be the people that expect you to let go of your own self-worth.

It's okay to be naive and believe that this world is better than what some people make it out to be... being hopeful is a *good* thing. We don't need any more pessimists. They will try to push you down to their own level, but you need to remember not to fall—*because pessimists won't catch you either.*

When you feel weak, just remember, *there's nothing wrong with you.* Read this again, and then reread it as many times as you need to remind yourself that you do not need to settle for anything less than what you deserve. You are not *"running out of time,"* and if people make you feel terrible about yourself, then *walk away*—leave them. Stop being petrified of the unknown future and wondering if you'll ever find anyone even half as good as the person you are currently with. If you are unhappy, if they restrict you from seeing your own potential, then they're not the one for you. *You will be happier on your own because you'll be one step closer to finding someone better when you are alone.* We keep making the same mistakes and expecting different results. Stop settling for less.

Say no, say no, please, my love, learn to say no.

At every step of the way, society and its people are going to tell you to *"take it with a pinch of salt,"* to *"get over it,"* to *"stop being so difficult,"* and at every one of those steps, you're going to wonder if something is wrong with *you. Am I too sensitive? Am I not enough? Am I wrong?*

That's when I want you to take that salt (don't use their stupid lemons) and add some fucking chilli to it instead. Cook a meal, make a drink, down a tequila shot—do whatever you want with it—but don't let that salt burn you. *Do not let it contaminate your sense of self.*

This is me, here, right now, answering that silly question you keep asking yourself—*what is wrong with me?* Nothing at all is wrong with you. Be difficult. If you feel like you aren't being heard, *shout.* Create a scene when it's needed. Leave if it's no longer satisfying you. And fuck the people that want to break your bubble. *You protect that bubble of yours.*

This is my task for you; it's the most important thing you will ever do for me: *protect your bubble.* Far too many people want to burst it, but there are going to be so many more womxn to come like you and me. They have been walking a very long time, fighting the same fight as us, sometimes even bigger ones, and if their bubbles have burst along the way, they're going to need to rest in your bubble for a while and feel safe again. We are going to have to protect them. If anything, make this bubble of yours bigger, so big that someday society will realise that *if they try to burst it, they'll be blown up with it too.*

Make a list of things they blame you for and ask yourself: is it really your fault, or is it because you're a womxn?

My Notes

My Notes

CHAPTER 15

CHOOSE A PARTNER, NOT A WINNER

A friend of mine dated someone who thought her skirt was too short and asked her to *"wear something else"* when she was getting ready to go out but later asked her to put on the exact same skirt in the bedroom that night because he thought she looked extremely sexy in it, which was why he wanted her to change in the first place—he wanted to save it for *himself.*

I say *"a friend of mine"* even though this has happened to at least 15 women I know, and easily three to four times to myself.

The only advice, based on my personal experiences, I could ever give you about finding someone in your life, is to find someone that loves you in a way where they *do not wish to own you.* You are not a trophy, you are not an achievement, you are not a burden or something your father has *given away* to your partner, nor are you an object. You are not less than him, nor are you his *responsibility.*

We often look at women as going from the father's responsibility to becoming the husband's responsibility, and I don't know what kind of life you want to personally live, but find someone that doesn't literally treat you like you are *his*.

You can be a partner, you can be a lover, a wife, a girlfriend, a soulmate, a mother to his children, the person he shares this life with, and hell, you can even be his dirty whore and his bitch in the bedroom if that's what you two find kinky, but regardless of what you are to your partner in moments and places *by choice*, the day you lose your own identity and become *"his"* is when your own decisions are *no longer yours*.

Most people in relationships are extremely insecure. Men and womxn both, in different ways. However, given that as of today, men are hierarchical and *usually* hold more power in relationships, they also have the tendency to be more controlling (there are exceptions). I know enough womxn that have at different points been told not to wear that short dress, or that top because the neckline is too deep, or even that colour of lipstick, don't go out this late, don't upload that photo—maybe you know some womxn too? Maybe you're going through it yourself? You'd be surprised at just how common this is.

There are plenty of men out there who will ask you to change your clothes because they think you look *too attractive* in your outfit, and turning other men *on* is somehow considered *your* fault/something you can *avoid* by changing your clothes. What they're really saying is that you can stop men from doing/feeling something by curbing your own desires and altering your own life, *but if you still choose not to compromise,* then it's *your* fault. A common belief, trust me. And if you don't trust me, look at religious customs and traditions—*any/most* of them believe that women's bodies are a distraction to men.

A man I briefly dated, who told me to go back and change, had this warped logic that if he found me attractive in my shorts and also ended up *with* me, *what's to say I won't end up with another man that finds me attractive too?* I often wonder what's more disturbing, the fact that he thought so little of himself that he didn't think I wanted to stay, or even worse, that he thought of me as just a piece of meat that any man who found attractive could take home—*like I had no say in any of this.*

Similarly, another very good friend of mine dated a guy for over a year who was so fucking abusive that it still makes my blood boil just thinking about it. If one night she didn't talk to him before going to sleep, he would call her/leave her texts telling her she's a whore and a slut every morning when she woke up. We had a sleepover one night, where we stayed up until dawn talking about our lives and our friendship. I don't remember when, but we both fell asleep watching TV. I woke up to cover her with a quilt and move her phone aside, which hadn't stopped vibrating, and *that's* when I saw all these *awful, abusive* messages. He left her texts saying *she's a whore, and she's probably fucking someone right now, ignoring him, because that's the kind of dirty slut she is.*

I couldn't go back to sleep. It bothered me that she *hadn't even told me.* I confronted her in the morning and asked her what was going on. Had she cheated on him? Because he still had no right to speak to her like that. I couldn't understand what was happening… Finally, she confessed that this was just his pattern on *most nights* that she didn't call before going to sleep. It wasn't a new development, and now that they'd been dating for half a year, she was almost used to it. I couldn't believe she was going through so much and hadn't said a word, simply because she thought we would all judge *her* for *his* awful behaviour.

Let's rewind to the first time they met. All my girls and I were out on a weekend. They met each other at a club and liked each other *immediately.* They had common friends and hung out most of the night. In fact, I barely saw her that night because she was with him the entire time. Turns out, they went to the same school and knew each other since then. At the end of the night, she said she wanted to spend more time with him and we should go home and not wait for her. She was so happy; we teased her a little and giggled about it in the toilet. I took his number just in case her phone switched off or her parents asked who she was with, and that was it.

Apparently, they booked a hotel room and stayed up all night drinking and talking and laughing. *She told us it was absolutely beautiful.* She said they really liked each other, which they must have because they started dating immediately after.

A few months into the relationship though, every time he couldn't get through to her—she could be sleeping, showering, watching TV, with family, out with her friends, working late—for whatever reason, if he couldn't reach her, he would start excessively abusing her because according to him, *if she fucked him the first night they met in a hotel room, who's to say she isn't doing it every night with other men?*

It was the most absurd thing I had ever heard. He couldn't trust her—because she slept with *him* the first night they met. It's confusing because they had been dating ever since they met and she was *always* with him; she never went out with us because he didn't like it. But if she did go out, or wasn't reachable, it was just evident that she was *"being a whore, the way she was a whore with him."* I could not believe it. I wanted to cry and kill him at the same time—a very confusing and confronting state of mind to be in.

What I just didn't understand was, why was he acting like there was only *one* of them who had sex that first night? One of them being *a whore* in his words? What about *him, didn't he sleep with her too?* Why wasn't he questioned or tagged *untrustworthy?* The fact that he took her to a hotel and paid for a room and spent the whole night *with her* seemed completely fine when it came to his own character, but it made her a slut. He wasn't held up (or down) to the same standards as her?

What the actual fuck?

This isn't even news to us, is it? Think about it. Even in the instances where men *pay* for sex and book hotel rooms and spend the night with sex workers, *we don't really judge the men that sleep with these womxn.* We judge those in the business of selling themselves because as a society, we've just accepted *this is how men are,* haven't we? *"Eliminate the sex workers, put a thick fat fucking blanket on the demand for supply. Make it illegal, that'll solve the problem. This way, they have no respect and no rights. Our men, on the other hand, well..."*

Never mind that he turned out to be a lying piece of shit who made up a story about his own mother having an affair in order to gain sympathy from us. My friend also caught him cheating on her, and when she confronted him while he was driving her home, he hit her head on the front seat car window and held her down, suffocating her all along while *driving the car.* She couldn't physically move or breathe properly, so in order to make him stop, she kicked him with her high heels and broke his nose. Shit really went down. Either one or both of them could've had an accident and died that night, but what got to me the most is that *this...* was not the first time he had hit her or hurt her. *This...* was not even the first time I was hearing of such abusive men in relationships. This man was not an exception to the rule. He wasn't like this because he was a *rare asshole.* Nope, he was, sadly, a very common stereotype. I've talked to far too many womxn who go through this sort of abuse on a regular basis in India, and it's made me realise that the only reason I know so many women's stories is because after I was abused myself, I chose to speak about it publicly. Had I not spoken up, *I may have never known the others.*

I was once contacted by a womxn who wanted to let me know that the man who shot my YouTube video about *eliminating the violence and abuse women face in sexual relationships and families* was her boyfriend, and he had been beating her up black and blue. She sent me all the abusive messages from him, showed me photos of her bruised, bleeding face, and said that she wanted me to know because after she saw the video he had helped me create, she couldn't keep it a secret anymore. She was in so much physical pain, she couldn't even go to work. She was petrified of him, and here he was, helping me talk about *violence against women.* He would actually sit with me and talk to me about how horrible it is that men abuse their power and it's about time we encourage more women to speak—while he was punching and beating her up himself.

When I confronted him, he ever so casually said, *"Dude, Saloni, she brings out the worst in me. She pushes my buttons. I can't believe you're so angry but you don't even want to know why I hit her?"*... I couldn't do it anymore. I told him that better be the last time he *ever* spoke to me in his life. I wanted to talk about him publicly, in case he'd done it to other womxn because we sure as hell had a lot of common friends in the film industry. But his now ex-girlfriend said she'd prefer to just erase him from her life and forget all about him, instead of taking more limelight for being physically assaulted. Given the sort of taboo around working in the film industry, a lot of women are not only judged but also called back home by their families for being involved in *such characterless things.*

And to think, I would've never known... had I not been so vocal about women and abuse myself.

There's another thing I need to say before I move ahead: I am so proud of that woman for leaving him. I am so proud of every womxn everywhere who walked away from abuse whenever she was ready to—*because it sure as hell isn't easy.* I'm so proud of my friend for finally deciding to leave. Abusive relationships can start to feel like a suffocating trap in ways that blind you from reality and make you so powerless that the truth is no longer that you *don't* want to leave, but you genuinely think that you *can't.*

My friend's abusive ex-boyfriend was the kind of person that once while kissing her in a lift, he pinched *my* breast and thought I wouldn't say anything. There were four of us in a lift, and he had the *nerve* to pinch me *while* he kissed *her.* I was so shocked and numb that as soon as we got out of the lift, I froze. I stood there and told my other girlfriend what had happened. She said we had to immediately confront it and so, on the way home, we did. What happened afterwards sadly set our friendship back for a few months. She said she didn't believe me and that I was only saying this because we hated him. She also said she would need to see the CCTV footage to actually believe that her boyfriend had done it, maybe we were just *drunk and mistaken.*

I can't say it didn't create a massive barrier between us... it did. We stopped talking for a while, and that's when I realised that if I disappeared from our friendship and let her become isolated enough to have nobody left in her life except for this awful human being, then *he* would've won. Cutting communication with her would only mean that he'd convince her *he is all she has, the real support system, unlike her fake friends.* I didn't want that, so I stayed in touch. I did my part while maintaining as much distance as I could. I made sure I kept telling her that the abusive messages every morning were *not* okay, and after almost a year, when she caught him cheating and he hit her in a moving vehicle, when *she left him*, I'm glad we were just a phone call away.

She might have still stayed. A lot of womxn do. She had to make one of the toughest choices she's ever made. She chose to leave and for that, I will always be so fucking proud of her, but I also know that *the decision to choose yourself isn't one that happens overnight, and it sure as hell isn't easy.*

The first time I met one of my ex-boyfriends—we were on our first date—he told me he'd seen me on Instagram (years before that blue tick) and that he saw a video of me counting all the abuses I had memorised in Hindi and could say in one go. He said, *"It was so cute, the way you were counting them on your fingers, talking in that accent of yours. It's the first time I have heard a girl say all these Hindi bad words so adorably. I think you're amazing, Saloni."* To which, *I* thought, *wow, a man who doesn't want to control me and tell me I shouldn't upload such videos but actually thinks it's cute, how refreshing.* Thanks to the low bars we've set for good men, he and I started dating. Other than a lot of awful issues in our relationship that are too exhausting to get into right now, but I will talk about eventually, what happened a few months later is what actually *got to me.* I was about to put up *Part 2* of that same video on Instagram when he turned around and said he didn't want me to upload it. I laughed, thinking it was a joke, and when I said I was going to do it anyway, *we had a big fight.*

At the time, I felt like someone was playing a ridiculous prank on me because I couldn't really understand what was going on. We met *because* of that video, yet here he was, telling me not to upload it. Was he going to pull out a *"you've been fooled!"* sign anytime now? He didn't. I, however, did try extremely hard to understand what the problem was, given that he wasn't very clear about it. He shifted between *"you just don't get it, do you?"* to *"it's inappropriate, Saloni!"* I thought I was losing my mind. Eventually, he yelled out the words, *"It was different then! You weren't my girlfriend, and it was cute, but now you're my girlfriend, yaar. It doesn't look cute anymore.*

How can you be so childish? What will people think? That I cannot even control my girlfriend… Oh, look at what he lets her upload!"

That… was the moment. I had wasted all that time trying to figure out what was wrong, and it turned out to be just age-old hypocrisy and toxic masculinity. It turned out to be the misogynistic ways in which we condition our men and women to believe that *anything* a woman does *after* she is in a relationship is a *direct reflection* of the man and *his* respect. It's *his* responsibility to control *her*. From what she wears to what she says in public to where she goes… it is all a reflection of how well-*tamed* she is.

But at least he hasn't hit me like the last one, I thought to myself. The low standards for men were still very much intact.

I was so hurt at that moment that I couldn't really fight back. My world felt like it had shattered, and I felt so weak. I started to see how controlling he was. I noticed the ways in which he controlled and restricted his siblings and what they wore. I suddenly realised that the fundamental reasons *why* I had liked him were all lies. I'd started dating a man based on his best behaviour, which was far from his true self. He said and did things to *impress* me, but in reality, he didn't even like who I was. Or maybe he liked it and wanted to tie me down and tame me. Keep it for himself, love it, live with it, let it entertain him, but also turn me into the good girlfriend/wife he deserved in front of the world. Well behaved, cultured, mannered, polite, poised, pretty, a trophy.

I didn't upload the video that night after all. I gave in because I just didn't have the energy to fight him when I was hurting that much. I waited until I could gather my thoughts and finally uploaded the video after a few months. I firmly believe that the periods of my life I've spent thinking *"why is this happening?"* in silence, without retaliation, are the moments that made me as strong as I am today. I needed time… I needed time to understand what was happening in my life, to figure out who I was, and to *believe that it wasn't my fucking fault.*

It wasn't that simple at all though. In those months of silence, I also stopped interrupting him when he was talking to people. I stopped voluntarily joining conversations that he was having with strangers because he'd say it was *"rude and disrespectful"* of me to involve myself in a conversation he was having with someone unless he'd asked for me to. *"Don't you know not to speak in the middle when I'm talking to someone? Do you ever wonder what they will think of me when you interrupt?"* he'd ask when we were all alone within his four walls, where he could *finally say these things out loud.* I learnt that we were so much happier when I didn't disobey. So, I did as I was asked to. I didn't speak much in public places or tell anyone our problems, or even dare be the sort of outspoken person that would cause him disrespect. At every step, he'd tell me to *"stop being so vocal, stop saying such things publicly, stop being so loud, stop being so you."*

I fought whenever I couldn't take it anymore and stayed quiet whenever I could because somewhere deep down inside whispered that very low bar, *"He's never hit me, what more could I want?"*

When it ended, I realised just how suffocated I had been feeling for the last year. I realised how tame and timid I had become, and that… is how I *exploded* into the me that had been buried under the me that *men wanted.* It wasn't as though I was just meaninglessly buried though. Inside, I was growing. Parts of me were becoming so strong that even I didn't know who I was going to become once I finally broke away.

However, unlike the movies, in real life, the journey to becoming a better you is not a consistent straight line. Because you make mistakes, you learn from them, then you make new mistakes, and often you repeat the old ones again. And all along, you're learning something new about yourself and the world we exist in. When you finally think, *"This is it, I know better now,"* you absolutely make another mistake, often a huge one too. This journey is especially tough when everything you stand for, you often stand alone. When you go *against* the tide, it's going to be harder and harder to swim through… and every now and then, you'll find yourself changing directions and going with the pressure simply because you're tired and exhausted. By the time you start fighting your way back in the opposite direction towards your destination, you have so much more to make up for than you did before. But if you hadn't gone along with the tide at that moment, you might have never lived long enough to try again.

Which is why even after all the drama and the bullshit, I made more mistakes.

I briefly dated someone for a few months who said *he wanted me to wear salwaar kameez every day of the week* because he didn't *like* me wearing shorts (I spoke of him briefly at the start of this chapter). So, I went over to my mum's house and got *all* my Indian clothes back home, changed my entire wardrobe: Indian clothes, every day. I made so much effort, and it lasted like five days. My five days of swimming with the tide. I think I could have maybe done five more before I broke. I was doing *okay* until one day, when he came home and tried to sleep with me because he was so turned on that I was wearing Indian clothes every day (it wasn't even a surprise or a gesture of some sort; *he'd very clearly demanded me to do it because my nudity bothered him*). I couldn't believe that the idea of *controlling* me and my life choices was *his idea of romance*. It actually turned him on. I realised that I felt suffocated, depressed, and unhappy every goddamn day as I put on my salwar because I didn't even know who I was anymore, and *he was turned on by it like it was some power trip. Sick fuck.*

That's when I snapped. I couldn't have known I was making a mistake at the start… you never can. People who tell you that *"you should've known better,"* like you would have *assumed* that all the men you fall for will be shit, well, they're low-key *victim-blaming;* don't listen to them. The desi girl vibes lasted for one whole week. After that, I was back to swimming against the tide, and honey, I realised that salwar swimming is *no joke—no wonder I was slower.* The bikini trunk had to be opened. I'm not even kidding, I broke up and went to Thailand with my best friend.

I think I'm an extremely stubborn person who can't seem to give up on my choices, nor do I easily give up on people until I snap and break and can't take it anymore. I don't leave while there's still time and it's healthy. No, I stay… and I let it pick me apart slowly until I know I've given the relationship everything I had, and *that's* when I leave. Also, that was just me testing you. *What I just did is victim blame.* Claiming that *"I'm stubborn and so I don't leave"* is harmful and self-destructive. People that stay in mentally and physically abusive and toxic relationships because *of power imbalance, taboos, and societal pressure often tend to blame themselves when they shouldn't.*

When I do leave, I leave with a lesson learnt and cognizance to share. I leave scarred, but also indestructible. I leave knowing in my heart that I was strong enough to leave, saddened with the realisation that in reality, not every woman out there is.

You know why *I think* women stay in such awful relationships for so long? Because our whole lives we are told that we're doing something wrong. To tone it down, to compromise, to change, and after a point, you don't know when you should fight back and when you should *actually* change. Because change is a good thing, right? You *should* stop smoking, you *should* stop screaming, you *should* stop being aggressively angry, you *should* change your bad habits as/when you're ready, but when you're continuously told to *"stop"* doing *everything* by your parents, your friends, your partner, your boss, your teachers, strangers on the internet, your neighbours, by an entire society—then you lose track of what is right and what is wrong. When do you say yes, and when do you rebel? When is it *okay* to stand up for yourself? What's too much? Especially when there are other womxn out there just like us, catering to these boundaries themselves and laying all the rules out for us. It isn't *man vs womxn*; it's *you vs everybody.*

Different ways of territorial behaviour

This chapter has been confronting to write, but I need you to know some of the different ways in which men are often territorial in relationships, commonly expressing clear ownership of the other person. Men are not raised to say things like *"I'm feeling insecure about your clothes, can we talk about this?"*; *"Can I try to convince you, or maybe you can convince me?"*; *"I find myself feeling jealous and I need to express it."* Forget *talking* about these issues to your partner, a lot of men won't even Google it in their own personal time or seek help to understand better *why* they are reacting the way they are or *what* can be done about it. In order to do that, one would have to first accept that maybe they are *wrong*. And if there's *one thing* I've learnt in an Indian household, it is that *men are never wrong; they're just misunderstood.*

Men are not the enemy here. It is their *upbringing* that I have an objection with. I don't think I can *change* men either. I would, however, love to reach out to the ones that *want to know how womxn are oppressed and why they feel so controlled,* the ones that *want to start a conversation and be more present and involved in this fight towards a better world with more equality,* men that are *aware* of their privilege, men that don't perpetually attack platforms for women empowerment with *"but what about men?"*

All I can do is share my stories and the stories of womxn that have spoken to me over the years. The stories I have grown up to. Words are all I have; they're my weapon and my strength. I feel like it's my responsibility to share them with you today—*find yourself a partner that doesn't control you or act like you are his property.* I know it's not going to be easy because you won't really know who the people are that will try and control you, until you are so deep in the relationship that you question your own actions and choices.

But you must *try your best.* Build a strong foundation with your self-worth. Have conversations. Ask questions. Don't hesitate to be who you really are around your partner. When you first meet them, ask them their views in life *again and again* without feeling like you're *too much for the first few dates.* It's okay to be too much—this is your *life* at stake. Be hectic. Challenge their views, and *let them challenge yours.*

As I said in the beginning, I don't really know *what* you want from your life. Maybe you're ambitious, maybe you don't want children, maybe you want to adopt kids like I do, maybe you want to travel or study further, maybe you like wearing clothes that are looked down upon, or you don't want to live with anybody's parents, maybe you don't want to give up your job or your friendships. Maybe you want to be married and be a mother, but you just want to be respected. *Whatever it is that you want, however big or small,* a person that loves you and wants a healthy relationship will *not tell you to compromise* on all the things you want in ways where they dictate the narrative of your life, nor will they think that they can *allow you* to live your own life. That doesn't make them progressive in any way. Instead, they would support your personal journey and your growth, or maybe you'll both realise that you're not right for each other, given that you want completely different things.

You have to try to evaluate a relationship or a situation for *what it is,* and not *what you wish it could become,* especially when the relationship you're in is abusive and/or controlling.

Patriarchy and conditioning

It took years to realise what was wrong with my relationships. The men I was settling for weren't in love with me but instead were winners who treated me like a trophy—or let's say an *expensive bird to flaunt in a cage* (my next book should be called *101 Metaphors That Don't Work*). I don't think all the men I was with were *terrible humans,* because some of them did good things for people around them, and they often made me laugh. But they were *raised* in a society where they are *taught* to be *winners,* not equal partners.

Only when I met Rahul did I realise that I actually had the potential to be wholesomely me, *as I am.* I remember the first few times (I still occasionally do this) when I asked him, *"Should I wear this? Is it okay?"* We would be getting ready to go out to meet his friends or his family, and he would oh-so-nonchalantly turn around and say, *"Why do you have to ask me every time? You can wear whatever you want to wear."* I realised I wasn't even aware that I was *asking* him, that's how conditioned I was for his approval; it had become a subconscious act. Now that he refused to partake in my toxic conditioning, I didn't know what to do with all this sudden freedom to wear whatever the hell I wanted without being told off for my neckline or the length of my dress or being tested and asked *if I thought what I was wearing was appropriate.* This new dynamic was refreshing, but also extremely uncomfortable at first. Suddenly making my own choices was unknown territory, one where I tiptoed, quietly wondering, *"Is he mad at me? Why the hell does he say I can wear whatever I want? How odd."*

Right before I met his mother for the first time, I wore a cute black dress and my mum angrily snapped and said, *"You just cannot wear that! Change!"* Now there's something I was used to. She immediately turned to Rahul, who she barely knew then, and said, *"Please tell her she can't wear this short dress. She can't wear it to meet your parents!"* Rahul laughed, standing outside my room in Adelaide, looking at my helpless puppy face that I often make, and he said, *"I can't tell her that... it's okay. I don't need her to be fake. She should wear whatever she wants to wear. She's still the same person in a salwar as she is in a bikini. They'll just have to accept that."*

My mother was *very* furious with him. She nodded disapprovingly and said I had met my match. It's a different thing altogether that she then somehow convinced me to wear a salwar kameez, which I've grown to regret until this day because when his family finally stumbled upon my Instagram, they were shocked and probably felt a little betrayed because I went to meet them in a *salwar*. In hindsight, our relationship might have had a smoother transition if I had just gone as myself, wearing something I was comfortable in. Mum, however, told me this was *"the best thing to do"*... because "first impressions mattered and later I could wear what I wanted," she said. Rahul, on the other hand, didn't like the idea of me going as someone I wasn't. He pointed out that his mother wouldn't wear a dress to fit into my life, so it seemed very unfair that I was expected to dress according to his family. *"What you wear shouldn't be anyone else's business."*

I know, right?

But, because my mother guaranteed this would give me brownie points in his family, I had to convince him that it was actually *I* who wanted to wear a salwaar and not the dress I initially said I wanted—do you see how twisted patriarchy and conditioning can be sometimes? My mother, who was worried about her daughter being accepted into a man's family, first convinced *me* to wear a salwaar, then she convinced me that this was extremely important for *my happiness,* and she guaranteed that if I did this right, made this *effort* as a *gesture* and cared about their culture, then *my life* in the future would be easier (FYI – false). So *I,* who *never wanted to* wear salwaar in the first place, found myself sitting on a sofa, trying to convince *my partner* that *he* had to understand *this* is what I truly wanted to do… oh, the irony.

I knew exactly what my mother was thinking at the time when Rahul said, "Saloni doesn't need to pretend." She thought he was wrong. A part of her believed that he *should* be setting certain boundaries for me, for the sake of *my happiness* in the future. She said, *"This doesn't last. They act like they don't care at the start. Eventually, when his family objects, he will tell you to remain within your limits. He should do so too, given how much you fly all the time."* Except it did last, it has for three years at least, and only time can tell what's in store for us in the future, but *my limitations are the ones that I set for myself.* She's right, I do fly a lot. I fly too high and I never want to come back down, and my mother may dismiss his unconditional support towards me choosing to spread my wings and be who I wish to be (err, a bird), but I also know that she can't help but give in to her own life long conditioning, what she was taught, *what she knows to be true.*

Was she happy? I think she would've felt the happiness if this brave world of ours allowed her to stop feeling scared for just a single second. Scared that he will change, that if his family doesn't approve of me, then he will leave and I will be judged. Scared that my bubble will burst. Scared that I'll one day have to learn to compromise. I knew as a mother *all she wanted* was to be happy that *her daughter is happy,* that she is free, and she makes her own decisions, but she also wanted me to be more than just an exception to the rule. Because exceptions are a gamble.

A life of having one's own worth should not only be a possibility for all womxn but should be the most *basic of things.*

Even today, when we're sunbathing on an island and I think I look extremely sexy in a photo he's just taken of me, but for some reason I exclaim, *"Ugh, I can't upload it because I'll get so many nasty comments, people will call me a slut again,"* he just turns to me and says, *"But you're not a slut. What even is a slut? You're dressing the way you like, why will you get hate? You look beautiful, just do it."* And I say, *"Trust me, I'll get randi hai comments,"* to which he responds, *"The girl I know doesn't back down from the fear of hate. That's not you, that's not who I fell for."*

I could be topless on a beach with my tits out, and he'll never turn around and say, *"Isn't this a bit much? Who are you trying to seduce? What are you trying to prove?"* In fact, he'll take out his camera and capture the way my eyes sparkle every time I conquer an internal battle.

He understands that my desire to be/feel attractive or look sexy has nothing to do with the people that find me attractive. People may find anything and everything attractive but that certainly isn't a good enough reason to limit women and their behaviours. People find cars in showrooms attractive too and not very often do you see them breaking in and riding off with it, proving that in our society, *actual objects* have more respect than womxn.

In conclusion

I often get told, *"You're extremely lucky and your partner is so very special because partners like Rahul don't exist."* Except that's not true; they absolutely do exist—*they are womxn.*

Womxn in relationships with men don't *usually* tell men to *"put on a shirt"* or *"you can't upload this photo because girls will look, why are you being a whore?"* *Women don't abuse* men when they show their body. Women are commonly *more supportive* of their partners wearing whatever they like, working however late/hard they wish to, studying, having friends, and living their lives without being restricted and chosen for because women have *always played the supportive role in relationships.*

Men, on the other hand, were always the leaders, providers, decision-makers, and we're *still* raising them to feel threatened, insecure, and territorial when *we ask for our freedom.* People think Rahul is an exception because *being a man, he's so supportive,* and we do not seem to know a great deal of men that are raised to be secure enough to *not* be threatened by a womxn and her freedom—*whatever her required freedom may be without the dictatorship of someone else.* Our expectation from men in society is so low that if he doesn't hit you/control you/tell you what to wear/stop you from working, then he is a *gift from God* and hence he's put on a pedestal because let's face it, *he's perfect.* I love Rahul; he's a great partner for many reasons outside of just behaving like a decent human. We both make mistakes, like everybody else. We both fight and say horrible things to each other too. And whenever we sit and talk about the way he's appreciated by people around us, we often wonder, "*Why is he always praised for not controlling me and doing things around the house, even though for generations women around the world who have done the exact same things for their partners, if not more, aren't appreciated for it at all?*"

Maybe we need to demand more from men? More than just "*he treats me like an adult and gives me freedom and so he's perfect.*"

That should be the most *basic* requirement from the men *and women* we date, not the *reason* why we settle.

This obviously doesn't mean that you shouldn't (constructively) criticise or question each other. Choose to talk about why you've chosen to be the person you are, where the desires come from. We ask questions and have debates and learn from each other's growth while also challenging it, and when we think the other person is maybe getting lost in their morality, we remind each other to stop and evaluate what *they* want to stand for *as a human being.*

I want you to find someone that respects you as an individual, and *that doesn't mean they won't make mistakes.* Of course, they will. The question is: *are you both equal? And are you willing to learn from your mistakes?*

Find someone that wants to love you and respects you as an individual human being, not a winner to whom you are a prize, or simply an extension of himself. It's easy to fall into a trap. If you're in one now, or have been in one, or feel like you're slowly falling into one... maybe you need to leave?

"If you don't like where you are, move. You are not a tree."

My brother sent me this quote once, and it changed the way I looked at life and relationships. Because once I knew I could *move* anytime I wanted, then maybe I wasn't as trapped as I thought I was?

Sometimes, the smallest of encouraging words are all the reminders we need...

Consider this your not-so-small, 7000-word reminder.

Write down the kind of person you want to spend your life with. Write the qualities you want in that person. What are the things that matter to you, and what are your deal breakers?

After every first date, every anniversary, every fight, and every break-up, I want you to come back and remind yourself of the things you wanted, be grateful for the ones you've found, and ask yourself if you need to leave for the things you still haven't found.

My Notes

My Notes

CHAPTER 16

IF IT HURTS YOU

I've lost count of the number of times something has hurt me, and I've been asked to simply get over it. It's usually *"you're overreacting"*; *"why are you so sensitive"*; *"that's your interpretation"*; *"it's honestly not that big a deal, you're blowing it out of proportion"*—or the worst, most basic, lacking any effort *"get over it."*

It's no surprise that people say it all the time... because I'm sure I've been in shoes other than those of the receivers. We all do it, but it only hits home when someone does it to *you*.

The truth is, we look at the world through a lens which makes us the centre of our every story—and fair enough, right? Why the fuck not? This is *your* story; no one can take that away from you. I'm just a writer in your story, the girl that inspired you to change your life in some small way maybe, and in my life, you're the reader (insert: cupcake). We're the hero of our own stories. We cannot feel the pain that people feel, and *they* can't feel our pain either. We are our own heroes—*as we should be.*

Over time though, I've realised that when someone tells us we've hurt their feelings, instead of listening to them, we react. We defend and we justify why we are right, even though someone else's pain *doesn't make you wrong;* it just means that they are hurt. Apologising doesn't make you wrong either. An apology often means that you never *meant* to hurt them, which, in all honesty, you probably (hopefully) didn't. You can always, at least, say that you're sorry they're hurting. *Lack of empathy does not make us strong; instead, it makes us weak.*

We have all been the person that has hurt someone without meaning any malice, and we need to look into the mirror when we behave a certain way and ask ourselves if we would want to be treated like that by other people.

And you're in luck today because *this chapter isn't just about their pain*—it's about *your pain.*

For whatever underlying reasons, most of us refuse to be the heroes of our own stories. We would rather tiptoe around other people in *their* stories, as though we don't deserve one of our own. I spent so much of my life being that person, I now know her like the back of my hand. Tiptoeing is an art, one that doesn't pay at all though, may as well have learnt ballet instead.

I remember being the girl that would feel like I've made a mistake every time I was hurt. Convincing myself that I was too much. *"Stop being so selfish, you shouldn't be so hard to deal with. Be more likeable. Feel less pain. Don't have expectations—after all, isn't that the best way to escape disappointment? Give it your everything. Expect nothing."*

Every time I was hurt, I thought I was just being oversensitive. I let the world tell me that feeling too much, too deeply, was *my fault.* A man I worked with once said what he loved about me the most was that I imploded... At first, that seemed so romantic. *"She implodes."* Except this man knew I had so much emptiness inside me, I felt hollow and sad from memories that felt like they were killing me slowly. Every time we met, he said he wanted to have a secret love affair because he wasn't *ready for the world to know about us.* However, he claimed to *really care about me.* Thanks to all the damage I've dealt with from men wanting to *hide me* from their families, I couldn't get myself to have this *secret rendezvous* despite his warped concept of romance. We agreed to be friends. I continued being the sad girl who imploded within; he continued to desire me for it. One day when he tried to touch me, I finally became the girl that *exploded*.

Facts: *Imploding is not sexy; it's fucking toxic.* This is not a tragic romantic movie. In the real world, you do *not* want to be Juliet. You want to be happy, trust me. You don't want to be with someone who loves you because they see the sadness in your eyes, or because you're the kind of womxn that implodes... there's nothing wonderful about him noticing that you're sad and glorifying your sadness through poetry and romance without actually helping you in any way. No, tell him to shut the fuck up and leave. Focus on *you* and help *yourself.* In fact, here's a suggestion... *stop imploding.*

Explode.

Your sadness isn't supposed to be romanticised. *It's supposed to be addressed.* It needs to be talked about, to be confronted. If we don't stop glorifying a woman's suffering, then how can we expect to see stories where damsels aren't helplessly distressed anymore?

I want you to know that if it hurts, *then it just hurts*. No questions asked. None of that *"but tone it down a notch."* No one else in this world should have the right to decide what hurts you. Neither should they decide the intensity with which you feel your pain.

When *Friends* ended, I bawled my eyes out for an entire day. I was just a little girl. I am not even sure if I knew I liked the show enough at the time... but I cried, and cried, and cried. A part of me felt broken because I knew it was over forever. The only friends I knew of, the ones that made me laugh, were gone. This was it; it was *over*. Strangely, I felt the same way about sunsets growing up. Before I began to love sunsets, I used to be petrified of them... the thought of something ending scared me, let alone a new ending every single day. It was scary, before it became hopeful.

I still cry while watching movies—a lot. Sometimes I cry so much that I cannot breathe... I really, truly *feel* the pain. When someone dies, when relationships end, when people leave, when feelings are shared, when a song touches me, when there is a fight, *I really feel it*. Even though I'm an actor and I know everything on camera is a performance, for a split second, I can't help but feel it. I relate it to my own memories. I feel it to be real, and for me, *it is real.* Stories are an extension of real life, and many of them, I resonate with. I don't know how else to explain it to you, but *I feel it.* Have you ever felt that ache in your chest? When your stomach churns and you try your hardest to breathe slowly, but you feel choked and tears just keep rolling down your cheeks...?

I feel like that a lot.

More than other people around me do. I feel too much, too often. For some people, that undermines my emotions; *"there she goes again, being so emotional."* But to me... it's a part of who I am. Just because I feel a lot simultaneously doesn't mean that it hurts less or that we get used to the pain. I'm just more aware of it at the moment, but it still hurts the same. It's like I can now watch myself from a distance *as* I'm feeling it. A part of me detaches, a part that knows I'll get through this, I'll be okay... maybe that's just my coping mechanism.

The reason I share things about myself in this book is mainly because I'm hoping you will realise that we are *all* flawed. So many womxn tell me every day that they want to be like me, but I don't think you need to be like *me*, when you can be such a great version of *yourself.* Maybe once you realise that I am heavily flawed and you still let me motivate you, when you can see my imperfections and my pain and yet love me, that is when you will know that *you too can be anything you want, not despite but with all that you feel.*

If you can know everything about a person and still believe in them, then you've got to start believing in yourself too. I am not better than you. I am not more capable, nor am I more deserving. I bet I've told a few people in fights that I am more deserving than them to hurt them, but that's exactly why I'm probably not.

This world is a scary place, you know? We must look out for ourselves. Don't let other people define your pain or its boundaries for you. Don't let them tell you that you're *too much*, or *too little* either. Don't overvalue or undervalue yourself. Know the difference between self-love and self-entitlement. I think two of the most important things to remember in order to be content in life are 1. have zero tolerance for bullshit and 2. the ability to filter out the things people say... I'm currently working on both. It's the only way you will ever be able to follow your heart or get where you want to be. Breaking rules, changing norms, altering social structures requires *courage*, and *courage* requires you to not give a fuck about what people say to/about you... Because people *will say things,* and you *won't* always be able to do anything about it, but if you let their words get to you, then you have already lost half the battle.

Listen to me, you cannot lose this battle.

Start small. Start with confronting the person who hurt you. And if/when they deny your pain, remind yourself that your pain is yours to feel. No one else can decide what is painful to you. However, let's add another extremely important layer of pain that people often feel. Sometimes, people are hurt simply because *you're living your life* and these people—parents, family, friends, controlling partners, neighbours, or society at large—want to have a say in *who you become, how you live, where you live, who you love, and what you wear.* That's when you can, if you wish to, apologise for their pain, but anything beyond that *is not your fault.* Don't let the world guilt you to a point where you *stop living,* please. Everybody always has *something* to say about someone else's life choices... you must try to distance yourself from their *opinions* of *who you are.* Don't let them decide what you should do with your one life. The pain they feel when they lose control over your life is not *your fault*—that is, in fact, caused by their hierarchical, toxic conditioning and their need to hold the power at all times. It isn't sustainable. People often feel confronted when you raise your voice, because it weakens their own place of authority. Don't be afraid of being a threat to their power.

Maybe unintentionally, but they're bullying you and it's abusive. Walk away. Say no to the subtle yet harmful forms of abuse that we give and receive daily purely because we've made it acceptable to disparagingly control people.

Your pain is real. If it hurts you, then it hurts you. Period (which also hurts).

My Notes

My Notes

CHAPTER 17

FULL-TIME MOM, PART-TIME HUMAN

I don't think I actually, properly understood what *mansplaining* was up until the day I was writing this chapter. I have heard it, I have read the definition, I have looked up examples, and I have seen men do it. But this feeling you get when you're being mansplained and are actually *aware* of it, instead of feeling like *"maybe I need help"*—it finally happened. It is a sense of sudden frustration that comes from a man patronising you, but *pretending* to be polite. Teaching you a thing or two, telling you what it's like, in this case, to be a mother. Somehow, he knew better than me, as he said, *"You're not a mother, Saloni, you don't know."*

I definitely did not know the same way he seemed to, I thought.

I woke up that morning being mansplained about what the troubles and considerations of being a *full-time* mother were. You've got to see the irony there. I, as a woman, never asked a man about the troubles in the first place. *I* actually never asked him anything at all, but I still had this obnoxious, narcissistic man (he's an ex, could you guess?) unnecessarily patronise me. After all, isn't that why it's called mansplaining? Oh, he's the same ex that also used to tell me *"stop your randi rona"* every time I cried in our fights. *He* went on to tell me in a huge argument that I was *exaggerating and destroying* our simple conversation. I swear to God, this is not the first time in my life that a man has felt the need to explain something to me that was never a question, to begin with, get offended when I asked him to back off, and then shifted the whole blame onto me.

That morning's experience got me thinking about a few things. For starters, I asked myself what a *"full-time mother"* means. Sometimes in life, it's necessary to be confronted and placed into a situation that frustrates you enough to ask more questions. For me, this was one such moment.

A full-time mother, I said the words out loud to myself later.

Such a strange term when you think about it. Is there a *full-time father* too? How do you choose to become a *half-time mother?* Or a *half-time parent?* Because once you're a parent, aren't you just always a parent? Where does the half-time/full-time concept arise from? Caretaking, maybe?

I think—and I insist, *I think*—the reason why *full-time mother* is even considered a term is because we live in a society where once a womxn becomes a mother, we are hell-bent on making sure that everything she does, she does as a *mother*.

There's nothing wrong with being a mother or even behaving like one. What I don't understand is, *what is a mother supposed to behave like?* Because as per the socially constructed little boxes, a mother is supposed to have somewhat inhuman, *mother-like* tendencies. When we talk about women becoming mothers in an Indian society today, we expect to see a woman that stops identifying with *anything* outside of her children. There is a special dress code that a mother must follow. She mustn't work out excessively because, after all, *this bundle of joy that's entered her life is exercise enough.* Running behind this child is *all the cardio she needs!* Eating whatever stale food she can find once she's finished her motherly duties is the diet she must maintain. She must maintain a certain lack of skincare and an absolute lack of self-love. Now you can't possibly be a mother and be exercising every day, going to the gym, eating right, spending an hour or two making salads and grilling meat, or applying beauty products, only to wear a nice outfit—*as though you're asking for attention.* You're not a *MILF* now, are you?

Drinks with friends? No way. You can't be whoring yourself out like that. You're a *mother*, after all. A *full-time mother* at that.

Do full-time mothers still go on dates with their partners? Do full-time mothers have sex and also scream out orgasms? Do they talk about sex? Surely, given that they have such little time, mothers must at least have dildos? I don't know if you need me to answer these questions for you given that you know this little voice inside you, called *"log kya kahenge,"* is screaming *"NO!"*

Louder for the people in the back thinking *"talking of mothers in such a derogatory way... chee chee!"*

Once a mother, you don't go on dates... married *or not.*
You don't dress in attractive ways.
You don't expect romance.
You don't devote time to a fitter body.
You don't put your career above your family if you have one.
Oh, sorry, there's no if. *You better have a family—how else did you become a mother?!*
God forbid if you're separated, divorced, or a widow, you don't go on dates, *ever again.*
You become a good *wife* [insert: cook, clean, look after the children, dress well, look good but not good enough to *distract* him, maintain a peaceful environment in the house for a man to return to, let him fuck you when he needs to, and be his emotional support].
Mothers don't have feelings, desires, emotions, ambitions, whisky, sexual demands, apprehensions, dildos, break downs, goals, tequila, or dreams.

And if you think this isn't true because you have girlfriends that are moms and have great lives, are working and balancing motherhood, and putting up stories practising yoga (yes, I have those friends too)—*those* womxn, those mothers, are an exception to the rule, and not the rule itself. Most of those womxn, if not all, would have had to *fight* for the life they are living today. They would've had to argue, stand their ground, set boundaries, tolerate taunts and judgements. These womxn that you see being #momgoals are rebelling against the norm. They are breaking stereotypes. They've chosen a tougher path so that they can live the life they think they deserve and also have the family they want. So their daughters and their sons can have a better future. Those womxn could set examples and break taboos someday, with our help.

The #momgoals are a minority, not a majority. Most Indian women today *do not* rebel/break some forbidden rules. They don't have the support, the voice, the education, or the financial assistance to stand up for themselves. In the big tree of privilege and oppression, most Indian womxn are at the *bottom* of this tree, unaware of their power. Unaware that *they are the roots holding the forest together.* Their growth and voice are limited because they are dependent on the men in their families. They're raised with the discipline to take orders. Most Indian women cannot even afford to put their foot down and say they will work, or convince their husbands to wear a condom, and we're talking about *fitter bodies and flax seeds.*

Our womxn raise children on their own with little to zero help from the man. They quit jobs, stay home, and raise children knowing that they will look after the entire house (and often the 10 relatives), while the husband goes to work, because someone has to. *Except, mothers don't get some sort of free grocery pass or a free monthly travel pass. Money* buys things, and womxn, once they become mothers, stop earning money and become *entirely dependent on men* for their finances while they figure out what to do with this new human being that's just popped out, under the assumption that they are financially stable and looked after. Mothers don't *think* they're becoming dependent; they're just dividing jobs in their head. But when you become a *homemaker* and give up the ability to have an income, are you not automatically giving up your *right* to make independent decisions even when you're disagreed with?

When we are children, we're told by our parents that it's *"their house, their rules"*—when you grow up and have a house of your own, you can do as you please. But if we grow up and become dependent on our husbands, does it not then become *his house, his rules?* Whether you choose to work or be a homemaker, shouldn't you *at the least* be *able to work to support yourself* if and when needed?

Our culture doesn't promote a lifestyle where men and women both work and simultaneously both raise children. Men go to work, because *what does a man know about changing nappies?*

On top of it all, womxn don't even have their own lives once they give birth. Mothers don't have the luxury or space to understand their postpartum depression. *Most* Indian womxn don't even have hobbies or goals that don't align directly with their children.

Most Indian women, once a *full-time mother,* are expected to become a *part-time human.*

Let's try to break the pattern and help our mothers. Make a list of things that your mother does every day as a routine. Observe what she does in her free time. Ask her what her hobbies are/were and find a way to help her include them in her life again. Tell her about your own.

If nothing else, you might even find something you love doing together…

My Notes

My Notes

CHAPTER 18

(IM)PERFECT GIRLS

It's absolutely true that men and womxn *both* have insecurities, but men are yet to stuff socks in their underwear and fake abs in their t-shirts *on a daily basis*—that is how excessively we promote push up bras and ass pads. I once knew a womxn who used to work out wearing ass pads because she didn't want her trainer, or anyone else for that matter, to know that she had a smaller butt than she portrayed… defeats the purpose of having a trainer, if you ask me.

Of all the womxn *I personally know*, it's safe to say *most* of them hate too much about themselves. When I say hate, I'm not even exaggerating, sometimes I mean it. You may call the insecurities womxn have harmless… but to me, the ones I've seen are absolute self-loathing.

I don't think most people really understand or grasp the intensity with which womxn hate themselves due to the social expectation of what they're supposed to look and behave like, and men might never understand it either. It's not entirely *their* fault. It's just that I don't think womxn speak to men the same way they speak to other womxn when it comes to their bodies and their insecurities.

Have you ever sat in a group of men and heard them talk? Even if you haven't, that's okay. Pick up any movie and watch the stereotype conversations men and womxn have, or go out, grab a coffee, and eavesdrop. Boys talk about sports, music, cars, gadgets, games, girls, and if they're geeky, then they talk about coding or science.

Womxn, on the other hand, talk about makeup, fashion, jewellery, brands, things that glitter, boys, other womxn they hate, their arms, their butt, their stomach, their calves, their hair, their face, their *toes, and the annoying hair on their tiny toes.*

Most coming-of-age movies for young men don't have scenes where boys are standing in front of the mirror, pointing out their imperfections. *Mean Girls* and countless other films for womxn do. In fact, I've actually never seen men talk about their features or their hair the same way. Even the extremely insecure, conscious ones don't really talk about their eyelashes, their lips, or their elbows and their toes. If we *are* making movies about this, then we obviously aren't making enough of them because I haven't seen one yet.

Is it not alarming that women everywhere, actually, genuinely, truly want to *constantly change themselves?* From daily little things like threading, waxing, and nail painting, to the more prominent, lifelong changes. I used to think maybe we as women are just insecure when we're younger, and with age, we come around. We change. We get used to this body, this hair, our skin… but no, instead, what changed with age were *the multiple new technologies and opportunities to change ourselves.*

There is liposuction, anti-pigmentation, Botox, fillers, jawline thinning, eyelid surgeries, nose/cheek/chin/lip/boob/butt jobs—*let's just combine the jobs in one.* There's fairness treatments, laser hair removal, vaginal bleaching, hymen replacement, nail extensions, and then the one I find most strange, eyelash extensions (you knew it was gonna be either this or the hymen).

I met a friend a while ago and she told me how the eyelash extensions she has have to be renewed every 10-15 days. *You can't wash them.* And because you cannot wet them, here's the catch, *you cannot cry.*

I apologise in advance if I'm about to hurt you, but *what the fuck, ladies? Tell me this is a joke!*

You-cannot-fucking-cry.

It's not that you *have to cry…* but are we now going to let the standards of beauty take away our *right to cry?*

Turns out, *"almost every second girl walking down the street has them these days, so it's no biggie,"* she said. The streets she referred to were Canadian, but still.

Do you ever stop and realise on a daily basis how many things we as womxn think are wrong with us? It was bad enough when our insecurities were related to our bodies. Because fat, skinny, fit—regardless of what the womxn is—in the end, there's always a hundred things she hates about her body. It's either that her stomach isn't *curvy enough,* or her legs are *too lanky,* or her butt isn't *that big,* or her breasts are *too big.* I've even heard women complain about their *foreheads and necks!* Legit things you cannot fix by *exercising/being fit.*

The shame we feel around our weight was bad enough, but then came these other insecurities, the ones that make us want to change all the tiny little details of the way we look because that's how much we hate ourselves. And this self-loathing is not due to some sort of *normal human behaviour. We just don't like who we are* because, in this big, somewhat bad, brave world, womxn are constantly reminded of *just how much they lack.* How they *aren't good enough.* They aren't *pretty enough.* They aren't… *enough.*

And that's what hits where it hurts the most—as a society, we hate women and the way they naturally look so much that *we feed them insecurities,* and then we eventually *judge them, blame them, and put them down for wanting to change the way they are. Because, ladies, buy a razor and fairness cream—just remember to #loveyourself #selflove*

"We used your hard-earned money to make you feel miserable enough to change everything about yourself so we could then tell you to love yourself, by becoming somebody else. Meanwhile, we're buying yachts and mansions, as we leave you there, stuck with a measuring tape and a weighing machine."

The only part of *empower* they're living up to is the part where they hold the *power* over how you see yourself. Society is not *one* person, and they don't even have to say it out loud in order to say it at all. Don't be fooled by what people don't *say* to your face because that's not what this is all about... it's about every billboard, every magazine, every fashion model, every advertisement, every actor, every fashion brand, every porn video, every angel and mermaid we draw and watch in cartoons, and every princess in every fairy tale.

Womxn are constantly portrayed as a certain *kind* of beautiful that has now taken over and become a stereotype. Tall, but shorter than the man, thin, but with big breasts, a small curved waistline, a big butt, long slim legs with good calves, of course, *naturally* fit, thin arms, collar bones popping, long eyelashes, big eyes, beautiful long black hair, a small little button nose, big lips, and fair, flawless skin...

Kill me now.

I'm not saying that the womxn who actually look like that aren't beautiful, I'm saying that they sure as hell are not the *only kind* of beauty there is in this world. And sadly, *even the womxn that fit into these stereotypes are extremely insecure about themselves.* Constantly starving themselves to look a certain way, maintain their bodies, comparing themselves to other womxn that they think are slightly better than themselves. The closer you are to perfectly fitting in, the more you worry about losing it all.

And then there's the rest of the women that don't fit into this category and spend far too much of their time trying to look different to themselves. I have met some of the most beautiful women in my life, but *they* genuinely don't think that *they are beautiful* at all. They feel flawed, they feel ugly, and they want to *fix* themselves.

Because we—society—tell these women that it's *their* fault. We tell women that are insecure due to socially constructed standards of beauty that they themselves are awful and shallow for wanting to change themselves. *"Why can't you just be happy with yourself? Why are you so insecure? Why do you spend all your time trying to be different? Is how you look all you care about?"*... even though we're the ones that have created this unsafe environment for them in the first place.

It is extremely harmful and unfair to expect *womxn* to stop being insecure overnight (or over many nights) when *we as a society* haven't done anything to contribute towards them feeling secure or beautiful. All womxn aren't going to, and shouldn't be expected to, *not* change how they look just because of *"self-love."* It's not that simple. I think we as human beings chase after everything that we're conditioned to desire—a house, a job, a family, a car, luxury, status... We spend our whole lives being miserable in a job just to pay a mortgage and own land that isn't even *really* ours. We give birth to children that we cannot afford to educate without being overburdened with loans. We live our lives based on what we've been conditioned to want from the moment we were born, *what we are told to want.* So, why the hell do we expect women to be unusually strong enough to break these desires that we've planted in the first place and practice *self-love?* Not everybody rebels against society. Not every woman is the kid that became an entrepreneur without finishing their college degree (my brother tells me my metaphors don't make sense), and the point being that *self-love should be taught as a way of life, instead of it being a rebellious act.*

As for the ones that *do* manage to be strong enough to break the stereotypes and live their lives without caring about the world—we don't praise them. Instead, we put them down. We shame them. We tell them they're ugly. We ask them *"who will marry you?"* We feed into their insecurities so much that these womxn then feel pressured into shaving their legs, losing their weight, using bleach to become fair, and starving themselves, because if they don't fit into the stereotype, then, of course, they become the outsiders. When we see a woman who is content with herself, we say, *"Thank God, at least she's smart, because she's clearly not beautiful."*

So, we shame the women that refuse to fit into the standards of beauty and rebel because they are tired of being labelled and want to live life on their own terms, but we *also* shame and judge the women that get lip jobs and boob jobs and take fairness injections and vomit after every meal. As for the ones that *do* fit into every category and are *considered perfect,* well, we don't spare them either. We objectify them to the extent that they're nothing but objects. *They're hot, and so their sole purpose seems to be to please the male gaze.*

Have you ever noticed that when a womxn from a typecast beautiful-womxn-profession (insert: model, actor, etc.) decides to talk about politics, the environment, or human rights, society shames her for being half-naked on billboards? We tell her to shut the fuck up and do what she's best at, which is looking pretty, according to us. *"Don't stress that little brain of yours, sweetheart."*

When a womxn that's considered "average" by society's terrible standards of beauty talks about the same topics? We tell her she should maintain decorum; *"she's beautiful, but she's too opinionated, she'll ruin her career if she doesn't stop talking so much."* Encourage her to wear high heels, get married, and shop. After all, if she did excel at her work, we're only going to accuse her of fucking her way to the top, aren't we?

And what happens when a womxn that doesn't fit society's bullshit standards of beauty *at all* talks about the same things? We don't even consider them womxn. *"She's a rebel without a cause, she's lost, she's just sexually deprived, she's probably really a man"* are just some of the many comments people pass. *"She doesn't even look like a woman. No one's going to marry her anyway, she's just an angry feminist. Does she want to compete with men, or become a man herself? Looks like one already."*

In the end—regardless of what women look like or how smart they are—*society shames them for having a voice.* People try to limit, threaten, control, change, stop womxn from speaking up about *anything* that doesn't align with *what men want.*

It's a *miracle* that so many womxn everywhere are even rebelling today, given that most of them weren't raised to be rebels. They were raised to be good wives and good mothers, but somewhere along this patriarchal journey, they unintentionally discovered themselves.

Women for generations didn't even know that they were growing up in a world where no matter what they did, they'd be questioned, objectified, be told to shut up and focus on something more productive—*something that doesn't threaten the masculinity of our society. Something that works in favour of men... "Oh, here's an idea, make it a taboo to not have children, that'll keep them busy. If it doesn't help, then throw in a few insecurities too—wait, do womxn grow hair? That's it, let's tell them that's disgusting too... it'll be generations before someone notices why."*

So, yeah, in conclusion, it's alarming. It's also extremely saddening and awfully true that far too many women everywhere *hate themselves*. They're insecure and unsure of where they stand, who they are, what they're supposed to be, in order to be good enough, and why are they supposed to see every other woman as a threat?

But that's precisely why I'm writing these words today—to remind you that *yes*, you are imperfect, you have flaws and bodies that vary and multiple shades of beautiful colours. You have eyes that sparkle bright enough to light up the sky on a moonless night, a smile that could stop tears from rolling down, and a magical mind that can be everywhere at once, even when people think it's nowhere at all. You are caring, and kind, and considerate, even when you're too hard on yourself. On most days, you don't even know all the things you are absolutely capable of. You underestimate your own power.

You are short, tall, and sometimes too small for that bra, often too big for that pair of jeans. You are imperfect, but you are so, so beautiful in your own way.

And I cannot force you to never change a thing about your body or your face. My job isn't to convince you to love yourself. No, instead I want to *remind you* that all the times you've changed the way you look in order to fit into the standards of beauty, *it wasn't really your fault.* I have been there too. *It's not your fault that the world has unreasonable, unfair, unvaried, boring standards set for what women should look like in order to be beautiful, instead of letting them flourish and be themselves.* It's easy to get confused and feel deflated when you constantly feel like something about you isn't good enough for this world.

It's not your fault. It's all of ours, as a society. *I keep saying we/us because "we" are the society we allow ourselves to become. If we cannot accept that we're all a part of the problem, then how can we even be part of the solution?*

I cannot force you to love yourself, but what I can do is make sure that you always, *always* know how absolutely gorgeous you are. You are stardust and magic, and without you, this world would cease to exist in the same way that it does. I want you to know that whenever you feel like you aren't good enough, you've got this page to come back to, to let me remind you: *you are enough, my love. You are more than enough.*

Write down a list of your favourite beauty/makeup/products and next to them, write down why you love them/why they make you feel good about yourself.

Do you love them because they make you happy, or because you feel like you aren't beautiful without them?

Are the products making you feel better or worse about the real you?

How you think, what you think, the way you think matters.

My Notes

My Notes

CHAPTER 19

MARRIAGES ARE (NOT) MADE IN HEAVEN

PART 1

"*Have you ever loved someone so much that you're scared your heart will explode, and still not wanted to get married to them?*"

Sure. My mother, my brother, my best friend, my grandmother, my dog—and my boyfriend. Apart from the last one, I'm not expected to marry any of the rest... unless I'm manglik, then a dog or broccoli, maybe.

People say marriages are made in heaven, but I am pretty sure that marriages were made in a room full of men, frantically talking about monogamy and different ways to build a society so diseases wouldn't spread, and men could keep working while still having children, and people could actually trick the system and buy a house together because two can do what one couldn't; however, three would be a legal mess. And very systematically, practically, there it was—*a marriage* (seriously, do your research, don't just believe anything I say). Before that, everybody was sleeping with everybody else as and when they wanted, and the fastest sperm survived and then the entire community raised all the children together. Polygamy? Oh, I don't truly know. I'm sure there are multiple layers.

Contrary to popular belief, my problem is not with the monogamous part of this ritual. I am, in fact, *conditioned* to be very, very monogamous. I am an extremely monogamous romantic. I'm all about poetry, love letters, romantic dates, and weekend cuddles with *one person*. I'm the marshmallow in the chocolate milk you order where there's only space for two in a cup, *so you either gotta keep this marsh alone forever or paired with one and only*. I want to spend *the rest of my life* with one person. I want to adopt kids and travel the world together and look after each other, and restrain from any form of attraction towards another human being because, in my head, that's just infidelity (hectic), and grow *old* together… I want to do everything and more with the man I love, even more than what married people usually do.

I'm not *"scared of committing"* either, as people would assume about anyone who says the words *"I don't believe in the concept of marriage,"* which I personally don't. I don't see the symbolic side of it. I never have. A lot of my relationships ended because that was a deal-breaker for me. I didn't want to *"get married"* and the logic was very simple: I didn't want to do something just because everybody else was doing it. I wanted to be convinced *why a person I love and I were going to go down that road.*

Everything I have done in the last few years, that I can remember, I've done with a purpose or a reason. At some point in life, maybe after doing *Girls on Top* and realising that my voice was being heard—that people were reading my words and it *meant something* to so many young womxn out there—I decided that I wanted my actions, my life choices to *mean something* (whenever possible). I didn't just want to live my life and be oblivious to the lives I was influencing with the decisions I made every day. I wanted my choices to *matter*. I knew that being in the public eye meant that everything you do makes a difference, whether you intend for it to or not, and I intended to.

My problems with marriages were trivial to others but important to me. I hated the way society viewed relationships that were anything outside of marriage. We didn't respect them. We didn't respect people that may have been together for five or seven years (or even longer) because they simply *weren't married*. You could live *like* married people, but no one cares until you sign a piece of paper. That, to me, felt like a massive slap in the face. How can *anything* that's created in heaven be this *stupid?* What about… love? Did God even create this sham? If God actually created marriages, then God clearly made a mistake because she also created love, and love sees no caste, colour, class, gender, religion—love has no restrictions. Marriage, on the other hand, has one too many. One couldn't marry outside their religion, they couldn't marry inside their gender, they couldn't marry into other ethnicities or a lower caste than their own, or have one ritual that was dedicated to all gods in every religion. It just didn't make any sense. She made so many beautiful things and then she just fucked them all up by creating marriage? *"This was definitely not created in heaven by God herself,"* I told myself. *"They're lying to me."*

I watched movies and saw adults having discussions about marriages being so black and white. Either people were absolutely *ready* for marriage, or they were *petrified* of marriage. Be assured that it is just socially expected for you to go through both emotions in life but in the right order, of course, depending on your age. You go from *"Marriage? God, no!"* to *"Let's get married! I'm ready now."* As though you just needed to be one or the other? Once again, I found this to be a big slap on the face of *love*.

What does marriage mean to everybody? Some people think it's really sacred, some do it to get their parents off of their back and they don't really care about the rituals, some do it for freedom, some so they can finally live with their partner, to have a child, some want the status, others just want it over and done with. Some people do it for legal purposes like adopting a child, buying a house, making sure if something happens to your partner, you're the spouse that can take decisions on their behalf. Some do it for citizenship or to migrate, some for money, and then there are others who do it because everybody else is doing it. Some even do it to get laid because they believe it's immoral to have sex before marriage.

People get married for multiple different reasons. But popular social belief? People get married *for love*. Pssst! That doesn't make any sense. *Love* has got nothing to do with marriage. *Love,* to me, is about respect and trust. And from what I know, we neither respect nor trust unmarried people in love. However, once you're married, no one cares if you're in love. It's *how* relationships are treated prior to/sans marriage that bothers me the most. Most parents and families in our culture—I can only speak of what I know—treat these relationships like they're not *worth acknowledging.*

Two people (in an Indian family) could have been together for *years,* but they'll still get told that they can't sleep in the same bedroom because, oh my God, *sex.* Sex in *unmarried relationships* is looked down upon. They make it sound like it's *impure,* or illegal—sans legality. All that goddamn love you feel for him/her/them, forget about it. No one cares nor respects it because you're *unmarried.*

That particular word really pisses me off. *Unmarried.* I'm sorry but what the fuck? There's single, separated, divorced, and *unmarried.* What? What about an actual relationship? What about being a live-in or a *de facto*? It's like you're either married, or you're *un-married.* Why does the "unmarried" once again feel like a slap in the face? Like, you're satisfied and *unsatisfied.* You're reasonable, *unreasonable.* You're loved or *unloved.* Married? Nope, looks like you're *unmarried.*

It's really frustrating to have society tell you, *"Yes, you're together, but up until it's marriage, it doesn't mean anything."* The benchmark for *"Are they really in love?"* is simply *"Are they married?"* and that's hilarious because most married people that *I talk to* aren't even happy in their marriages—or *in love for that matter.*

As a teenager, I saw male characters in movies getting all creeped out with how a womxn wants to marry them and they're not ready because they just want to *"have fun"* in life. I thought, *this doesn't feel right…* That's like saying everything I do with a man until I get married is him secretly not actually wanting anything with me in the future? But what if womxn just want to *have fun* too? If you're going to marry *"the one,"* then what is everyone else you were once in love with? Weren't they the one, *back then*? I always wanted the man I'm dating, his parents, my parents, his friends, my friends to *respect our relationship for however long it was to last*, instead of acting like it's something impure. I'd tell my mother, *"Marriages could fail too, and often some relationships last longer than marriages do, so who decides that we must respect one and condemn the other?"*

My mother would just nod disapprovingly and tell me I was going down a very tough road with all these rules that I wanted to break.

Maybe you can understand now why I didn't have any friends or boyfriends for most of my teenage years. I may have come across as a very *hectic girl*. Most boys my age liked girls that were more… well, *fun*. Light-hearted. That hasn't changed. I'm still too hectic for most people, and gladly. *My life is too short to not be hectic about my rights.* You could always tell when I'm flirting with a man at a party because my idea of flirting would be discussing religion, gender-based roles, and equity. It would be an absolute disaster. My friends would take me to a corner and say, *"Why can't you just chill, Saloni…"*

How do I explain to them?

This is me *chilling!*

PART 2

My second issue with marriages… (if you haven't guessed it by now, then where is your focus?) *drum roll* is how *God-damn-fucking patriarchal it is*. From the *ceremony* to what a marriage *stands for* to most people, to why women want to get married since their childhood, all of it is so directly associated with making womxn dependent on their husbands, so heterosexual, so orthodox, *that it makes me want to vomit.*

"These are just traditions" isn't good enough on some days because our culture and traditions also shape the way we think, and this isn't a one-off event. Instead, it's how we raise womxn to desire and prioritise a *wedding* their *entire life* over other milestones and goals. We prepare young womxn

to become good wives and mothers, never *once* being honest with them about just how much they'll have to give up in order to become one. We sell it like a Hallmark card, and then when the time comes, *the actual day that they've dreamt their whole lives about,* it turns out to be the biggest fucking patriarchal event in the world. But by then, they're too blinded by the glittering lehenga and dresses, the mehendi, the makeup, and the jewellery to even *notice* what the fuck is going on. It's a trap, ladies.

We trick womxn into thinking this is what they want their whole childhood, and by the time they realise that curbing their freedom isn't what they ever wanted, they wanted to be independent, we then tell them to remember who's paying their bills.

In a lot of Indian weddings, there's a ritual where the groom's family *changes* the bride's name, in order to give her a new identity as she enters the family. Like taking away the surname that she was born with wasn't bad enough, *we actually erase her whole identity and give her a new one,* because now the man's family owns her? *She's ours.* Her real life has *just begun,* as Mrs [insert husband's name forever]. When I asked my mother about this, she said, *"But it's not forceful... you have a choice to say no."* A choice given to people that believe from the bottom of their heart that a daughter is to be *given away.* Kanyadan – *Kanya-daan* – donating the girl/daughter – WTF?

Are you still with me? I hope I haven't lost you.

So, when I fell in love with my partner, Rahul, we talked about marriage within the first few weeks (turns out he likes hectic girls). Rahul asked me if I ever wanted to get married, and I was like, *"Nope, don't believe in it, but feel free to convince me if you feel so otherwise."* There wasn't so much *convincing,* but he really did raise the topic more often in the most beautiful of ways. I felt like I was debating life with my best friend over drinks. No expectations, no pressure, just conversations. He would constantly send me articles to read, and we'd ask each other questions and talk about our opinions on the topic, an open discussion. It was pretty much understood that *in order for marriage to be on the table, one of us had to convince the other*—whoever wanted their way or had a better argument had to make a good enough point that could convince the other person.

There was no *"if you don't marry me, I cannot be with you,"* which is what *all* my other relationships would eventually turn into at one point. It was always *"my parents won't agree,"* and I was like, *"Well, that's too bad because neither will I."* It was a draining and exhausting process to go through with every man. I knew I didn't *want* to get married and Rahul knew that too, but no man had ever asked me if they could *try to convince me* before. He didn't pressure me or make me feel attacked. If anything, I liked knowing that in order for us to never get married, *I had to try and convince him too.* It was exciting; we were open to either/or, as I believe love should always be. One day, when we decided we both wanted to adopt children together, we realised that marriage now *might* have legal benefits. The conversation was definitely then on the table. It went straight into our ongoing *To Be Discussed* folder.

Being the hectic girl I am, I started looking into weddings, customs, rituals to see where I stood with my beliefs when it came to a *wedding.* Little after doing my research, I thought my brain would explode. *It wasn't as simple as signing a piece of paper in court at all; that now felt like a blessing in disguise.* I would furiously pace up and down and rant all day about how ridiculous it all seems, until I couldn't breathe anymore because I was stressing myself into horrible anxiety attacks. *While this is not the end of that story,* first, I'd like to share the things I learnt, so you can be on the same page as me (yes, still chilling). Here are some different rituals from different parts of the country, some of which we do in almost all weddings, and I can't wrap my head around *why we do this to the women we claim to love.*

1. *Kanyadan* – the father gives the daughter away, as though to say, *"She's your responsibility now."* I'm sorry (I'm not sorry), but why is she anyone else's responsibility? I know the father walks the daughter down the aisle in Christian weddings too, so it's evidently not something that exists in isolation in Indian cultures, but maybe that makes me even more uncomfortable. A lot of Indian weddings don't even happen without the *kanyadan* because giving away the daughter is one of the most *important* rituals.

2. *Haldi* – I'm all for glowing skincare routines, but in a lot of cultures, the haldi that is applied on the girl has to first be applied on the boy, rinsed off, and sent to the girl's house because *she* must apply the haldi that has first washed *his* body in order to purify her. Thankfully, a lot of people realised that this was not only disgustingly degrading (can't guarantee they actually ever realised that) but also extremely unhygienic. So, now a lot of the families don't do this ritual anymore. Instead, they just ask the boy to *touch* the haldi powder before it's sent over to the girl's house—because him having put his blessed hand in the haldi just once is enough to purify her. This, to me, is still sexist. I don't know if any of you know this or have seen it, but if you're ever having a wedding in the family and you see the groom touching haldi in a bowl before it's sent away, *do something.* Even if it's just tripping and falling on the bowl of haldi to drop it all… or, like, ask the family *if his fingers are so magical, shouldn't he be using them to do other things with it that satisfy his wife?* But don't quote me.

3. *The Pheras* – without getting into far too many details of what they're saying in the pheras, we are all well aware of the fact that the vows that are read out are *often* sexist and conservative. The wife must obey the husband and look after the family and comply with his needs, support him, and cook for him, while the husband must earn for his family and always protect them. Fair enough, whoever wrote it back in the day, I don't know like 4000 years ago, was very smart and did well (pat on the back). I think it's about time we edit/alter these vows and add some new ones, don't you think? Why are we still reciting such gender-biased vows that are all about unequal power and dominance, of master and slave, vows that are extremely derogatory and controlling towards women, while also putting so much pressure on the man?

4. *Mehendi* – this broke my heart because I absolutely love mehendi. The smell, the colour, and the patterns. If I could, I'd just have perpetual mehendi on my hands throughout the year because of

how beautiful it is. What bothers me is the *ghisaa pitaa* belief that *if he loves you,* then the mehendi will turn out really dark brown. Why don't we put mehendi on our men also? And why aren't we telling them that the darker the colour, the more their wives must love them and hence they are so lucky? Or is it just a given that she loves him, except it's not luck *because he deserves all her love?* The *"hiding his name"* and making him find it later, sorry, I'll just go barf and come back.

Ask a man to hide his to-be wife's name in his mehendi before his wedding… people will laugh and wonder *if he is even a man* because, you know, toxic gender roles. So, what truly makes a man… *a man?* Being arrogant and confident? Not insecure about his partner's love? Being born privileged? Physically strong, and less emotionally available? Less sensitive? Bread-earner? Master? Because for generations, that is what we are raising men to be, and maybe you don't mind, you're allowed to decide for yourself, but *it sure ain't working for me.*

5. *Mangalsutra* and *Sindoor* – regardless of what these two customs symbolise for you and however excited you've been for both, the only thing I keep wanting to know is, *why only our women?* Why does the woman get a bell around her neck that the husband puts on in the name of protection from the evil eye, and why does he cover her *maang* (partition) in red sindoor (a lot of which has multiple health risks involved because they often contain high levels of lead), yet the same ritual isn't applied to him? Marriage is still a union of two, isn't it? Unless we've digressed from love to ownership and worship at some point, this is still two people, vowing to love each other until death do them apart? So then where's his *mangalsutra and sindoor?* If men had to apply it, we'd have probably found a sindoor substitute that doesn't have heavy metals in them, *just saying.*

6. *Domestic Abuse* – I have spoken to a few people, I've asked friends who've gotten married, but by no surprise at all, most of them had

no idea what any of the rituals meant. They did it for the sake of family and couldn't care less about the meaning of it all. There's a custom where the womxn's brother/male member comes and partakes in throwing rice and other things in the fire as he stands next to her, while the pandit speaks out the mantras. Apparently, this one is to promise that *the brother will protect his sister from any domestic abuse.* For starters, I just want to say, if this is true, then I'm so proud that we've made this part of our customs—that is actually cool, huh? That at least during the *wedding we* accept that our women may be beaten up. We accept it enough to add it in a vow, even if we choose to turn a blind eye to it forever afterwards. But we do acknowledge it.

We don't have the groom's brother come and do the same though because, once again, I guess *maybe* men don't get beaten up by their wives as often? *I don't know, you tell me.*

7. The Rice – I don't think as a kid I even noticed that the bride is awkwardly throwing rice behind her head as she's leaving. Definitely didn't realise it's not cooked… imagine cooked rice… Anyway, I learnt that it's the bride's way of saying *"thank you for everything you've done for me, for having looked after me, and I can never pay off your debts, so here I am, showing gratitude for everything I cannot repay as I leave, as I am no longer your responsibility…"*

   Yes. Thanking our parents seems like a *wonderful* ritual, and why not—that's so beautiful, right? I was waiting for this one. Only the daughter does it though… for some odd reason, the son isn't grateful for everything his parents have done. She's the only one starting *her new life.* He's just continuing his previous one. *He's just bringing her home.* At this point, I'd like you to know that this is really hard for a man to deal with too, okay? *Because he will now live with two mothers (see, chilling and cracking jokes).*

After reading all of this, when I told my mother how furious I was about the things I'd just discovered, she was obviously disheartened. She almost seemed a little disappointed that she had me for a child. It was like I took all her dreams and shattered them. But as my mother always does, she picked up that disappointment and she threw it in the bin very quickly. She turned to me and said that the rituals were beautiful to her, but yes, *maybe they should be performed by both the people getting married instead of just one.* "*You could both throw rice behind you, beta, because you're both thankful to us,*" she said. However, she also ended that conversation with, "*But, beta, my only advice to you is that don't get married. If they try to put pressure on you, please just say no because it would any day be better for you to say no to a wedding ceremony, than for you to say yes and then object to all these customs. Do you want to kill someone else's parents, beta? Just say a flat-out no. Why do you want to put someone through this? Sign a paper and finish it off, don't give someone else a heart attack, please.*"

And I said, "*But, Mum, you also agree with me...*"

To which she responded, "*No, not always, but you're my daughter, so I don't have a choice. They do.*" Brutal honesty aside, the thing is, *they shouldn't have a choice over who their son chooses to fall in love with.*

PART 3

After all these years, what shaped my thoughts was also a conversation I had with my brother. He asked me why I didn't want to get married. Though he knew; *he's always known.* Hell, a huge part of it was because he once said he didn't believe in the idea of marriage, and no, I don't agree with *everything* he says. There are a lot of things we disagree on, but the aversion to marriage resonated with me. I'd felt a detachment from what everybody else felt, but I didn't have the words to express it. So, when he said them out loud—*they hit home* (my mum's going to kill him). Yet, here he was, ten years later, asking me *why* I didn't want to get married... so I turned around, confident, ready to give my *already-repeated-for-a-decade-speech* which went somewhat like "*One day I am going to have children, and I want to raise them to know that they can be whoever they want to be.*

They don't need to be someone they are not just because society expects them to fit into a little box. They don't have to be scared of who they love or be pressured into getting married. How can I change this world for them if I make the same mistakes? How can I look them in the eye and say 'follow your heart' if I didn't follow mine? I want my kids, and the womxn that look up to me, to know that they can live their life the way they want to, and still be respected"... I'm personally *very* proud of this one. It's taken years to phrase and it comes from the heart. It's honest and it's vulnerable. I think it makes for a great monologue too. (So narcissistic; don't date an actor for precisely these reasons.)

My brother then casually nods like he's been there, heard/said that before (ugh, older siblings), and says *casually,* "*If you don't want to get married, that's fine. You should do whatever you want to do, but to say that you don't want to do it because you want to change the world, that's not necessarily how change works. You can't change the system from the outside; you have to be a part of the system to change it. People don't listen to other people if they consider them an outsider.*" With ease, he destroys years' worth of my work and then continues, "*For example, if you suddenly decided you want to speak for Muslim women's rights, Islamic women are more likely to listen to a woman that wears a hijab or believes in God herself, instead of listening to someone that isn't even one of them, doesn't live like them, dress like them, or have the same belief system as them, because what would she know about their struggles? You can't preach freedom if you don't even associate with what freedom means to a certain set of people. That applies to underprivileged, religious, orthodox, oppressed, and all other kinds of women. They will most likely trust and look up to a woman that they can resonate with, and not one that is nothing like them. To change the system, you have to be inside the system.*"

I know I should've said something at this point, but all I really wanted to ask was how many years *he spent on this monologue, and would I be able to steal it?* Ugh. "*Thousands of girls look up to you,*" he continued, "*if you don't get married, you might encourage a few of those women who didn't want to get married in the first place to fight for their right too. You may be able to help them stand up, or maybe not. Because patriarchy is injected so deep into our societies that eventually those few who don't want to get married might also give in to the pressure. Not everyone has a great support system or the courage to break that many rules at once. As for the others that look up to you, most women actually want to get married. That's how they've been raised, to want it, so they won't resonate with you at all. They can want to break away from patriarchy but also want to get married. Those women still love you and look up to you, but they'll also accept that you're different to them in this aspect, or you have a different upbringing, or a different lifestyle or culture. That's why you wouldn't want the same things as them. Even though, in your head, you're doing this to change something for them. If you really want to change something, then instead of taking the extreme step of not getting married, you should actually get married, and do it in the way you think is right. Break the rules, change the norms, rebel—let them know that they can too. Get married, but don't change your last name. Get married, and don't do your kanyadan. Get married, but say no to sindoor or all the rituals that you personally think are sexist. Adapt the customs with your partner. Be a part of the change in a way where they can still relate to it. A lot of women may want a wedding but might also hate these sexist rituals, and this way you will impact their lives by letting them know that it's possible to bend the rules and adapt our culture to fit it into our own lives. That's the real change we're looking for, isn't it?"*

I almost burst into tears. Unsure if it was because of how casually he destroyed my beautifully articulated reasoning, washed away my arrogance and pride, or because once again, like many other times in our lives, *he was right*. I am pretty sure I didn't tell him he's right at that moment. I would've argued my way through that conversation and said I disagree before letting his words sink in later.

The truth remained—he is right. *If I wanted to change the world, I had to first be a part of the system.* If I wanted to encourage women to stand up for themselves, I had to take baby steps because we're all fighting a fight that's too big, and every little step we take towards a tiny change is a victory. And maybe the real victory is not to erase our culture, but instead, adapt it to fit our lives.

My family in Lucknow once told me about a wedding that became the talk of their town. During the ceremony, the father of the daughter *refused to do a kanyadan.* He said, *"We are not giving our daughter away to anybody. They're both getting married, but she is still our daughter, and she has her own identity, as she always had."* I had goosebumps when I heard this, in 2017. I couldn't believe this was a story I was hearing about a wedding in *Lucknow* of all places. And then I heard about it again on Twitter, and again, and again… I smiled; the winds were changing.

A year later, I read an article about a wedding that went viral because the groom bent down and touched the bride's feet. *"Why should she be the only one to touch mine?"* he asked. Soon after, I saw an article titled *"5 Indian weddings that have broken stereotypes"*… Isn't this how change happens, after all? Step by step—customs, rituals, upbringing, and then people's mindsets change. You can't wake up and *change the world in one day,* but if you keep waking up and doing what you believe in, you're contributing to a much bigger change.

The same way that far more women today don't change their last name, dowry is *(mostly)* unacceptable and illegal, kanyadan is beginning to be looked down upon (in some families), mothers-in-law don't check for bloodstains on white bed sheets the next morning anymore, and haldi isn't reapplied from a man's body. Customs are changing and adapting, and that change is not happening out of nowhere. They're not changing because of the couples that simply agreed to all rituals to get it over and done with. They're changing because of the people that decided *"let's get married, and let's do it on our own terms."*

Marriages are not made in heaven. Marriages are made right here on Earth, with often the most regressive rituals and customs that have not been adapted to respect the history, the culture, or even the women we come from. These rituals often cause harm and glorify misogyny. *Tradition* is too lazy an excuse to not change the way we do things. Our behaviour often mirrors our society and its values. If you believe in marriages, and you want *a wedding,* remember that marriages are also about love and companionship; the wedding, however, is debatable. Do it in a way that works for you and your partner. If you want to change the rituals, know that you're allowed to. The vows that you're saying, claiming to love and respect each other for the rest of your lives, get to know them, mean them, and who knows, even write them yourselves (or at least hire a good writer).

I say this to you after having spent the last one year having extremely ugly fights about weddings in my own life. It hasn't been an easy journey, and the pressure is *very real*. It was never going to be easy trying to carve your own path in this world that prefers for you to follow a straight line. I hope you have a partner that loves and respects you enough to have the patience to fight it with you. There will be times when you want to give up, let go, or maybe even give in… that's when you're going to need someone that looks at you and tells you that *they're proud of everything you fight for every day*. I know I've needed to be reminded every day for the last year. I have fought, I have cried, I have yelled, and I have bawled my eyes out, and I am here to tell you to *choose yourself*. Remember that if you got married, it would be *your* wedding to share for the rest of your life. Everybody else is just the crowd in the photo album. *Do it your way.*

I'm low-key pushing for a female pundit… Just saying.

The one thing I've learnt is that "I don't want to" isn't often going to get us what we do want in life… but our reasons, our patience, and our ability to communicate with the people we love help more than you think it does. Whether it's our parents, lovers, or friends—everybody wants to be loved and be heard. So, let's start from within ourselves.

I want to know if you want to get married, or if you don't want to get married.

I want to know your reasons. Tell me why. Maybe once we know what we want and why we want it, we can take baby steps towards explaining it to others too.

My Notes

My Notes

CHAPTER 20

MY DEAR NON-FEMINIST FRIEND

How are you? You don't seem to check up on me, so I thought I'd check up on you. We don't talk as much as we used to when we were kids… when our experiences of life were exactly the same. We've lost touch over the last few years, and I'm not too sure what happened. It seems to me that my life experiences seem to bother you because you seem very, very angry at me for wanting to speak up against the wrongs in my life. You say my problems aren't *real,* and I really sometimes wonder when our lives went in such different directions, and where/when you were told it's okay to bring someone down, for simply having different opinions? I must've missed a few classes that you made it to because I don't remember anything else that we did without each other.

The last time we talked, we argued about violence and abuse, when you said to me, *"Don't you think it's unfair that a man can't hit a womxn, but a womxn can hit a man?"* And I replied, *"A womxn absolutely shouldn't hit a man, and it shouldn't be acceptable either, but the impact and outcome of both situations are completely different."* You shook your head and scoffed in disbelief, claiming that *this* is why you aren't a feminist—because *what about men?* *"How is it okay for a womxn to slap a man, and say that the man shouldn't slap her back?"* I listened, patiently, wondering how I could explain to you the different ways in which patriarchy affects gender imbalance. I never said that womxn should hit men. *I agree with you*—they shouldn't—but I also stand my ground when I say that *men should be discouraged from hitting women back.*

You don't seem to agree with me. You repeatedly say, "*That's* the problem with womxn's rights, they're not *fair."* I'm surprised you say so, even though you were the first one by my side when we were just 12 years old and I got into a fight with those boys who said horrible things to me in the garden under my building, about my parents, about my body, and how *nobody would want to love me.* I remember being angry and crying. I remember pushing him back and yelling for him to stop. I used up all my strength, and he barely moved an inch, but then he pushed me too, and I fell on the ground and scraped my elbow. You were right there, furious, yelling, *"How dare you push her?"*

What changed?

When we were 21 and drinking at a house party, we saw your friend get into an aggressive fight with her husband, and we went to save her from this yelling, drunk, abusive partner. I remember pushing him away from her along with a few other people. I took his collar and asked him to *back the fuck off,* and in the heat of the moment, he slapped me hard, and I fell to the ground. *You* came with me to the police station. *You never spoke to him again.*

...What changed?

After that destructive, toxic relationship with an extremely abusive ex-boyfriend, I finally confessed to you that he was hitting me, and I didn't know how to ask for help because I perpetually blamed myself. I told you about this one time amidst the abuse and the pain, when I stayed up all night rewinding and repeating all the terrible ways in which he had abused me, used me, and bruised me... and how I went straight into the bedroom where he was lying down, and I slapped him. He instantly got up and slapped me back. I fell down to the ground, and he dragged me to the front door, pulling me through the entire house while I was still on the floor.

When you found out, you cried. You said you didn't know what you would've done if you had been there, to witness someone treating me like that. You've always been there, at every step.

What changed?

My dear non-feminist friend, I wish I could explain to you why the impact of a man hitting a woman is so different from when a woman hits a man. Maybe I'll try to explain it anyway, and hope you stick with me until the end. I want to begin with saying that I still agree with you, *and I always will*, that we shouldn't make it acceptable for a woman to raise her hands on a man—*that is not okay*. However, the thing is, there is a huge imbalance in power dynamics between men and womxn culturally, socially, traditionally, genetically, and financially. Men are usually physically stronger, have more privilege, and hence are more powerful, financially more stable, socially more accepted, culturally more respected, and hence more included in our society.

If you look away from *individual* exceptions, you'll learn that *stereotypically* men's lives are not at the same risk of domestic violence by their partners. Men are not being raped, killed, threatened by the womxn they're with. Men aren't tortured by womxn in the name of dowry, pleasure, culture, or tradition. Men are not bruised black and blue, bled, or burnt through the violence of their wives.

Women, however, are.

When women hit their partner, in most cases it's self-defence and/or helplessness, unlike when a man hits a woman, more commonly from an aggressive place of power and control.

In our society—where womxn are already underprivileged, and not only are they statistically poorer than men but also less likely to be hired, more likely to be raped and abused, less likely to be educated, less financially independent, more likely to be judged, and less socially credited—*when a man hits a woman, the impact of that abuse does not begin and end at that one slap; it becomes an act of oppression and control.*

Womxn are, on a daily basis, assaulted and abused by the men in their lives. Punched, choked, throttled, slapped, beaten up in order to be *controlled*, to *obey*. *Most* of them cannot/do not fight back because they're physically not strong enough to fight back. The physical imbalance is one of the first reasons I noticed; these men abuse women who are weaker than them in strength and cannot defend themselves, even if they wanted to. The second reason women *don't fight back* is because they're conditioned to accept this abuse. *No one says this out loud, it isn't something they teach you in school, but we absolutely condition womxn to compromise in relationships.* We exist in a society where womxn are less likely to be educated than men, paid less than a man, sexually objectified and molested at a far higher rate than a man, and hence perpetually need to be *protected by a man*. Womxn are expected to focus less on their work and more on starting a family in order to look after the children, and therefore they are extremely dependent on men for survival. When we condition women to *need men* in order to be respected in society, we're automatically teaching them to *obey* the breadwinners, the man of the house, *their husbands*.

In relationships and equations with so many imbalances in power and structure, *domestic violence* becomes a far bigger problem than just *"so you mean to say a woman can slap a man but a man can't slap a woman?"*

And a part of me feels like *you used to know this too* when we were younger, but at some point, our lives went in entirely different directions where your experiences were extremely different to mine, your inequality different to mine, and we formed opinions and ideas that began to clash. The only thing I didn't ever understand is why your ideas promoted the dismissal of my rights?

I will always hope that you get as few hurdles as possible and may you never have to see the injustices I have seen, but I will also *hope* that you learn to sympathise, if not empathise, with other people's journeys in this world.

So many womxn everywhere—white womxn, womxn of colour, womxn with disabilities, queer womxn, trans womxn, cis womxn – **womxn**—have *stories to share of inequality, abuse, violence, and being unfairly excluded from a society we claim is for "everybody"* and yet you decide to turn a blind eye to it all, just because you've personally never felt the imbalance?

Feminism isn't about you and me, and it sure as hell isn't about the people that identify themselves as one yet do nothing but cause harm. *Feminism* isn't the people that take advantage of the system, nor the ones that pretend to care about lives while they abuse their own rights. Feminism is *equality and equity for all.* For womxn, for men, and for everybody else.

Feminism promotes uplifting womxn and gives men an opportunity to be more vulnerable. Feminism says why shouldn't we have more stay-at-home dads and househusbands if that's what men wish to do with their time? Why shouldn't we have two people earn in a relationship to take the load off of one? Why shouldn't queer rights be the same as heterosexual rights, and why don't we give equal respect to the trans community? Why shouldn't people be allowed to identify as *they* instead of *him* or *her*? *Feminism*—because everybody deserves more than just the right to speak; they deserve an audience, *they deserve to be heard.*

My dear non-feminist friend, how are you? You don't seem to check up on me, so I thought I'd check up on you. We don't talk as much as we used to when we were kids… and I just wanted to remind you that I'm still here… I'll always be here if you're ever ready to start a dialogue again. I'm here because I know deep down inside, you believe in the goodness of people, and I know you care. I know you're the same little girl that would fight for my right to speak in debating class. You'd shout at them all, regardless of whether you agreed with me or not, *even when we were on different teams.*

Maybe the world has convinced you that feminism excludes men, or maybe you haven't lately explored the stories of abuse against womxn around the world. Maybe society does a good job at convincing you that womxn collectively, all around the world, just like to complain even though they've got all the equality they need. Maybe you've just been busy.

I don't know your reasons anymore, but I do know that this fight is incomplete without you. What I do know is that regardless of whether we agree or not, I will always fight for your right to have your own opinions, like you would fight for mine, and *that makes you a feminist*. I know you say you're not a feminist at all, but every time I think of you, I see a feminist. I see a woman who genuinely believes that everybody should have the right to live the life they wish to but also hates to be labelled as a *feminist* because you think feminists are a killjoy and anti-men, but if there is only *one thing* I could ask of you, it would be to stop letting men, other womxn, or this entire world define the cause for you. We are not the definition of *feminism,* but instead, we identify as *feminists*. When a feminist does wrong by its cause, please don't let that ruin the cause itself for you. We as human beings, as feminists, aren't always *right*. Sometimes people slip, maybe you do too?

When you're ready, friend, I want to ask you to *be a feminist*—be the kind you want to be, believe in the equal rights *you* believe in, but please don't be afraid of *saying you're a feminist*. Because this world needs more little girls that fight back when little boys violate their space, and in order for that to happen, I need the little girl inside you to raise some more, and teach them to take up more space, so that one day they can proudly say *their mother raised a feminist.*

Maybe you have a friend that you'd like to write to?

My Notes

My Notes

CHAPTER 21

THERAPY

I go for therapy. I have been on and off for ten years, and I plan on making it a more consistent part of my lifestyle.

I just wanted that to be the very first thing I say to you in this chapter. I have also been on antidepressants in the past—once for a few months. It was right after my abortion. The pressure of dealing with something that had such a huge impact on my physical and mental health and yet not being able to openly discuss it just because *society thought I didn't deserve control over my own body* took a very big toll on my state of mind. I felt like I couldn't breathe. That's when my psychiatrist at the time said that I should go on antidepressants for a few months. A few weeks in, I realised my panic attacks were only getting worse. The meds weren't really working out for me, and he agreed. He said in the past I'd responded better to different forms of art therapy, writing exercises, yoga classes, and so I went back to trying to find different ways to express myself (really, this entire book is just a therapy exercise).

My partner, Rahul, and I go for couples' therapy. We've been together for three years, and no, *something isn't always "wrong" in order for us to go for our sessions.* Instead of going when things are wrong, we try to make therapy a lifestyle choice *so that things don't go wrong.* Having said that, we've been there and done that too. We've been a mess, and we've avoided getting help, and we've learnt the hard way that life is just better and we are so much kinder and healthier when we're regular at 1. going to see our lovely therapist, and 2. following the lists of things and activities we've discussed to do regularly in order to maintain better standards of life.

If there is anything that I am extremely sure of to an extent where I won't say *I think* anymore, it is that *everybody needs to get help.*

Therapy is for absolutely everyone. Regardless of how happy you are, or how beyond help you think you are. You are never too good for therapy, nor are you beyond the point of help. *Therapy is for everybody.*

Normalise the concept of getting help, by getting the help.

We don't seem to mind getting help when it comes to fitness, medical aid, physical health, or education. We are regularly taught something new. We take help from others who know better/are experts in the field that we're trying to familiarise ourselves with. We don't turn around and say *"I know everything, I don't need help in order to pass this test, or be promoted, or fix my broken knee,"* but when it comes to therapy, everybody seems to think *"I'm absolutely fine. I know myself better than anyone."*

Just because you drive a car doesn't mean you can fix it. Getting a degree doesn't mean you can teach, and knowing enough about a human body doesn't mean you're a doctor. So why is it that when it comes to mental health, we don't care that we lack the right amount of knowledge, we just think we know *everything?*

Therapy, oh the taboo.

Mental health itself is given far less importance than it deserves. You don't tell someone with a broken leg to just *"get over it."* Instead, you tell them to see a doctor, to take medication, regularly exercise and stretch. You tell them to get help. But when it comes to depression, society often acts like people just need to *"Get over it. Be stronger. Stop being weak."*

When we see famous people talk about depression, we are quick to judge—*"So bloody rich. What are they so depressed about?"* Being rich doesn't spare you from getting diseases, illnesses, it doesn't spare you from breaking your bones or even dying, so what makes us think that money buys out depression?

Absolutely *everyone* needs help with categorising our cluttered thoughts into the right compartments. *All of us* need to nurture our minds. Therapy is not something you should go for when you hit rock bottom, because people at rock bottom often tend to lose hope. Therapy should be a consistent part of our life, on good days and on the bad days. Because the bad ones don't exist in isolation, and in the happiest of your moments, it's important to know that this too won't last forever, but hey, *neither will the sadness.* The erratic mood swings, the phases, the feelings, and the numbness—everything *can* change from time to time, and we've got to start talking about it to people that have studied so hard about how our brain works, *in order to make our mind our safe space.*

Over the last few years, what therapy has taught *me is* to create balance. I tend to fall headfirst into a thought process where my happiness and my sadness both feel like *this time, it will last forever.* But it never has, thank God. I've learnt to calm down and breathe through each phase of life, and it's successful on *most days.* Every time I overcome a tough phase, and not only do I see the light at the end of the tunnel but also run straight out under the bright blue sky, is when I know *I can do this.* I try to remind myself even on the happiest of warm sunny days that just around the corner could be another tunnel or a sad cold day, and quite frankly, that's okay. Maybe we'll get through it. Sometimes I'm right, sometimes I'm terribly wrong… but I'm never ever alone because I always have a safe place called therapy.

Talk to your psychiatrist and/or your psychologist about your goals, your childhood, your memories, what makes you happy, what makes you sad, your worst moments, your hobbies, your loved ones, your ideas, your repeated mistakes, and your regrets. *Why* aren't we willing to get the help we need in order to be more *content?* What are we afraid of? What is so embarrassing about it? The stigma around mental health is by far one of the most damaging things we have done to ourselves as a society because regardless of what gender, caste, religion, or country we belong to, we have chosen to self-inflict pain and force ourselves to go through so much trauma—all because our egos are too big to admit that sometimes *we are not okay*. And you know what? That… *should have been okay*. We stigmatise mental health, we judge the people that choose to do the right thing, and we cease to exist in a better world.

I was talking to a friend of mine who told me she thinks her father is maybe mildly autistic. Another friend overheard us and he said, *"Really? I think mine is too."* Then both of them said that they didn't even know what was actually going on with their parent until they had accidentally stumbled upon Hollywood movies and TV shows that addressed mental health and types of behavioural changes. People, generations before us and our own, are autistic, dyslexic, bipolar, depressed, they suffer from PTSD, OCD, personality disorders, and we need to start saying *that's okay*. Instead of having the knowledge of *how to* deal with the people who are struggling and suffering, we are oblivious, existing in a society that isn't mental health-friendly at all. Psychological help has been looked down upon for generations and so people continue to suffer, without their own friends and families being aware of it. We brush off human behaviour and their cry for help with *"get over your tantrums, what is this mood swing, stop creating a scene, don't be so emotional, so much drama, this is just your habit, oh it's that time of the month again"*…

These people are real, and their problems are *real*. So many humans spend their whole lives not knowing what's wrong with them, and upon getting no guidance or help, they begin to think this is who they are. The only thing they *are* is misguided. We don't acknowledge that they need help, or we keep pushing them beyond their capacity to do more, and it really, truly needs to *stop*.

I think I have PMDD, and it's crazy because up until last year, I didn't even know that such a thing existed. I just knew PMS, which has such a huge impact on our hormones yet is often made into a mockery, but PMDD? I had absolutely no clue. I had to find out from a girl ten years younger than me that such a thing even existed and can be diagnosed, so I decided that I would get myself checked by the end of this year.

We are constantly learning new things—everything we believe to be true, everything we are, is based on *what we think we know.* There is a lot inside our minds that we cannot even access at all times, but it still continues to contribute towards who we are, how we feel, what our lives become every single day.

Getting therapy is a *good thing.*

Seeing someone to understand *yourself better* is the best thing you can do for yourself.

Quite frankly, I don't even know why therapy isn't mandatory growing up, in school, in workspaces, and in relationships? How have we turned a blind eye to the fact that nobody really knows how to deal with life? No one knows shit about how to be an adult, clearly. No one knows how to breathe when they're panicking, or how to be happy or content. They don't teach you this in school because they themselves have *no clue what's going on;* they didn't fix themselves either. So, why not therapy for everybody? For the heartbreaks, for the long hours working, for the hobbies, the family drama, the internal chaos, the life pressure. Wouldn't this world just be such a better place to live in if confronting our thoughts in order to figure out the right box to place them in was mandatory?

I could write you a hundred books on what *I think,* and the things I say may not apply to you, be right for you, or even resonate with you. No matter what you read/hear/are told, know that those are the things that *people choose to believe for themselves.* The only real way you can know what your truth is, what you believe in, what you *need* in your life, is through therapy.

Don't wait until you're feeling really miserable to do it. Do it because you're happy, do it because you're a little sad. If you ever thought you would listen to me, *then do it because I said so*, but whatever you do, normalise therapy.

But be prepared that not all therapists are going to be the right ones for you, the same way not all doctors are either. You'll meet some amazing ones and others that may cause more harm than help. Please be prepared to try a few before you settle in for the right one, and don't let the ones that aren't right for you exhaust you from the process altogether. Do your research. I know it's a lot to ask of you, to make yourself vulnerable again and again in order to find the right therapist, but believe me, it's worth it. The results are, indeed, *therapeutic*. Finding the right one is like falling head over heels in love—only this time, with yourself.:)

Give your mind, your heart, and your body the right to express itself and live life to the fullest.

Allow yourself to paint, to see colours, to experience them, to create, to nurture, to live in the moment, to love, and to give yourself the gift of balance.

"People in therapy often go to therapy to deal with the people in their lives who won't go to therapy."

I read that on the internet (no attributions were found), and it really resonated. Far too often, I've needed to get myself in a room with my therapist because people *around me* refuse to get therapy themselves. I'm not only dealing with my own issues and struggles to survive and get by in this world, but also *other people's unresolved issues* because *they refuse to get help themselves*.

Don't be that person. Don't be an idiot, and do the right thing—*for yourself (and really, for everyone you love too)*.

Make a list of things you'd like to discuss in therapy.

My Notes

My Notes

CHAPTER 22

TIT

"We minimise a woman's worth to her body parts,
but demand that she plays no part in owning them."

— Me

People always ask me, *"What's feminism got to do with vaginas? Why are you always talking about tits and underwear? This is not empowerment,"* and my question *always is, "Why isn't it?"*

Who decides what's empowering for womxn? Society? Men? You and me? Because there's barely anything *empowering* about snatching away a womxn's right to decide for herself—that, in fact, is control.

What does feminism have to do with vaginas and tits? Well, if you ask me, *a lot.*

For starters, men need to stop getting horny at just the mention of those words. If you're one of these men, then put the book down. I'm about to ask a lot of confronting questions in this chapter... or on second thoughts, keep reading; by the time I'm done with you, you won't feel aroused anymore.

At an absolute foundation level, the reason womxn are deprived of many rights, opportunities, and freedom of choice in our society is *because they are womxn.* Our body parts have *a lot* to do with the unfair treatment we receive. As I've mentioned in other chapters, I meet a lot of people who say, "*If you want to empower womxn, then make them doctors and engineers instead of talking to them about breasts,*" but breasts are a part of their bodies, so why shouldn't we be talking about it?

And how can you say that when *India's daughters,* who had those degrees, *became* doctors and engineers, and should have been empowered as per your standards, were still brutally raped and murdered, *for being women?*

Most womxn in our country are uneducated and poor. When a family has more children than they can afford, the sons get the first preference for education because, after all, *they're the ones that will get a job and earn money.* The daughters would be married off and you don't need a school to teach you to be a good wife. If, by chance, young women *do* get an education, many of them stop attending school once they get their periods because of fear, lack of awareness, discomfort and pain, zero access to sanitary products, hygiene, and shame.

Growing up in our society, girls are extremely conscious of their breasts, their bodies, and their mannerisms. I know a young girl whose mother used to tape her breasts down inside oversized t-shirts, just so the boys at school couldn't see her growing breasts. After all, there's a reason why *dupattas* exist, isn't there? Plenty of school uniforms make it mandatory for girls to wear salwar kameez and dupatta and/or a saree. The only purpose of the scarf-like fabric is, well… *breasts.*

Tell me, how in the world do I ask young girls to dream of becoming engineers, doctors, scientists, and athletes when most of their childhood is spent trying to cover up their body parts, as though being born with a vagina or breasts is a fucking crime? While boys are taught to weaponise their penises and their desires, girls are taught to hide away, to protect, and to find a way to *survive.*

Make sure you don't bend too much while serving food at home.

Wear appropriate clothes.

Cover your cleavage.

Don't spread your legs when you sit/sit appropriately.

Don't dry your lingerie in public.

Hide your bra strap.

Don't expose your legs. Cover your shoulders.

Smile less. Stop frowning.

Have long hair. Don't have body hair!

Don't study too much. Don't smoke—because it's bad for *women*.

Don't wear anything tight. Don't step out late at night.

Don't run because your breasts will bounce.

Don't wear revealing clothes in summer. Don't wear revealing clothes, period.

Don't keep your hair open. Don't wear a bikini. Don't come out in a towel!

Don't – Don't – Don't… because you will provoke men, and you will either a) get assaulted/raped, or worse, b) become a characterless slut.

Let's get *one thing straight.* Womxn in our country are not raped for being doctors and engineers. Womxn are raped for having breasts, and a vagina. Womxn are raped for *the exact same body parts* that we are told are *petty things to discuss,* even though they've created industries built on the pure *sight* of a woman's body.

I know that men are afraid of being out on the streets alone as well. The difference is that men are afraid of being punched, pickpocketed, stabbed, robbed, or worse, killed. Men are not afraid of being *raped.* Every time I ask a man if they've ever been scared of being raped when they're out at night—other than the few disappointing, disgraceful homophobic slurs—most of them say they've never even thought about being raped as an outcome; it's truly never crossed their mind. *Womxn, on the other hand, think about it all the time.* Being alone at home, walking late at night, walking at any hour of the day, if you're in an isolated street in the presence of 1-2 other men, at after-parties, while travelling, in trains, I could go on...

Robbed? That's not something I've thought about... I would any day give up everything I have. But rape? *For us, the fear of rape is as common and real as it gets.*

If our bodies are not the problem, if our bodies are not sexualised at every step, then why is it that most fathers and brothers don't buy lingerie for the womxn in the family, even though mothers and sisters very *often* do the underwear shopping for men? I've done it a thousand times for my brother too. My mother makes me carry a new pack of underwear whenever I visit him because, you know, maybe Spain doesn't sell any underwear. Not that I mind shopping for him at all, but what I do mind is that our society sees *his need* for underwear as a necessity, but *my need* for lingerie is overly sexualised.

None of my friends has gone bra shopping with their dads, but their brothers go underwear shopping with the mums all the time. Why do you think young girls are told to close their legs and not bend so low while putting the dinner out in their own homes? I don't see a lot of boys being told to put on a t-shirt, and I don't see boys being told to fold/cover their legs and sit appropriately either. Boys don't get yelled at for bending like that at dinner tables.

The most confronting part is that *this is a family environment.* We are asking our daughters to maintain a certain body language in their *own homes*, in order to not arouse their own fathers and brothers. *Are we normalising the fact that if a girl walks around her house in a bra, then the men in her family could want to rape her, and that it is her fault?*

Do we ever suspect that of women? Do we think that if a boy is shirtless, his mother and sister may get aroused or behave inappropriately with him, let alone that it would be his fault? I don't think we even raise womxn to imagine such things. We raise women to believe that there's something wrong with their bodies, that *they need to behave appropriately in order to be safe,* while we normalise the crimes of men.

Every time I upload a photo on Instagram that society thinks is controversial, I am asked, *"Would you roam like this in front of your father and brother? Why don't you flash your tits to them and see what happens?"* And I am always so confronted by the sort of upbringing people must have had in order to ask such questions. These men have *raised me.* What, in their head, is supposed to happen if I were to flash my father and/or my brother? Are the men of our families supposed to be sexually aroused by us, or are they supposed to act upon it and teach us a lesson? *Is that all a womxn is worth in our society? Bodies existing for the sole purpose of satisfying the desire of men and reproducing? Bodies that themselves feel no desire of their own, of course.*

Instead of addressing that we're raising men *wrong*, we victim blame and minimise a womxn's worth to... *nothing.*

Why do you always talk about breasts and vaginas, you ask?

Because I would be lying if I told young women that a lot of the battles they'll face in life *aren't going to be about their bodies.* I am not here to lie. When I'm groped in the middle of a street, when someone brushes their hand up my thigh while I'm waiting in an auto on a crowded street, when I feel a hand up my skirt pinch me in a crowded bar, when a man gropes my breast in a train, when men twice my age rub their boners against me in busy lines, when I'm not able to exercise because my clothes bother them, and when I walk down the streets every day, aware of the way they're raping me in their minds—I know that this isn't about me becoming a doctor. It's *always about my breasts and my vagina.*

I choose to discuss these body parts often, because I am sick and tired of being groped, touched, pinched, grabbed, and assaulted. I am tired of being threatened to be raped every time I talk about politics, religion, humanity, the environment, minorities, body positivity, or *absolutely anything under the sun.* I am tired of watching two men fight by claiming to rape each other's mothers and sisters in order to hurt their ego—because, apparently, a man's ego lies in his mother's and sister's vaginas. I'm tired of watching Indian men threaten to rape cricketers' wives and underage daughters when they lose a match. I am tired of perpetually being told I'll be raped for crossing the boundaries *they've made*. There are sick men out there that think raping womxn is the punishment that teaches her a *lesson*, and makes them more of a *man*.

Here I am, announcing that I am taking your *ego* out of my clit and my tit, and reclaiming my body as what it is supposed to be, *mine*. If that makes me a radical feminist, then I'm proud to be one.

Over a thousand different incidents in life when I have been pushed and shoved and touched all because of this body, I have wanted to strip naked and scream, *"Here I am. Is this it? Tell me when you are done staring, so we can finally move the fuck on and you can treat me like a real person!"* but the answer lies in the gang rapes and lives lost of the daughters of our country… they won't stop until there's nothing left.

It's a constant struggle, every single day. Wear a bra, but it shouldn't look like you're wearing one. Cover the strap. Don't wear anything too thin, too transparent, too light, too tight, too short. If anything, I feel like society is perpetually telling us to *focus* on our vaginas and our breasts. Focus on how to cover them up, focus on how to make them perky and hairless, how to use them to our advantage, how to keep them intact, how to be sexy, *but also how to be safe*. The moment you decide to say *"You know what, they're just a pair of breasts, and I'm tired of everybody making such a big deal out of them, here they are,"* the same society loses its mind. There's chaos and lack of control. Everyone is petrified of this unnecessary, unacceptable, radical behaviour of a characterless woman.

Suddenly, you're labelled as the womxn who thinks *feminism is as petty as boobs and vaginas*… but if nobody gives a shit about breasts, then why is my desire to let mine loose even a topic worth discussing?

Men do it all the time. They're shirtless *all the fucking time*, but no one tells them that they're being *petty*. They're just being fit, or inspirational, or silly, or feeling warm, and nobody cares. But the moment a womxn takes her top off, it's like there's a war, and the only enemy is the one they all desire.

I also understand that a lot of women *don't* want to show their tits, and that is absolutely *fine*. There are a *lot* of women out there that want to *cover their breasts,* or their faces, their legs, or maybe all of the above, *by choice*. Let them. Let women decide for themselves what empowers them. Wearing a dupatta empowers some, wearing a bikini empowers some, and the burka empowers some—it is neither your place nor mine to decide for any womxn *what they want*.

We constantly talk about cultures where women cover their heads, claiming that they shouldn't have to, and you are right—*womxn shouldn't have to cover their heads or their faces if they don't want to.* The same way that womxn shouldn't have to wear jeans, or wear a bikini, or wear *anything* that doesn't make them comfortable.

How about we stop forcing womxn to cover their faces, and we stop forcing women to cover their tits, and we also stop forcing womxn to uncover the parts they wish to cover? How about *we let them decide what they want to do?*

Why is society so threatened and confronted by a woman *choosing* what she wishes to do with her body? Some don't want to have sex; others want to have a lot of sex. Some womxn want to upload topless photos because *owning their own body empowers them;* others want to have nothing to do with exposing their bodies because *that empowers them.*

But to say that every womxn has to become a doctor or an engineer or a scientist to be *empowered* is a load of *bullshit*. Some women feel empowered by talking about their own bodies, *that's about tit,* you know?

I'm also aware that you and I can't eradicate the problem. We cannot change the world in one day, and we definitely cannot change the way women's bodies are seen in our society overnight, but what *we can do* is be here, present, through our words and our experiences for the young womxn looking for us. Be here, be ready for when they're looking for you—because they will stumble across these words one day... and when they do, *when you do,* I want you to know that your body is nobody else's but *yours*. Your body is your home. Cherish it. Stretch it. Love it. It is yours to do what you wish with it.

It's OKAY to want to explore your body. It's OKAY to want to empower yourself with it, to experience it, *to own it.*

There sure as hell is a lot of feminism in your bra and your underwear, and it's powerful enough to shake the whole goddamn system—don't you ever let them tell you otherwise.

Love from,

my tits.

My Notes

My Notes

CHAPTER 23

SEXUAL OBJECTIFICATION VS SEXUAL EMPOWERMENT

I have been thinking about this for almost as long as I can remember, and before I jump right in… you and I need to talk about how we see the world around us first. It's tricky, because if you don't understand the two terms, then you automatically confuse them both, which can be harmful to you, your growth, and the people around you. *I know from experience.*

To think that "*objectifying womxn is empowering them*" or to think that "*womxn who are empowering themselves are sexually objectifying their bodies*"—how quickly the misunderstanding of the terms could escalate social stigma, judgement, control, and damage the way we see womxn in general.

Unfortunately, this is not a *possibility* in some distant future, but our reality today. We as a society have already misunderstood the two terms, confused them, mixed them up, and cooked up an awful meal that stinks. Everybody is eating it, even though it tastes so bad, and *no one really likes it*. It's like the whole damn world has an upset stomach, and for those of you that think feminism is cancer, well, let's talk about food poisoning first.

I, much like you and the others like us, felt very confused about the difference between sexual empowerment and objectification. I still do sometimes, because our social conditioning is extremely influential. It's embedded in our minds, fed to us in our daily lives, and to stand against patriarchy and the injustice women go through, we must consistently do our homework of reading, educating ourselves, sharing our views, listening to other womxn, apologising—because it's okay to be wrong and make mistakes—and being more *aware* of the way womxn think/feel around us, being more *aware* of the prejudice they are naturally prone to.

I know it's a lot to do at all times, and a big chunk of *"changing the world"* consists of changing *yourself* because *the only things in your control are your own actions.*

I look at so many womxn around the world *choosing* to expose their bodies *more than others*. Women that wish to wear bikinis, upload photos of themselves that are considered seductive, womxn who think they are attractive and aren't afraid to show it, women that flaunt their ass and their cleavage, womxn that have built an entire empire for themselves and are now multi-millionaires. Some of them are stereotypically hot, and they're smart too because they *know* they're attractive *as per the male expectation,* and hot womxn sell like a new iPhone in the first 24 hours *(sorry, a reference made purely because the new one is out since months and I am thinking about it all the time. I promise this chapter does not lead to comparisons of women to jewels and bank robberies).* And these womxn only care about getting rich and building their own empires. They're not worried about the damage they've done to other women and *their self-worth,* because they're in it for the showbiz and that's an entirely different conversation… But then in contrast, when I see womxn who are *not* your typical standard (whatever that means) of *hot* but are curvy, plus size, big, thin, short, socially tagged *"imperfect"* womxn with vitiligo, women with different skin and disabilities, and womxn breaking stereotypes and *owning the goddamn internet* and creating their own legacies and inspiring other women like themselves to believe that they *are worth it*… I am blown away. When you think about it, *real women* are not perfect and perfection can't possibly be the aim on the journey of *self-love.*

Let's talk about the women in the media that have built their own empires. I often feel like those that judge these women are judging them for all the wrong reasons. We're not talking about the unachievable goals they're setting for young girls, or the toxic society we have created where we *normalise* all the work womxn feel forced to get done in order to *look good.* It's strange, when you think about it, *our bodies are a business capable of selling on its own.* If you are a woman, and you have a body, well guess what? *You are very much a product that can be sold because there's a demand.*

Whenever I talk about personal choices womxn around the world have made for their bodies, there's a certain *shame* and *stigma* attached to what they do. I mean, *the top 20 most famous womxn* in the world might have the highest amount of Instagram followers, fame, and success, however, let's not forget the leaked sex videos and looked-down-upon career choices and how badly *they* were shamed until they became as big as they are today. *Today,* they are an empire. *Today,* they are the exception to the rule.

Except, we can't have it both ways, can we? We can't say *"what an ugly body, only hot women should get naked"* while simultaneously saying *"stereotypically hot women that expose their bodies are making young girls insecure"* because *that's* the society we're currently creating ourselves. *We've made "hot womxn" popular, successful, desired, and in the same breath, we're saying "what a shame, these womxn are harming young influential minds."* I promise you, amazing womxn with real bodies and a voice will stand up and say *"hey, look at me as well, this is real,"* and society will respond with *"shut up and go work out, you're not even hot."*

Do you see the problem?

We don't respect the hot womxn, and we don't respect the womxn we don't find hot either. When it comes to womxn… the word *respect* is categorically saved for personal relationships. Every other womxn is either fuckable or… *unfuckable.* Why don't we respect the ones we think are fuckable? We love them on the internet but they're not what your family wants you to aspire to become. Your own boyfriends and brothers will double-tap models on Instagram but simultaneously think it's unacceptable for you to follow down that *"obscene"* path. Do you think society is worried about the makeup, the insecurities, the surgeries, the disorders? No, in our society, *it's* the *nudity* that makes them shameful, characterless women. *Get as many boob jobs and nose jobs as you like, ladies, as long as you keep the jobs strictly for the bedroom, cover yourself up in public... after all, who else did you get it for? Not yourself, of course...*

I see many young womxn following the footsteps of celebrities (insert: models, actors, singers, porn stars, dancers, etc.) who simply like to *show off their bodies,* whether that's in a gym or on the beach or casually when they're at home. These womxn, regardless of their profession or age, *are shamed for what they choose to do with their own bodies.*

Because womxn that sell their bodies and want to *objectify themselves* and make money are considered *characterless.* We don't respect women that use their bodies to make a living. We, in fact, don't respect women who even *like* their bodies, period. The tone of the conversation is somewhat like: *"What do you expect from men? If she wants to objectify herself, then she's just asking for it";* *"She puts up photos of her ass, she shows her tits, she bends when she smiles, she wears white, can't you see she wants the attention? Such women are sluts, and they get what they deserve."*

Raise your hand if you've ever heard someone say that to you/about you/about another womxn.

Raise your hand if you've ever been confused about how to counter-argue that point because deep down inside, thanks to conditioning, you often judge women yourself for doing those things. *It's okay to accept that by the way.* There is no shame in accepting when we are wrong because that's the first step to change. It's also completely normal for your *first* reaction/thought towards things to be one that arises from conditioning. That doesn't make you a bad person. *What may make you potentially "bad" is when you breed that thought and believe it to be true instead of challenging it.*

We, as womxn, judge other womxn for being attractive, for showing their skin *by choice*. But we *don't* judge men for being attractive or topless or *any of the same choices*. Men could be supplying or demanding, the blame automatically falls on womxn.

Oh, the number of times and places I have encountered men shirtless and not even thought about it twice. Bars, parties, beaches, drunk on roads, marching on the streets, friends' houses, riding bikes, an after-work party in a sports bar—cheering their favourite team and exchanging t-shirts, pepping each other like they're the ones playing the game, *"testosterone"...* *"boys will be boys"... "they sweat when they play sports, you know, give them a break"...* The gym, the park, near the pool, in the pool, at the traffic light on big billboards, driving the car on a warm summer day, walking their dogs, on a tram after the beach, running—the list is endless. I actually saw a man shirtless at the airport once. He spilt hot coffee on his t-shirt and then he casually took it off, and the waitress immediately got him some tissues and directed him to the toilet. I didn't even once, for a split second, think *"wow, what a fucking whore, he's so inappropriate... as if this slut just took his shirt off, there are children here!"*

But as I boarded my flight, I thought, *damn, imagine if that was a woman...*

I've seen womxn be escorted out of places for being *"inappropriately dressed"* even though I have actually never seen a *topless womxn* in person anywhere in the world, except for the Barcelona beach. Makes you think *"inappropriate"* is just something we measure based on our mentality, *or what we think will distract our men*.

Two years ago in Portugal, I was at the beach and we walked on the sidewalk from the beach to a cute little Indian restaurant *by the beach*. I was wearing a long bohemian skirt and a bikini top, and as we take a table *(outside, by the beach, not even inside the restaurant)*, this waiter walks out looking extremely irritated, and he tells us we can't sit at the table unless *I* wear appropriate clothes. I wasn't naked... in fact, I was wearing a full-length skirt. In a moment of shock and embarrassment as other guests looked up at us, I nervously said to Rahul that I should wrap a scarf, but he seemed far more offended than me. He said there was no way we would be insulted like that, so we left (after giving the staff a piece of our mind).

I realised that when confronted out of nowhere, my first reaction was to *obey* because a part of me is just conditioned to believe if I'm being told off by a man, *then it must be my mistake.* Having someone with me who saw the situation for what it was, absolutely sexist and unfair, helped me gather my own confidence to stand up for myself. But it was jarring, to say the least. The waiter, the people sitting there quietly eyeing me, probably judging me themselves, the mindset of those that first noticed— *the discomfort society feels when they see a woman's body.*

Another time, in Croatia, after being at an island all day, I got onto a ferry that would take me from Hvar back to Split. I was wearing a pretty, red frilly crop top style bikini/bralette and, once again, a long skirt. Honestly, I didn't even carry other clothes. It was my *outfit of the day* because when you're sandy and have spent all day in salt water, it's the most comfortable thing to cover yourself with because it dries off and doesn't stick to your legs (look at me, trying to justify my choices), and this middle-aged male staff who checked my ticket *first checked me out top to bottom shamelessly, then asked me where the rest of my clothes were.* As though I was *naked.* Behind me was *an entire line up of shirtless men* that boarded the same ferry without being scrutinised or objectified the way I was. They weren't judged, ogled at, insulted, or commented upon because they weren't, evidently, *asking for it* the way I was.

A number of times in life, I have been treated with little to no respect simply because people around me think that *I am disrupting the society we live in due to the choice of the clothes I put on my body.* I'm basically distracting men, so I must be *characterless.* With all honesty, far too many times, I've looked at other womxn and had the exact same thoughts about them—especially when I was much younger, out with a boyfriend, or if I was feeling particularly insecure that day.

News flash: On most days, thanks to the different ways in which we oppress womxn, I wake up feeling quite insecure about my body, and therefore often doubtful of my entire existence. It's bad enough when you're not what they tell you you're supposed to be all day—a beautiful, curvy but not fat, light-skinned woman, that never has her periods, never poops, never farts, is ambitious but puts family first, looks gorgeous when pregnant and has thick black long hair (only on her head), loves your parents and dresses well enough that you can see she's attractive but never inappropriately, is a trophy that you show off to all your friends who are jealous of you, except she's not a slut because she's gorgeous in a respectable way, she is calm and poised, composed, smart, and yes, gives the world's greatest blow jobs, even though she must have never ever given one before you; she's just a natural, you see.

Now, imagine waking up bloated, with frizzy hair and clogged pores, luckily not pregnant but PMSing with back pain and no energy to shower, let alone shave—and having to live up to those goddamn standards. There are multiple reasons why I'm such an "angry feminist."

Anyway, coming back to the point: I have judged other womxn that I think are beautiful, attractive, or confident. *A woman that exposes her body, or is outwardly sexy by my standards, which are really originally a man's standards, is automatically being a whore and seeking attention*—that's the thought process our society teaches and normalises.

So then *what* is the difference between sexual objectification and sexual empowerment? That thought right there—when you judged her—*that's an example of objectification.*

Unfortunately, we have made ample amounts of space for *objectification* and little scope for *empowerment*, which is why the latter is so hard to digest. We sell womxn's bodies in porn, in music videos, in movies, in magazines, on billboards. There is an unspoken understanding that at *any point* if a woman's body is visible, it is for the purpose of evoking men's desires, not because *she likes it*. And so we ask women to *"cover the fuck up"* politely. We tell them to dress appropriately. We judge the ones that break the rules because if she's not doing it to distract a man or steal our boyfriend and also isn't *"asking for it,"* then what the hell does she possibly want?

When *men* expose their bodies, we don't think that they're doing it to distract or pleasure womxn—*because, hold on, what pleasure? Womxn and pleasure? That's not a real thing, that's just feminazi propaganda.* Men expose their bodies to build muscles, to have fun, to play sports, to inspire other men to be healthy, to become bodybuilders and trainers, to become models, to be fit, or because the weather is unbearably hot and they're at the beach. A man's body is not supply and demand, because womxn all over the world are not paying for it, and so an attractive topless man is just an attractive topless man. Who knows, maybe some women want to capture him to *marry him* and *have babies with him* while *she still can.* Evidently, according to society, womxn don't like to just *fuck.*

This has taken me so long to explain only because it's *extremely important* that you understand the difference between the two terms and how they have affected our society. I've had to take a long scenic route on this road trip with you.

The only difference, as I understand, between sexual *objectification* and sexual *empowerment* is who holds the *power* in that situation. If she's wearing the shortest shorts because *she thinks* her ass is *sexy* and *she likes it*, that for me is sexual empowerment. If you're passing unrequired remarks on how *you* think her ass looks or taking photos of her to send to your friends and circulate on the internet without her knowledge, that's *definitely* sexual objectification, and also *illegal*—it's a form of abuse and harassment. If *she's* having sex on a webcam or recording it with you because *she* wants to experiment or see it later, *that's sexually empowered.* If she's doing it because *you* forced or coerced her by telling her that you'll break-up with her if she doesn't do it, that's objectification and, once again, also sexual harassment. If *she* uploaded a sexy photo of herself on Instagram because *she* thought *she* looked hot, that's *her* sexually empowering herself and owning *her* body. If *you* took that photo and made a fake account or sent her a picture of your penis just because you follow her and you think she'll want one, that's sexual objectification and *drum roll* *harassment.* If *she's* sitting in a tank top without a bra at a cafe and *she's* comfortable with *her body,* that's empowering. If *you,* in return, make that all about how attracted *you* are to her because *you* can see the shape of her nipples and start passing remarks, that's objectification and… good guess, harassment. (And if you've done all of the above, congratulations, you've won harassment bingo!)

There is nothing wrong in finding a womxn sexy or attractive, but to lose all respect for her the moment she's attractive to you because from then onwards she's no longer a human being with feelings, desires, or her own decisions to make, she's simply a piece of meat to you *that's asking for it*— that's where things go wrong. Womxn find men attractive/unattractive *all the time*—in bars, streets, beaches, and all other public spaces—and usually, womxn do not scream out "*Yuck, cover that body up, you fat ass*" or "*Baby, that damn ass, come on, baby, smile, wanna ride?*" I mean, can you even believe how ridiculous that would be if men couldn't get out on the streets without being spoken to the same way by women, while simultaneously being threatened to be raped, groped in crowds, and gang-raped regularly?

We respect men and what they choose to do with their own bodies. *Not only do we disrespect womxn for the same, but we also limit their ability to choose for themselves.*

A perfect example of this are sex workers and womxn in the porn industry. I am making a choice not to get involved in the *"why do they do it"* and *"is it by choice"* discussion. I want to talk about how, universally, we as a society don't care if womxn *chose it or not,* we simply don't respect womxn in those professions; we look down upon them. Yes, even the ones that *had no choice* in the first place. *Why don't we respect them when there is a huge demand for womxn and sex in our society—enough for womxn to be trafficked, sold, and forced into it? Where does this demand come from? Men. Who usually goes to sex workers? Men. Who watches porn? By the ridiculous way it's been portrayed, I'm guessing in a lot of cultures and societies, openly more men than womxn. Who gets lap dances in strip clubs? Mmmm, usually men. Who buys magazines and wanks off to the photos in the magazine at night before hiding it under their bed? As of now, mostly men.*

Hence, the demand for a woman's *body* in the sex industry is *huge*, but these *women* that are contributing to men masturbating, orgasming, cumming, ejaculating, climaxing—whatever you wish to call it—they are looked down upon. These womxn are disrespected, even though the *men, who are the reason for these industries existing in the first place, are not looked down upon.* Technically, we've just socially accepted that men have high testosterone and are extremely *sexual* animals that'll bone whatever they can lay their eyes on. So, as a womxn, if you happen to *be there and be attractive,* well, *let's take your incident of abuse and set an example of what other womxn shouldn't be doing.*

Every man I have ever known or met in my entire life has seen porn at some point or the other. You and I don't start disrespecting them for watching porn at all. However, the womxn that act in the porn being watched by everyone are considered characterless. We don't want them in *our* societies. Shouldn't we at some point then boycott the men that watch these womxn too? What the fuck are we smoking?

Situation: A womxn uploads an attractive photo in lingerie on Instagram, gets 5,000 more followers, and ends up with 30,000 likes. Everybody says *"what a whore"; "Girls are selling their bodies"; "She's doing it for the fame"; "If you're a woman, then it's so easy to become famous. All you have to do is show your boobs and your butt."* While on the other side, she's getting rape threats, unsolicited dick pics, extremely graphic texts about what men want to do to her without her consent, and of course, multiple abuses and death threats. Throughout this process, no one turns around and asks the people that made her *famous... "why are you following her then?"*

We tell girls to make their accounts private in order to not get harassed on the internet, but are we simultaneously checking to see the accounts of our boys to make sure *they aren't harassing*?

Why do we think it's acceptable to treat a womxn like an object, simply because she's attractive? If she's using her breasts to become famous, who are these people that are *making her famous* in the first place? Why are her breasts objectified all the damn time? And who decided that anything that men find attractive should be hidden away? And for how long? *Where does this stop?*

When I have a photo that *I think* I look extremely sexy in, *I* upload it knowing that if *I* have the power in this situation, if *I'm* comfortable, and *I* love the way *I* look—then it doesn't matter if men want to wank off to it or not. It doesn't matter if society wants to call me a slut or not, because in that particular situation, *I hold the power,* and hence, *I'm empowered.* I try to apply the same rule to other womxn that I see. If her breasts are out and *she doesn't mind it* because *she wants it that way,* then that's her life and her choice to make. Ladies, go raise those temperatures. I am nobody to judge you, and why the hell should I or anybody judge you for loving yourself?

Men and womxn that want to objectify you will objectify you even in jeans and a full sleeve t-shirt. If your hair is beautiful, or you laugh in an attractive way, or you part your lips and eat ice cream, whatever you do, they'll objectify you. You cannot stop people from being assholes, but if you love the way you look, or in fact aren't even sure of what you feel about the way you look but *you want to flaunt it*—do it. Do it for you. Do it with power. Do it on your own terms. Don't let them objectify you when you're uncomfortable and feeling used. Don't wear short clothes because that's the only way to impress a man or because everyone else is doing it. Don't wear clothes that cover you because you think you'll be judged for showing skin either. Don't do any of it under *pressure.*

Spend time with yourself, find out what makes *you* feel comfortable (and it's absolutely okay for your comfort level to change every day), and choose that. Sexual empowerment is the freedom to choose for yourself. To look at yourself and *know* that you feel sexy, or that you're working on feeling sexy, regardless of what the *standards of sexy are.* To walk into a bar and know you'll turn eyes but still leave for the night with the freedom to *choose* if you want to go home alone or with someone. Without being judged, touched, catcalled, harassed, abused, groped, threatened, raped, or killed.

Basically, a right that *every man* is born with.

Ask yourself, what sexually empowers you? And allow other womxn the space to exist in this world without constantly being a threat to you and your well-being just because you think they are attractive. We are not a threat to each other, ladies—we are not competing here. If you're having to *compete* for a man, then the problem is not the women around you; the problem is the man. This is not a race; it shouldn't feel like one either. We need to do a better job at this, we need to learn to *coexist*, to *support* each other, to *trust* each other more often than we stab each other in the back.

Next time you see a womxn that's confident and sexy in her own element, I don't care what your first thought is, have another thought, and smile at her. *God knows we all need the support.*

Write down what sexually empowers you and what makes you feel objectified.

My Notes

My Notes

CHAPTER 24

ENABLERS OF PATRIARCHY

Believe it or not, but it was *rotis* that made me aware of the fact that I'm an enabler of patriarchy, *good old rotis*. I was talking to Rahul about our cook one day, and how I need to have a chat with her because it's either the atta (flour) or she's slacking because the rotis were just *not right* the last few months. Casually, without even once looking up from his laptop, he says, *"Rotis are absolutely fine. What's wrong with them?"* And because I couldn't believe the words coming out of his mouth, frustrated, I replied, *"Are you serious? They're either not cooked or too thick or too dry. How the hell do you not —"* Amidst that sentence was a light bulb moment that literally changed a huge part of my life, because I realised, *of course, he doesn't know... after all, how would he?*

I have had a subconscious habit of putting the best rotis onto his plate and taking the okay/bad ones myself. I don't think I could even tell you how long I'd been doing this for because I had no idea I was doing it at all until we were in the middle of this discussion where he didn't even *know* the problem because *I* made sure that the *problem never reached him.*

For as far back as I could remember, I was unknowingly doing something that I have yelled at my mother for doing my whole life; *"Stop feeding us the good ones and eating the old stale ones yourself. This self-sacrifice is not love, it's lack of self-love. Stop it, Ma."* It felt as though I didn't even know who I was anymore. I was moments away from snapping at my partner for being so absent-minded and ignorant, for not even knowing that the rotis have been bad when he had actually, in reality, been having good rotis for the better part of the year. *We were living different realities, and that too with my help.*

My entire life, I have seen womxn make excuses for their sons, brothers, husbands, and fathers. I've heard Indian families talk about the daughter-in-law and how *messy* she is, how she doesn't *cook or clean after she comes home from work, the kind of clothes she wears and how she cares more about her stupid job than she does about her children, she's even worse than a man.*

Someone very close to my heart was abused by her own cousin brother when she was barely 9 years old. Her mother found out and *begged her not to tell the father* because that cousin was from *the mother's side of the family*, and she knew that if the father found out, he would blame *her mother.*

So, she didn't speak, in order to protect her mother and her family. Year after year, she went for vacations in a house with her abuser, in order to protect her mother.

Another womxn I know was with someone who was a compulsive liar, and she was unsure of their marriage, but then one night, he forcefully had anal sex with her, and she bled. When she told her mother what had happened and why she wanted to leave, her mother said, *"Men are all the same, beta. Your aunty says your uncle often used to force her too, and eventually, you get used to it."* That uncle was her mother's brother.

Another womxn I know wanted to leave her husband because he had been doing dodgy things behind her back with her finances and she didn't trust him anymore. She would always tell me, someday she'll run away and come live with me. When she tried to tell her parents that she didn't want to keep doing this, she wanted a divorce, they asked her to get psychological help and go on antidepressants instead of ending her marriage. Because *she* was unhappy, *she* had to fix herself, or just have a child because *that* will solve the problem. So, she took the pills, and she had the child to put a blanket on all her problems. She wasn't the first, and she sure as hell is not last.

A young womxn I know was raped by a boy she *knew*. She went public with her #metoo story on Facebook because she wanted people to *know*. I asked her how her father reacted to it, to which she said he didn't even *know*. The entire family, including her mother, blocked the father on Facebook and found a way to deal with it in his absence because his presence would've meant pain, and not telling him was the *"right thing" to do*.

Another woman I know had been molested by her own cousin, his friends, her neighbour, and a man she met on a date. She refuses to speak about it publicly because she knows if she did, *her mother would tell her it's her fault.*

A man I dated grew up in an environment where his mother didn't allow his sisters to eat food until *he had finished eating*. Only after they'd served him food and he had finished, would the sisters then sit to eat. When we were dating, I noticed he didn't understand the concept of sharing food or checking if other people in the house had eaten or not before finishing *everything* in the fridge. After I met his mother, I finally understood why.

These stories don't even make up for half of the womxn I know, *not even close.*

Growing up in an environment mainly driven by culture and tradition, I have seen womxn time and again not only enable but also *protect* patriarchy. We make excuses for the men we know and we love, and we protect gender roles with everything we've got *like our lives depend on them*, which for far too many womxn, it maybe does.

If you want to really change the world, then the very first thing you need to do is look in the mirror because *you and I are often the enablers of the very system we wish to eradicate.*

Womxn enable and protect patriarchy. As *Shirin Ebadi* once said, *"Women are the victims of this patriarchal culture, but they are also its carriers. Let us keep in mind that every oppressive man was raised in the confines of his mother's home."*

Every single time that you've watched your mother make an excuse for your father's abusive behaviour, every time that you've allowed a man to yell, abuse, insult/assault you or anyone else around you, every time you've given reasons for why he drinks so much or why he has anger issues, why he raises his hands but still loves you anyway. Every time you tell a womxn to cover up and if she doesn't, then *she sure as hell had it coming,* for every *"she deserved it,"* for every time you cage and restrict the womxn in your family in order to protect them, every time you say *"who will marry her if she cannot cook?"* and every single time you convince yourself that *"I'm doing this to maintain peace in the family"*—you are enabling patriarchy.

Yes, womxn are victims of their conditioning and hence the vicious cycle continues, but who said that a victim cannot also be the perpetrator for another?

Womxn in families that know no better than to live the way they have been raised are the ones still protecting the patriarchy and raising a generation of people affected by it.

Some don't have a choice while others genuinely believe in the system. Regardless of which one you resonate/live with, you must also know that unless we take the first step and *accept* that women are also *enablers* of patriarchy, we will never be any closer to eliminating it.

It is this hole that men and women have dug for decades and generations before me, and even though I don't *want* to be in this hole, as a womxn, I was born in it, and every day I just keep digging deeper and deeper. It's almost like I'm not digging to get anywhere, I'm digging because I don't know any better.

For example, there was a time when my partner's parents didn't like the kind of photos I uploaded on Instagram (surprise, surprise) and a part of me, unknowingly, would make whatever little compromises I could in order to not hurt them. It was never as black and white as *"okay, I'll change."* Instead, I'd limit the number of times I uploaded controversial content—as though *balance* would make any difference in their outlook. If I had done an interview or a debate about sex ed or female bodies, then I'd go out of my way not to share it on Facebook, because I didn't want to *actively* be disliked by them. The strange part is, I never *force* myself to do these things or make these gestures. I don't even *realise* I'm making compromises until a month or two later in hindsight I think, *I'm living my life in order to accommodate someone else's family and their feelings even though I tell my own family to just deal with it.*

Why was I giving his family the importance I never gave mine? Well, don't forget, finding a man who loves you and a family that accepts you is literally *the most important thing in a woman's life.* So, of course, with that not-so-subtle social conditioning, *it had an impact on my thought process.*

It's only *after* I'm aware of the compromises I've been making for months that the problem really begins—which makes you think about how so many womxn probably never even get to *this step.*

I start feeling extremely snappy, sad, and upset about my surroundings. I feel a sense of loss, lack of identity. I feel pressured into having chosen this path to *avoid* conflict, as though *I* have done something wrong and *now it was my job to fix it.* My only two options end up being *"be the real me and deal with the drama that follows"* or *"don't be me, and avoid the drama."*

Here comes the dramatic, filmy part of all Hindi movies where the *hero saves the day.* My partner notices how this situation is affecting me. He offers to speak up on my behalf and tell them to back off. He says he can fight with them because *"his family shouldn't be sitting there passing judgements on my character."* And then when the first argument takes place, an even bigger rush of sadness and guilt takes over me because I have now suddenly realised that *I'm* causing conflict in *his family.* Where does *that realisation* come from? Well, of course, *patriarchy.* Years of hearing families talk about that *"terrible daughter-in-law who tore the family apart"* and being raised with phrases like *"if his parents don't accept you, he will eventually one day leave"* and people saying things like *"after she came into his life, he was so distant from his parents, she broke their bond"* mixed with of course his own family throwing shade on *how difficult it is that their son has changed since he's been with you.*

"Why couldn't she just not create this mess if she truly loved their son? Why would she pit him against his own?" So, I beg him to stop fighting. Because let's step back and face it, he did *ask* me before he picked this fight, and so when I tell him to stop, he will most probably stop fighting as well. The only person he is doing this for is *me*.

Does abruptly ending a fight without any conclusions help? No.

Are you still the bad guy? *YES.*

Not only that but you're now also sandwiched between living your life on your own terms vs wanting to keep his family together. Is living *your life* according to *other people* the only way to *not spark a fire?*

When you really think about it, women only hold so much power to *"destroy a family"* because that power goes hand in hand with their character and their choices. *If people stopped caring about what womxn were doing with their lives, half this power would go away.*

This feeling—this particular scattered state of mind—is possibly one of the saddest moments, because you're well aware of the fact that *you haven't done anything wrong*, but you're also aware that if you stand up for what *you believe to be right,* you will be encouraging conflict. As long as you stay silent and ignore the insults and adapt to their lives, *you will be okay.*

You are expected to mourn the death of *your* desires, without the slightest cry.

But that shouldn't be too hard, given that it's exactly what you've seen your mother and grandmother do your whole life, right? What you've had to do when *"dad comes home"* at night. You've made plenty of compromises and you have watched the womxn of your families make them with ease too. If anything, the womxn that raised you don't whisper *"you won't have to do what I did"* at night. Instead, they prepare you for the misogyny because *"they want what's best for you."* They are parents, and they know that the sooner you understand your place in this world, the happier you will be. After all, ignorance is bliss.

And that is how you enable patriarchy. You give the women of the house the power, not all the power of course, but just enough power to be right under the man, and then you let them dictate and decide a decorum of behaviour. What's the purpose of their life? To be validated by their husbands, his family, and this society. And how do you get validated? By always doing the right thing by society.

If I were to become the womxn that constantly compromised on my own self to keep a man's family together, I could maybe see myself 20 years later thinking that *this is the way of life.* How else do you convince yourself to give up on *you*? So, you convince yourself that what you're doing is the ultimate *right thing,* and you raise your daughter to know well enough how to compromise. And god forbid if your son brings home a girl who lives her life on her own terms regardless of how little it fits with your own values. You remind him that *"she doesn't actually love you or belong in our family. If she did, she would change."* And he believes you because he knows the sacrifices you've made for your own family, and he loves you enough to know that a woman should be aspiring to be as strong as his own mother, oblivious to the fact that *strength never meant compromise.*

Generations down the line, this is how family *values* are sworn by and cultures are kept unshattered, and womxn continue to protect the patriarchy they were conditioned under and enforce it further onto the women their sons bring home.

When you grow up and fall in love and start a family, there are three kinds of womxn you could become if you were raised the way I was:

The kind that was conditioned to take up less space and accommodate the people around her, but grew up wanting to live her life according to what *she* thinks is right, regardless of whether it creates conflict or not, because at the end of the day, this conflict isn't *her* fault; it is the fault of people that are patriarchal enough to demand her to change *for them.*

Or the kind of womxn that is torn between her desires and her responsibility. Who after a point doesn't want to fight the world every day. There are only so many battles she can fight and win, without feeling exhausted and breaking down. It's her against society, and when her independence and freedom is at stake, it's maybe better to have *some* freedom than none at all.

So, you enable and protect patriarchy and demand that no one tries to break the very rules you gave up everything to sustain.

Or lastly, the kind that is torn yet again, between her desires and her responsibility. Only so many battles she can fight and win without feeling exhausted and breaking down. So, you sacrifice your own self to make sure that the children you raise get every opportunity you didn't, and you whisper to them every night that they won't have to sacrifice their dreams too.

They will grow up to shake the system.

Focus with me for just a second: there are children out there, many of whom are like us, in fact, we are those children, and we are *proud of the patriarchy that suppressed our mothers their whole life. Mothers that wanted to sing, dance, become doctors, work, run a business, teach, or maybe write poetry.* We actually admire this system *for killing her sense of self and putting her husband, her/his relatives, her children before her own identity.* We continuously glorify the sacrifices womxn have made in order to become wives and mothers. To give up *everything* and live for *others.* If you *respect* the sacrifices your mother has made, that also makes *you* an enabler of patriarchy, whether you like it or not.

It's one thing to understand these sacrifices, and another to admire them. There is nothing *admirable* about letting go of yourself and continuously putting up with abuse. She shouldn't have had to, and *yet she did.* She surely deserves an award for doing it, but what she also deserves is *support* and *help.* What *she deserves* is for you to remember to give her *her voice* back. She deserves for you to treat her with *the same respect as you treat your father* instead of occasionally snapping at her because mothers are *soft-hearted and god-sent, unconditionally loving creatures that love their children and would give up everything for the happiness of their family.* Mothers, unfortunately—to be damn good ones at that—are required to stop seeing themselves as individual human beings with passions and desires and opinions, as working womxn, as bosses, as human beings. Mothers are set up to fail because once you're a mother, *everything else* doesn't seem to matter. In order to be a *good* mother or a *good* wife, a woman has to first let go of *herself.*

And you can't blame them for doing that, can you? That is what we raise our children to expect of womxn.

We don't respect mothers for the same reasons we *respect* our fathers. We don't respect women for leaving a loveless marriage or for working late nights to build their careers. We don't respect womxn for getting remarried as many times as they fall in love or for standing their ground/leaving when they feel disrespected. *We encourage women to have no identity outside of being a wife and a mother.* How often do you see boys in an Indian society growing up daydreaming about their weddings and becoming dads? No, they're being told to be masculine, be strong, get a job, and be successful. Women are being conditioned to be good wives and mothers. Most conversations around the house are *"learn this, beta, one day when you're a mother, you're going to need it,"* but we've conveniently skipped the whole section of upbringing where we teach the same things to men because one day *they're going to be fathers and husbands* and should they not know how to cook, clean, change diapers, wash clothes, respect womxn, stay hygienic, learn to stitch a button, be vulnerable, and forgive with compassion, maybe?

This gender-based conditioning is precisely the reason *why* young womxn are faced with the choice of having an identity and ambition versus having a family, and far too many of them choose the latter, not because *they want to* but because *they've been well prepared for this day from the moment they were born.*

We encourage women to become martyrs because their respect is tied to how many sacrifices they make for us, equivalent to the way soldiers sacrifice themselves for their country. So what if they practically kill themselves in the process of keeping us alive, we clap and praise the things they did to help us get to where we are today, even though we're fighting against the very norms we're glorifying in the first place.

So, are womxn victims of patriarchy? Yes, of course, they are. But can victims also be the perpetrators? Yes, they can be. It's a systematic problem with a vicious cycle that probably won't end unless we use our voices to start a discussion and until *we accept* that even though we are *victims* of this system, we are also actively *protecting* the system that limits our abilities, with every single choice we make.

The world doesn't change because the people in power wake up one day and realise they would like to share their space. It changes because of the noise people with less power are making. It changes because those that have been catering to a system for far too long realise that they have a voice and *they can use that voice to make ripples in the water.* No matter what your journey or your story, it doesn't take away your ability to *change something.* Even if you chose to never speak up again, you'd be contributing towards *a change* in this world... Your silence may be the path that silences other womxn who are to come after you, and if that's not something you're ready to fight for, it's okay. The first step is to acknowledge the space you hold in this systematic oppression and inequality.

Knowing that you occupy some space in this world—is a change, to begin with.

Take a moment and think about things you might be doing to enable the patriarchy, and what can/will you change to stop doing so?

My Notes

My Notes

CHAPTER 25

HERO

I want to watch more movies with female protagonists. But that's not possible till more womxn become the protagonists of *their own lives* because these stories are being *written by men, for men.*

I want to see young girls grow up to fairy tales where the princess was never saved by a prince at all. Maybe they dealt with the struggles, maybe they went and rescued a dog, or better yet, they got help, saved themselves, and then rescued the prince as well.

I want young women to grow up watching stories of other women who aren't stereotypes. To *know* that womxn fall in love with womxn, and not all womxn have breasts and vaginas, not all womxn love men, not all womxn can/want to have children. Some womxn don't know *what* they want and they're allowed to build their own journey in life as they find themselves, love themselves, and if they never play with a doll or make a single roti their entire life, *it would be absolutely fine.*

The thing is, I want *you* to be the *hero* of your story. I am so sick and tired of watching movies where the female actor is always tall, beautiful, thin, with long hair, and big breasts. You know why they're cast? Because these stories are being *written by men, for men,* so they go with the stereotype that *they find sexy.*

But not all womxn look and behave like that. Not all womxn have zero interests in life outside of giggling and dancing around trees in high heels while the hero saves the world. If movies were being written by womxn, *the least* we'd do is make sure she at least wears comfort clothes when she's on her period (surely, she bleeds, doesn't she?) and puts on a bloody sweater in the snow, instead of her being in a saree. I mean, who wants a love story with pneumonia as the highlight?

Women in the real world are versatile, varied, flawed, ambitious, confused, confident, pleasant, angry, sexual, asexual, and all sized so differently, with each one having a different mess to handle—much like the men in these stories who actually are quite flawed, but the womxn they fall in love with are always *like an angel.* Women have alopecia, vitiligo, eating disorders, depression, anxiety, insecurities, acne, PCOD, endometriosis, UTIs, hormonal imbalances, disabilities, and a shit load of other struggles on a daily basis, but we don't see these in our stories, do we? We don't find out about their hormones or how their bodies change, or their struggle to find the right bra size, their first period, or when their hair fall. No one's talking about this stuff because stories are being *written by men, for men.*

Womxn in our movies don't have flaws because they are not the protagonist; they're just the love interests. The protagonist is the man, and that by the way is one of the biggest *justifications* for the pay gap between male and female actors in the Indian film industry. The male hero has *more screen time, hence is working much more. So, it's only fair, isn't it?* No, it isn't. It's a blanket on the real problem: *womxn don't have enough screen time.* If you really want to juice out the female character in your movie, *add item songs and scenes in bikinis,* the audience will definitely come to whistle at her waistline on a big screen before they go shag themselves in the bathroom after. These are the same people that then say *"look at the modern era and what all women can now wear and not be slut-shamed by their audience. We allow this, what more equality do they want?"* I don't know, maybe the kind where you *don't shame womxn for wearing that off-camera also?* The film industry creates what sells. Womxn's bodies, sex, coming-of-age stories, flawed male heroes, love stories, religion, and fantasy—*this shit sells*. I'm pretty sure the majority of the men and womxn who watch movies with so-called empowered-female-characters go home and say vague ignorant things like *"what more equality do women want?"* They are the people that *won't* let their wives, daughters, sisters, and girlfriends wear those clothes. Is it even equality if it's only real *on your screen* and not in your life? Because that's not equality. *That's a product, that is a sale.*

If we do not accept flawed characters in our lives, then the flaws of our hero *are just another sale*. If we do not accept womxn in bikinis in our own lives, then aren't these women's bodies just being used to get an audience to the cinema? A woman's body sells. It's a product with a *lot* of demand, as already established, and there is nothing empowering about the fact that womxn all over the country have zero control over *their own bodies*.

Stories are being written by men, for men—and the only thing they're selling you is a dream to *find your hero*. Nobody is teaching young womxn to *become heroes*. I don't know if you've ever thought about this, but guess what? If you're looking for a hero in your life, then *you are automatically just another character in your own damn story, aren't you?* Are you sure that's the dream you want to sign up for, where you're not even an equal protagonist with the same screen time? This isn't a multiple cast film, no, what we're buying as *life goals* are just stories where our life *revolves around a man, marriage*, and *the happy ending*. Shockingly, this happy ending has to happen before 30, because, wait, when do we ever see stories of women finding love or feeling alive at/after 40? The only time we make stories about 35+-year-old womxn is when they're divorced, widows, mothers, sisters, and wives. Or the *lonely womxn that missed her youth, as a lesson to be learnt*. Where I come from, we don't make stories inspiring women to *become something*.

I once had an acquaintance-friend that I used to hang out with over drinks. We had the kind of relationship where one of us would randomly call the other person with almost no notice and ask if we were free. We never met at restaurants, nor did we really hang out with each other's friends that often. We just sat up all night at his place and talked until morning. It was actually quite beautiful, *for me*. We would talk about everything under the sun—marriage, love, cinema, feminism, patriarchy, religion, poverty, people, life… my life. He knew a *lot* about me.

I remember he'd always tell me that I'm still young and naive, and with age, *the naivety will fade*. I would laugh. I *hated* being told by people "*once you're older, you'll know better*" because it feels like they're slapping you with their words, very politely. Like "*it's not your mind, it's just that you're too young, so nothing you do or say will matter.*"

I, on the other hand, don't think age has much to do with it. It's about experiences. A 12-year-old boy on the streets, struggling to make his ends meet, might know far more about life than a 30-year-old privileged, sheltered, rich man living with his parents. I genuinely do think that sometimes, *age can't help you learn things, and neither can it stop you from learning things* (also, I notice that most of my examples are always of men).

This friend of mine and I grew distant because we both got busy. When I met him one night after almost two years, he told me how he'd written a whole script and he was pitching it to production houses. I asked him to tell me more about this story of his, and that's when he said, "*It's actually inspired by you, but like you in the future. The conversations we had made me want to write something meaningful…*" At this point, I thought, *I inspired him to write a script? Who knows, maybe he likes me too? I've clearly had an impact.* He went on to tell me more about this story with a female protagonist, and as it turns out, his *film* was about a girl who was *stubborn* and "*too independent.*" She didn't want to change her values for anyone. She was "*too ambitious*" and as she hits 30, she realises how alone and miserable she is. She realises that she's made mistakes, she's lonely, and maybe she should've done things differently.

I don't know, I stopped listening after a point because I felt the ground beneath me shift. I was so numb that his voice started to echo. All I knew was that I had opened myself up to someone about my life, my dreams, and my goals, and he had broken my trust and betrayed me by *writing an entire story about the future me being miserable in life because I was independent, refused to be disrespected in relationships, and cared about my values.* In his story, I would grow up to regret being the womxn I wanted to be in my future.

At first, I was very upset. Eventually, that sadness and betrayal turned into absolute rage, before it eventually, slowly turned into pity. I never said much to him. At the time, it didn't feel like a battle worth fighting, but it was also the last time I ever met him. He never made that film either. He went on to make many others, ones I actually liked.

The bottom line is, I think it wasn't entirely *his fault.* It's all of us as a society. We have different labels for womxn who are ambitious, independent, strong-headed vs men who want the exact same things. I have never seen a movie about *a man at 30 who regrets the same life choices.* In fact, he's portrayed as the *eligible bachelor* who has womxn throwing themselves at him. He's charming, and he's *successful.* Women, on the other hand, are *lonely, intimidating, and depressed.* Men are not throwing themselves at successful women in our stories. Instead, they are threatened by them because these women seem to *lack family values.* The male hero is usually just *having fun, meeting women—mama mia, he's a casanova.* God forbid, you have a female *hero* do the same things at 30, there's a huge social outcry about *the wrong kind of feminism that's being promoted to ruin young womxn in India.*

While these sure as hell are *stories written by men, for men,* they are also a reflection *of our society and its values.* We do not value a woman's career, her independent growth, or her financial stability. We value a woman's fertility, her ability to cook and look after a man's needs. When it comes to womxn, we want her to be nurturing, sensitive, caring, and *adjustable.* As for men, we want them educated, strong, powerful, and successful. I can see why right at the start of humanity, some odd person somewhere thought *this would be the right thing, one will complement the other,* but it isn't *working* anymore. It hasn't been working for generations. It's suffocating us.

You, if you're not a *man,* are taught to be the sidekick character in your own story, which is why your whole life is about learning to make rotis, to be accommodating, to get a degree but not be too ambitious at work. Don't stay out in the sun because you'll become dark, don't frown you'll get wrinkles, and *definitely* find love and get married in your early/mid-twenties, because *it's all downhill from there for us womxn.* Men, on the other hand, will reach their *peak.* We teach men to be the centre of their own worlds, while we *also* teach womxn that men are the centre of their worlds as well. Boys aren't raised with dreams to find the perfect woman, get married, have a baby, build a family—those are just things that will eventually happen once you have your career in place. Women, on the other hand, daydream of their wedding dress their whole life. They are not told that if you just focus on being successful, *the rest will fall in place.*

In order to *see a change* in this world, in the stories, in movies, in fairy tales, I need *you to be the change you wish to see.* As corny as it sounds, *be the hero of your own story.* Instead of growing up/raising your daughters to one day find a rich husband or an eligible bachelor, raise them to *become "the rich husband,"* or maybe just raise them to be independent womxn? We should also stop asking womxn to be more like *men* when we are encouraging them to be rebellious. Maybe we should ask them to be like *themselves* and still be deserving of the same respect. My friends and I say it to each other all the time when someone has a break-up, *"Go on and have sex like a man,"* and I always think to myself how odd it sounds after we've said it. It takes away from the actual fact that *womxn too can want to have casual sex without being told that they are behaving like men.* We could also probably stop saying *"Boss Lady"* and just say *"Boss"* because it sure as hell isn't *"Boss Man."* The problem isn't that we have different terms for men and womxn, the problem is that we've invented and continue to invent terms/labels where the *default is man,* and you find a variation of the default for the *woman.* Ironically, even the etymology of the word woman is *wife of man.*

Be the hero of your own story. Focus on yourself. Your life goals, your ambitions, and your dreams. Take time out for your hobbies and interests. Travel the world or to the city next to yours, but step out of your comfort zone and grow as a person; *do it for yourself.* Dream multiple dreams, and yes, falling in love and getting married to a man and having children can be a *part* of those dreams if that's what you want from life. But that possibly shouldn't *define your whole existence*. That dream shouldn't be then injected into every young girl's mind so that she never sees another dream again. Not every womxn wants that life. Some womxn cannot conceive and others choose not to because they just *desire a different life*. Some womxn are queer and *don't* want to have sex with a man. Some womxn don't want to have sex *at all*. Be the hero of your own story, take time out for the people that love you, and love them back. When and if you dream about falling in love, dream about *respect and boundaries and a relationship without abuse, control, or any other forms of misogyny*.

Stories are being written by men, for men. I want to see the stories of the women I personally know, the ones I meet and talk to every day, the ones in their 30s and their 50s, the womxn that are achieving so many crazy goals and inspiring others by living their life on their own terms. In order for your and my story to be told, we have to raise our voice and share it with this world. For our stories to be told, we have to demand to hear other stories like our own, and simultaneously help create a world where more womxn and men can exist without catering to their stifling gender roles. When stories of women's lives and years of their oppression and struggles are shared, and the stories of them being independent and able and successful are shared, they won't be written *by men, for men. These stories will be written by womxn.*

In order for that to happen, we need to become those womxn, and then raise them too.

I want to know what you will share with the world if you are the hero of your own story.

Not the love interest, not just the daughter/sister/mother/friend/wife. Tell me your story, exactly as you would tell the world about the hero. Tell me about your dreams and your desires.

This one is about you.

My Notes

My Notes

CHAPTER 26

CREDIBILITY

Backtrack to a party, where I'm talking to a group of people (come to think of it, a lot of my epiphanies have taken place in such environments). We're talking about why so many female actors in our industry are silent about #metoo. *Why haven't they said anything?*

And one man—there's always this one man—turns to me and says, *"Well, because most of them have slept for work themselves, so how can they? You don't have the right to cry #metoo if you agreed to sleep with these men and made a career out of it. Because then you are just as much at fault. You sold your body and became a millionaire, and now you want to cry about it? Well, you can't."* I could tell from the way he said it that it wasn't the first time he was saying it out loud because there was a level of confidence that only comes with either A. stupidity or B. knowing that many people agree with your opinion, and it's safe to say in this particular incident, he was A & B. Within seconds, he had nods and agreements. A womxn chimed in, *"Exactly, these women who sleep for work can't have it both ways. You can't give into casting couch and then say it's unfair when you are also benefiting from it."* The man next to her leaned in, *"You're setting a precedent of behaviour that is then acceptable, making it hard for other women to enter without it, and technically it's your fault if you've said yes."* I have to say I did agree with one thing he said: many of the womxn that do end up saying yes, for whatever reasons, are *part* of the foundation due to which the system still works. But there's more to that than meets the eye; *it's just not that simple.* The first guy then says, *"Why did they give in? Just to become successful? Suck dicks and get famous, and then cry? Sorry. If you give in to the bullshit, then you lose credibility to speak against it."*

Why is that? I thought. No one tells the customers complaining in Ikea or Shoppers Stop that *"you bought it, now you don't have the right to complain/review. You've lost credibility."* If anything, we want to hear from the people that have had the experience.

Why don't we as a society give credibility to womxn that have been through something terrible and uncalled for and still come out successful?

We should listen to them because they're the ones that have gone through it, right? There is a massive imbalance in power, and that power is abused by those on top. Casting couch, demanding any sort of sexual favours from womxn in return for work is *wrong.* Whether those womxn choose to take up the offer or not is not what the conversation should be, because the person *looking to be hired* may have multiple different reasons for saying yes—some need the work, some have run away from home to make their careers, others need the money, some are just simply desperate. This shouldn't be about *"Why did these women give in?"* Instead, this discussion should be about *"Why aren't we focusing on the men on top abusing their power?"*

Would it be better if these womxn didn't give in to the casting couch and then raised their voice? Because, look around you, many womxn do raise their voice on a daily basis; I have too. It's either *"she didn't get work, so she's doing this for attention"* or if she's famous, then it's *"she's become so rich from sleeping with her bosses and now she wants to complain."*

As a society, we don't listen to the people that aren't *immensely successful* in the field, and if they become successful, then we say they've lost the right to speak. *How does this work?*

I think we need to give credibility to womxn that have gone through the experiences and come out of it stronger because *they* are, in fact, the ones that can change the system. Just because they were in a situation where they chose to give in to the abuse of power in order to get work doesn't take away from the fact that they are still *victims of abuse*. If an A-list female actor had to sleep her way to the top or was coerced into sex, *instead of judging her for having said okay under whatever circumstances she was in, shouldn't we be talking about why they were put in these situations, to begin with?*

Are all these womxn supposed to sit around and wait for you and me to *change* society and *change* the power imbalance before they make themselves successful? Should they give up on their dreams? Aren't we missing the point if we're not addressing the power imbalance here? Aren't we victim-blaming? To say that *these women should have said no* is *victim-blaming.* How about we say that *the men with power should not be demanding these favours and that, as a society, we shouldn't accept it?*

The whole *point* is that womxn who give into casting couch are *powerless.* No one should have to sell their body to be cast as an actor, a director, a dancer, a waiter, a nurse, a writer, or simply be promoted. People should get the jobs that they are *worth and deserving of,* not because they were ready to blow a dick for it; that shouldn't even be the *criteria.* It is evident that the women applying/asking for jobs are in need of the job. Some may give in to the abuse and others may not. The ones that give in and become successful shouldn't be *attacked* for choosing their futures. If anything, *attack the system, attack the sexual favours and behaviours we've made acceptable, and attack the abuse.*

Instead of *blaming* women, we should be *encouraging* them to *speak up* about abuse and not saying that they've lost *credibility* because they did it themselves. Of course, a lot of womxn have given in to their abuser's demands. What else do we expect them to do? Just because someone *does* something, does not mean they should've *had to* do it.

Allow the women on top, the ones that are successful, the ones with voices to *share their stories.* Give them the credibility to *speak.* They're not the ones who took advantage of the system; they are a victim of their own atmosphere, of patriarchy, and their choices. I wouldn't call being *sexually exploited as* an advantage.

Give credibility to women that speak up against the casting couch, even if they slept their way to get on top. They've been through it and they have *every damn right* to say they *shouldn't have had to.*

Give credibility to womxn that have been in abusive relationships long enough to then speak up about the abuse once they feel *safe* enough to do so. Give credibility to the womxn that have gotten breast enlargements and cosmetic surgeries done to speak up about self-love, and why they think it's important, instead of telling them they went under the knife, so they are hypocrites. Womxn who have been at a level of insecurity themselves have every damn right to tell other womxn to love themselves—maybe they wish someone had been there to remind them to love themselves. Maybe they're trying to love themselves in the process of helping others. Maybe getting something done made them feel accepted enough by society to finally focus on loving themselves better. We leave no space for change and growth if we keep saying *"you love your natural self, so you wouldn't know how I feel"* while simultaneously saying *"you're so insecure, you changed how you look, so who are you to talk?"*

If you want to change something, change the way we treat beauty standards, change the notion of *sexy,* and the stereotype of a beautiful womxn. Educate people about eating disorders and makeup and real bodies. The reason a lot of womxn go under the knife is because they *just want to be good enough.* If anything, they're probably the ones that have been there and done that, and they *should, in fact,* be encouraged to talk about self-love if they wish to.

If you want to change anything in this world, change the direction we throw blame in. There is a huge market that cashes in on insecurities that women feel. There are men (and women) that hold the power in industries where womxn are required to be skinny, fair, pretty, flawless, and big breasted. An industry where women are required to have sex, be attractive, and be single in order to be successful at work, and all we do is *blame* the ones that choose the only path they're given in order to *become something in a man's world.*

Once womxn are successful and actually hold enough power to implement a *change in the system,* once they have a *voice,* we tell them that they aren't *one of us anymore,* that they're hypocrites, that their voices *don't have any credibility* because *they sold out and cashed in on it.*

Instead of asking successful womxn to join the tribe of people that abused them in the first place, why aren't we asking them to help others once they've reached on top? Why aren't we asking them to speak up against the abuse they went through, the power imbalance, the unfair beauty standards? Why aren't we asking them to change the system once they're *inside* the system? If anyone *can* raise their voice, it's them!

The successful ones are the ones that can create awareness, start a movement, become inspirations, hire more womxn themselves, expose an industry that abuses their power over young womxn. They're the ones that can *make a difference*—and it breaks my heart to see that *they're the ones that we take credibility away from.*

My Notes

My Notes

CHAPTER 27

RAISE BETTER MEN

We live in a society where we raise men to be abusive and controlling, and we *demand* that they behave in toxic ways that limit women—women who are expected to be *controlled* first by their fathers, then their husbands, and eventually by their sons. If she's too vocal at any point in her life, it's because she *doesn't have a man controlling her*. Well, *uncontrollable* me is going to tell you that *maybe we need to raise better men*.

Stop raising men to be abusive and demand control. It isn't their job to be the gatekeepers of the womxn in their lives. Stop raising men to have so much power that they know no other way to live than to be abusive. Stop raising men to believe that their strength lies in their *masculinity* and their honour lies in a womxn's vagina.

It doesn't matter if you're a mother or not, it actually doesn't even matter if you're not a parent at all—we have young human beings all around us that need to be raised better by *us* as a society. *Especially* men.

Yes, we should raise our daughters to be more independent, have more self-worth and confidence, but what good is any of it if we're still teaching our men to *allow* their women to work? There is already a huge shift in how womxn are unintentionally being raised because all around me, I see young girls trying to break free of the shackles they're put in. They're confused, scared, and vulnerable. Every day, I get messages from womxn – studying to be doctors, teachers, dancers, accountants, and entrepreneurs. Young womxn who are suffocated by their surroundings because they are finally beginning to realise that they want their *freedom* and they don't know what to do—where do they go from here? From late-night curfews to being told what to wear, what to study, and whom to marry—everything is decided for them. And they're trying extremely hard to *break the rules.* The shift in upbringing needs to happen in all children simultaneously because no matter what we teach our daughters, it isn't going to be good enough if we aren't changing the way we raise our sons.

I often hear people say *"feminism is cancer because even independent womxn aren't happy. Look at them in their 30s – single, successful, independent, rich, but ultimately, lonely. This is what they wanted… So, what happened now?"*

No womxn said she wanted to be in her 30s and be alone. *We did, however, ask for independence.* There's a huge fucking difference between the two things… because I look all around me and *men*, independent or not, are not *alone.* A huge population of older, independent womxn aren't happy because they're being asked to choose between their career and a family. They're taught that they cannot have both, and if they wish to be successful, then they will have to do it all alone. Independent womxn are "unhappy" because we're not raising *men* right. We're still teaching boys to be threatened by a woman's success and achievements in life instead of teaching them to be encouraging of it. We're teaching men that a woman shouldn't make as much/more money than him, she shouldn't work as hard as him, and she should pick up after him and raise his children, while womxn are unintentionally growing up with bigger desires and life goals—and both their goals aren't *aligned.*

Far too many women I know give up on their dreams and get married into families where their basic rights are taken away. They sacrifice their own desires in order to *fit into our society.* And the womxn I personally know in their 30s and 40s who are still single, the ones that haven't given in, are single because men are looking to marry *mothers and cleaners, not equal life partners*. It's 2020 and men still want a womxn that'll take his socks out of his shoes and wash them, iron his shirts and know where his wallet is, have his children, raise them, cook for them, be kind to his regressive and overbearing parents, make an income but not enough to hurt his ego, fuck him well, nurture him like a mother but be sexy enough for him in bed, maintain a family, and don't forget, find the way to his heart *through his stomach*.

Except, womxn aren't just looking to be stay-at-home mothers anymore (and the ones that are deserve to be treated much better too). Some womxn don't even *want* children, some want their own companies and are working damn bloody hard towards it, and what we are teaching men is that these womxn aren't *wife material*. So, a lot of older women are lonely, yes, but they're not lonely because of *feminism*. They're actually independent and successful because of *feminism*. *The* reason they are *lonely* is because we still promote misogyny in the name of tradition. We raise our men to have authority and power over womxn financially, emotionally, and physically, and if you're hoping that maybe we could just reverse back a few steps and go back to a time when womxn were being raised to be obedient wives, then that ship has already sailed… fortunately, *it is too late for that*. We, the angry feminists, are here to stay.

It's too late because it's a revolution. It's called *breaking stereotypes* for a reason. Womxn aren't being *taught* to have the dreams they're dreaming. No, a lot of them are doing it all on their own. They're breaking free because they've had enough and they demand a better life for themselves. Much like myself, a lot of other women I know weren't *raised* to have a voice. We weren't *taught* to take up space, but we found ourselves waking up every day *wanting* the life we thought we equally deserved.

Maybe this wasn't a part of your plan, but it's definitely the environment we're going to raise our children in, whether we (you) like it or not, so *raise your men better*.

Raise your son to be a feminist.

Raise him to be an active father that's present in his children's lives.

Raise him to be supportive and equal as a partner, instead of raising him to be the breadwinner.

Raise him to be equally independent within the house, to be able to cook for himself and his family.

Raise him to be able to stitch his own buttons, draw his own curtains, and make his own chai.

Raise him to understand that bringing a child into this world is not just his *right,* but also *his responsibility.*

Raise him to know that parenting is the job of two equal and consenting adults.

Raise him to respect people, regardless of who they are and where they come from.

Raise him to know that respect is *not his birthright, but instead, it is something to be earned.*

Raise him to know that his honour doesn't lie in the women of his family, and so it cannot be taken away when they choose *themselves* above him.

Raise him to know that womxn too deserve to take up as much space as him in this world.

Raise him to believe in equality but also in equity because for generations, *men* have had rights that others haven't, and in order to fix things, it's going to take a lot more than just a 50-50 equal division.

Raise him to understand that *he can be pro-life* and still have *no right* to decide what a womxn wants to do with her own body. Nobody decides but her.

Raise him to understand that *pro-choice* is what *pro-life* should have been in the first place.

Raise him to be nurturing, caring, and paternal.

Raise him to know the meaning and importance of consent.

Raise your son with the awareness that womxn deserve to choose a life for themselves, and the reason history is filled with *men* is because womxn were oppressed, controlled, sheltered, and often *anonymous*. Not because men were better, but because men had more power— power that they abused, power that *should have been equally shared*.

Raise your son with the knowledge that the way to his heart *is through his heart—through kindness, humanity, and companionship—not through his stomach.*

Raise your son to be aware of the sacrifices womxn have made for generations just to be the wife of men, and *they shouldn't have to anymore*.

Raise your son with sensitivity and the ability to express himself, to be able to cry, hug, and be emotionally available. Raise him to know that opening doors and paying bills doesn't make him a gentleman. It simply makes him ignorant and privileged enough to be able to do so, and ignorance is no longer bliss, while privilege now needs to be shared.

Raise him to know his privilege.

Raise your son to know that sometimes it's okay to take the back seat, to be wrong, and to be corrected.

Raise him to understand why so many womxn everywhere are so *angry*. Raise him to know that his core purpose in life isn't to get a job so he can earn for a whole family, but instead to be caring and present towards the people he loves.

Raise him to know it's okay, and often very necessary, to ask for help.

Raise your son to know that womxn's rights issues are as much his problem as they are hers. That he need not rescue or save a womxn any more than he may need to be saved because, as humans, sometimes we all need to be saved from our own surroundings, regardless of our gender or sex.

Raise your son to be a feminist.

Tell me, how would you raise better men?

My Notes

My Notes

CHAPTER 28

———

MY GRANDMOTHER,
AND WINTER

Yesterday, my grandmother looked at me on FaceTime, covered in a turtleneck, shivering slightly as I shut the door behind me after I was done showing her the view from my terrace, and she said, *"How beautiful, you should always come visit us in winters. You look so pretty when you're fully dressed."*

I laughed and made a joke about how *if only she came to visit me in summers, wearing bikinis and tank tops, sunbathing too.*

Every now and then, Nani will tell me to *change* my WhatsApp profile picture to something she likes, and there's no surprise as to why she's requesting. I don't give up either, because every now and then, I send her photos and stories of 80+-year-old womxn, feminists, warriors, fighting for equality, posing topless, and owning their bodies.

For every single time I've told her *"Nani, this is who I am,"* she's told me she wishes I were a little more like her, and for every time she's said *"we are old, we have different values… not like your generations,"* I go on to show her a woman her age and older owning the #freethenipple movement.

Do I have fights with my mother about the photos I upload?
Yes.

Do they support me?
Not always.

Do they wish I covered myself more?
Hell yes.

Do they hate the photos in underwear and make it a point to tell me every time?
Yes, every time.

Do I purposely do it again out of frustration?
Often.

Do they disapprove?
Yup.

Do they know that they have no final say in what I do?
I'm sure they do.

Do they understand and still send me a message every time they don't like it?
Yes... without fail.

Do they fight with me?
Ugh, yes. A lot.

Do they occasionally object and throw taunts that are hurtful?
Yes.

Do they tell me they're proud of me?
Also yes.

Do they try their best to understand what I say?
So often, yes.

Do they still not understand it?
Absolutely, they don't.

Do they love me anyway?
Always.

Will they fight for my right to be happy always?
Yes.

Are they victims of their own conditioning?
YES.

Are they ever going to change?
Nope...

Will they still love me?
Absolutely.

...Is it okay?
Yes, I guess so.

It's always okay if there is space for some form of respect. It's okay because the aim isn't to *change* them, it is to convince them every day that this is the right choice for *you*. Every family has conflicts, every family fights—we are no exception to that rule. I often get told *these aren't the values they raised me with,* and *why have I chosen to disappoint them,* or *not everything is about feminism* (even though the moments when they say that is when it's *always* about feminism*)*.

The difference between my approach as opposed to many other children's approach is that I don't give up. I never have given up at home. I've always stood up and fought for what I believe to be right. When I was barely eight years old, I took my father's chappal (slipper) and I hit him with it. He turned around and beat the crap out of me afterwards. I didn't know then what the consequences would be. The eight-year-old me didn't know the hierarchy and patriarchal rules. All I knew was that there was a man standing there that I called my father, and he was hurting my mother in ways that made her scream, shout, and bleed, *and I had to do something to protect her...* So, I hit him.

I've always put up a fight. When I was younger, I didn't always get my way. I would be punished or told to stop being so disobedient, but I was also *dependent* then. If parents could, and while they can, they'll cut off your internet, your pocket money, and/or ground you—until you do what was required of you. I think maybe you and I would do the same thing, as parents. But as an independent human being, *I have space to walk away from toxic conversations at home and then go back to them later, after we have all had some time to breathe.*

Children in Indian family dynamics don't have those rights, but as adults, we can allow ourselves the *space* as long as we are *independent.*

I don't give up, and while at times I am grateful for the fact that they give me the space to have the freedom to choose for myself and have the fights I wish to have, there are other times when I feel cornered, exhausted, misunderstood. *"If my own family doesn't get it, then what's this fight worth?"* Except, that's the whole purpose behind this fight, isn't it? To create an environment for men and womxn to grow up in a space where they have equal rights, to create *families*, where maybe *your children* will be lucky enough to have what you might not have had; to do better, to do more, to try harder.

If all our families *got it*, then what would we be fighting for?

Then we would have won.

I like to believe that every single time that I am brought down by patriarchy, it is a sign that I need to keep fighting harder. Every single time that I am slut-shamed, misunderstood, accused, told to take up less space, told to cover more and talk less, to be more respectable, it is a sign that I am not alone, that there are other womxn out there who wake up to the exact same lives as mine, some worse and others better. But they are consistently told to take up less space, and every single time that I write, I am convinced that you need me... as much as I need you. Because without each other, we couldn't possibly do this.

So, I laugh a little as Nani tries to subtly tell me that she hates it when I show my body on the internet, and she laughs a little when I not-so-subtly tell her she and I will one day sunbathe on an island in bikinis, and we both laugh, well aware of each other's stance and stubbornness. In my head, she's regressive, and in hers, I'm beyond help, and we both blame each other's generations.

I continue to shrug off the weight they try to stack on my shoulders, and once again, I wake up the next day, ready to face the world—prepared, to say *more*, and say it *louder*, for those at the back that have missed all of life's classes and are flunking.

You can either let the hurdles get you down, which they will, and it's not always in your control, but once in a while, you can even let them *inspire* you. Yesterday was my sign, my motivation, my reminder… Yours may not be my grandmother, and it may not be winter, but you'll find something that pushes your buttons, something that makes you wonder "*is this all even worth it?*" And when you do, remember, the reason that you feel deflated today is not the reason to give up, but instead the reason to *keep fighting.*

I have fought so hard, and most of it has only been possible because I am financially independent. No husband, no parent, and no relative pays for my needs, and so I answer to nobody. They're welcome to give me advice, but the final decisions are always *made by me.* I am independent, and hence I am able to sustain a life where I work towards building a healthy relationship with my family, while also living life by my own rules. I love them oh so dearly, and they love me back *enough* to fight with me every day, while we try our best to give each other the space and time we often need in order to grow. We don't abandon each other when we disagree. We don't give up on each other when we are embarrassed by each other's views. We don't disrespect each other's choices. And we sure as hell fight for each other's rights to express themselves. We are all outcomes of the environments we were raised in. I have the right to fight so vocally today, *at my age, as a womxn—they didn't.*

I have seen my mother fight with me about my *indecency* with the same amount of passion that she fights with strangers on the internet for telling me *what to wear*. She thinks she has every right to tell me she disagrees and disapproves of my choices, while simultaneously believing that I *deserve* a world where I can *choose* for myself.

Now that is the kind of environment I would want to raise my daughter in. With compassion, conflict, and the ability to be one's own identity.

There is no better place to start than with the people you love. Make a list of things you would like to change within your family.

My Notes

My Notes

CHAPTER 29

IN BED WITH SOCIETY

The very first time I realised that I was in *bed with society*, it was when the man I loved tried to change everything about me that *I* loved… then it happened with another man and another. It often happened at home with my family, it sometimes happened at work, and occasionally with the people we call our friends.

It's the little things at first, things you don't notice, things that don't actually matter in the bigger picture… but then again, all big pictures are made of little details, so maybe it matters?

Growing up wanting to *change the world* in some way didn't eradicate that naivety in any way. I remember the little girl with big dreams, adamant at getting her way in life. The young adult, stubborn about her desire to make a difference. The womxn, bruised but stronger, certain that she wanted to reach out to other young womxn like herself and remind them that *they're not alone.* The very first thing I learnt at the start of this journey was that we're always *in bed with society.*

The people you claim to love, the ones that claim to love you back, the world that you want to change, and the world you cannot stand to associate yourself with, you're in bed with it all.

Of course, it's a figure of speech. You're not literally having sex with them all, but you are absolutely in a relationship with them. The world that you so often wake up being disappointed in is the world you also claim to love and can't live without. This fight against social prejudice and inequality is going to be harder than you think, and there is no such thing as a "safe space" (if you think that it's a space in which you *never* get hurt).

The people you call your parents, siblings, best friends, and the partners you love—they're all flawed, and they're all going to let you down in some way or another. The people that you claim to *despise* out there in the world are someone's best friend and someone else's parents… we're all in this, together. The truth is that the human beings you've put on pedestals because you love them and expect the best from them might be despised by someone else too.

While you may blame a womxn for breaking your family, maybe someone you love was blamed for breaking another's. In this really brutal, complicated world, someone else's abuser could be your lover. It took me a while to wrap my head around how my abuser could have become someone's lover today—and eventually, I realised that wasn't my journey anymore. The only thing in *your* control is to aim to be the best version of yourself. Be a good human being. You can draw your boundaries with things you disapprove of, but there will *always* be things you *do not know*, things you cannot change, things you may find out someday, and hope to be strong enough to deal with them.

I used to sit up all night, talking to my first ever boyfriend about how it *broke my heart* to see people leave each other because of religion. I'd tell him that I would *never let my children go through it…* he left me for his family because I didn't think I could convert for love in the end. He left me, or I left him, because we were both young and conditioned to do what our families (society) wanted.

I'd often bawl my eyes out to my ex-boyfriend about how sick and tired I was of the patriarchy in our society. He'd hold me in his arms and tell me it's going to be okay, even though he went onto become the same person that asked me to change myself in order to show the world that he *does* know how to control his woman.

I opened up about my deepest fears of violence to a man who claimed to love me, who then went on to hit me himself. And I'm often so mad at the mothers in this world that have made me feel so small, like I wasn't *good enough* for their son, hours before I fight with my own mother for making me feel similar.

You and I are constantly in bed with society. We are in bed with the same people that we wish to change. This world, your home, your relationship, your "safe space," and even you are *flawed*.

People will disappoint you and it's never going to be *us against them*. There's very little of *ours* that we can say is *against the rest of the world,* because the world is made up of us all and *nobody* is perfect. We are all made up of deep-rooted conditioning, patriarchal upbringings, and inherent prejudices, and while some people try really hard to work on being better, others just don't—that's where you and the people you love might be different. But when push comes to shove, everybody will disappoint you in some way. Just remember that's not *your fault*.

I am flooded with messages from young womxn every day who seem *so* disappointed, so disheartened by the fact that their own families don't understand them, that their own partners try to control them, or their own brothers won't take their side. And I just wish that I could tell them all that the biggest fight you ever fight *will be the one you have with your own people.* That's the hardest one, the one that'll hurt the most and take the life out of you, but it will also prepare you for the rest of the world. We need to stop living in a bubble where we think our *family will always support us.* They probably won't because families are made up of the same people that set those boundaries for us in the first place.

I tell you this closer to the end because this doesn't necessarily mean that you give up, or you stop trying to change the world, or that you don't fight for your rights. No, this just means that, hopefully, you're more aware of the people around you. Everybody makes their own set of mistakes, and people have certain limitations. You don't have to love everyone for their flaws, but what you must do *is to be prepared for them to be flawed.*

You will most likely be body-shamed by someone you call your friend, be told what not to wear or when to work by your own partner, be expected to maintain your boundaries and be more accommodating by his parents, and be prepared to be a good wife by your own mother. If none of these things happens to you, then you're an exception to the rule, but there's a huge chance that it *will happen.* That the people you love *will disappoint you.*

It isn't always just going to be a sexist boss or a stranger on the street. Sometimes, it's the people you trust the most, and for some odd reason, we are raised to believe that they'll always be on our side, even though half our battle is against the side that we were raised to be on.

Choose your battles so that they do not exhaust you, and know that the fights you are going to have for the rest of your life will not just be with the world outside of your "safe space" but often also within it. Learn to eliminate people that are toxic, and filter the words that you do not need. Breathe in as deep as you can, every little chance you get, because this world *will* exhaust you.

It is brutal and it is scary, and when you let your guard down, know that you are still in bed with society. You are in a relationship with the very people you wish to free yourself from, and so maybe it isn't the people that we wish to change, but the mindset instead.

And in the end, don't shy away from giving yourself the credit you deserve for getting through each and every day, for staying alive and rocking up every morning, ready to face the world again.

The very first step to changing your life is to acknowledge what you want to change.

Make a list of the problems you face and how they make you feel restricted. Be honest with yourself. Then tell me the things you're going to do to be part of the solution instead.

My Notes

My Notes

CHAPTER 30

TOO MUCH TROUBLE

I remember one particular night in 2018 as though it was yesterday. I was sitting with a bunch of my girlfriends at home and #metoo had somewhat, just, become a hashtag—or maybe like most other trends and releases, things reach home a little later than the rest of the world.

We sat there talking about just how many womxn had come out with their stories. Womxn I'd worked with, womxn I'd known briefly, women I'd known too well, cousins, friend's sister, friends' girlfriends—everywhere I looked, there was a #metoo. I remember a few nights prior to this, I was talking to a man who said that his Facebook feed was filled with stories of women's assaults and he couldn't believe that it was *this* common. He wondered if all of it was *actual assault* because of the *quantity* of incidents.

I told him that they must be real, unless hundreds and thousands of womxn from all across the world had collectively decided to *plot a lie,* which is a little unrealistic… to which he responded, *"But maybe all of these womxn are confused about what assault is? It's too many to be true."* I couldn't help but smile; the denial was so jarring that I didn't know any other way to react, anything other than a smile would hurt too much. So, I asked him if it was possible that *maybe* far too many men didn't understand/weren't taught what *sexual abuse and consent* is, instead of *womxn not knowing when they were being assaulted?*

He somewhat agreed and said *maybe* that's possible. I had learnt by then that I was probably not going to get an outright approval on the topic by most men. This would take time, and struggle, and if that's the only way forward, then I guess that was the only choice I had.

The reason I remember the particular night with my girlfriends is because a few wines and whiskeys later, when the topic of sexual abuse came up, I talked about my story briefly, and another friend spoke about hers, when one of my friends turned around and said, *"It's so scary, you know, that these things have happened to so many womxn. I've personally never experienced anything like it."* And we told her she was really lucky. Another friend then said, *"I mean, I wouldn't really say I've been sexually assaulted or anything, but reading all these stories of womxn, I realised I'd completely blocked out some really disturbing memories of my own childhood. I had a cousin who would always try to touch me at night. We were all young and the house was small, so the kids would all have to sleep together, and he would keep touching me. I didn't even know at the time that it was wrong, I just knew I didn't like it. Then as I entered college, I would take the sharing auto to the train station, and this one time, a man sitting next to me would keep bringing his hand up to my breasts and pressing them. I was so confused about what was happening. It was cramped and dark, and he just sat there, pressing my breasts again and again. I was so bloody petrified and scared. I just cried silently, but I couldn't say anything. I couldn't scream. I just froze… and I know that doesn't count as like sexual assault or anything… I mean it's not like I was raped or abused. It's nowhere close to what other womxn have been through, but it happened, and my brain blocked it out because my whole life I've thought nothing has happened with me."*

Before I could say anything, my first friend jumped in, *"Hold on, does that count? Because, I mean, my father had a friend who would always come over and take me into the room and make me sit on his lap, and he very obviously had a big boner that he would keep rubbing on me. I must've been six or seven years old. I would keep fidgeting, trying to leave, and he'd keep rubbing me with his dick, telling me it was our little secret. But, like, I wasn't assaulted. Hence, I said I've never been through it because, surely, that doesn't count... does it?"*

Three other incidents were shared, all of them as per their understanding *"probably weren't assaults."* I realised my male friend was right about one thing—womxn were definitely confused about what was considered *an assault*, and because far too many of them didn't even know what counts as an assault and what doesn't, the stories of sexual assaults were actually not accurate. They were, in fact, severely *underreported.* Womxn that were a 100% assaulted somehow believed that it *didn't count.* I couldn't believe that I sat there in a room of educated, independent, wonderful, ambitious, modern, smart, empowered 20- and 30-something womxn who had *all* been sexually harassed/assaulted yet didn't think it *counted as assault.*

It took a hashtag movement for womxn all around the world to actually recognise abuse and speak up, to start a conversation about their stories of assault, and even then, anything less than the gruesome act of being raped was often considered *not bad enough* to acknowledge.

That night, I realised that we as a society attach so much shame and judgement towards womxn when it comes to assault that far too many womxn would *rather believe that it never happened to them.* I asked my friends if they would ever speak publicly or tell their families or their loved ones about these incidents, and most of them said they'd rather not do it because it's either been too long and it didn't matter anymore, or it was too much trouble. *Too much trouble.* One of my friends said she'd have to explain why she *suddenly* remembered it, or why she was only speaking up after so many years. She would be told she's looking for *attention*, and she didn't want to feel like she was *taking away* from the stories of other womxn who had far more horrifying experiences. Another said that her family would be really disturbed if she told them. She would be told to move back home or stop taking public transport, probably even be forced to get married. She didn't think her loved ones would be very open to hearing these experiences without questioning if she was at fault—what was she wearing, was she encouraging it, what hour of the day was it, was she sexually active at the time?

Too much trouble.

I felt sick in my stomach hearing her say the words *"I wouldn't want to start some pity party for myself, you know? Like, oh hey, I've been somewhat sexually assaulted, I don't know, like, it's not that bad, but yes, I was touched and woo hoo, look at me, I'm a victim. I'm not a victim. I haven't really gone through anything. I fought so hard to go to college even though they were against it and to now tell them that I was assaulted at the time would be like telling them they were right for not wanting me to study further. They'll tell me that if I'd listened to them, if they'd been stricter and stopped me from going to college and hanging around boys, then this wouldn't have happened. It would rightly be too much trouble to go through when my life is going perfectly fine right now."*

Too much trouble... the words really got to me.

We've created a society where it's too much trouble for women to speak up about their stories of assault. It's too much trouble because these women aren't treated like the victims/survivors of abuse but instead like the ones instigating it. They're questioned, doubted, judged, cross-questioned, undermined, married off, and controlled... womxn are caged in order to be protected, as though it was their fault. Like their right to *freedom* was the problem.

It doesn't matter that it was their own cousin at the age of 10, or an uncle in her own home at the age of 7, or a stranger in a public transport at the age of 17; it doesn't matter if it's a boyfriend, a husband, or her own father—what matters is, *what was she doing at the time for this to happen to her?*

There is a lot of shame attached to assault, but this shame isn't attached to the perpetrator; it's attached to the victim.

I know a girl in her early 20s, someone very close to me that's helped me look at this world with a different lens, someone who's taught me more about love and patience. She was molested from the age of 7 to 9, then from 11 to 13, from 16 to 17, and again at 22. Whenever she's shared the incidents of her assault with people, there's this constant discomfort in the air. The discomfort doesn't come from being disappointed in our society, or from the guilt of how we've raised our men that they're capable of such disgusting acts. No, instead, the discomfort is often people automatically wondering *if it really happened. Why her? What did she do?*

Every now and then, an impolite, sexist person will say these thoughts out loud and ask, *"But are you sure all of these happened? You weren't just imagining them after the first one? Because I can imagine it's hard to go through something so traumatising, maybe the other incidents were… in your head?"*

I say she taught me patience because in those moments when I want to jump in and yell at such people, I see her calmly looking for the right words to explain to this very ignorant human being *why* it wasn't all in her head. Of course, she also has moments where she asks people to go educate their misogynist selves or shove their *imagination* up their ass, but she doesn't ever lose hope in humanity because of those that have failed her. She shares her stories the way she wants to share them, without the fear of judgement from the world. *She shares them in the hope of changing at least one life along the way.*

But she shouldn't have to prove to society that she didn't dream these stories of abuse. She shouldn't have to recall the time, what she was wearing, how old she was, the details of things around her. *She shouldn't have to first be doubted, in order to prove she isn't lying.* We, as people, as a society need to do better at listening to the womxn that finally find the courage to come forward with their stories.

I was watching the news once, where in a panel (of mostly men) discussing sexual assault, someone turned and asked, *"But why do womxn talk about their stories of assault after years, after decades? Isn't it weird that they're not talking when it happens? Isn't it strange that they go on to live their lives for years and years? They have sex and get married or get jobs, and suddenly they say they were molested or assaulted five years ago? Why don't they just speak when it happens? How can we know?"*

For starters, that's not an innocent question asked out of curiosity and general knowledge. It's accusatory, it's malicious, it's misogynist, and it's an unacceptable way to treat the womxn that are finally speaking. But I'll answer the rhetorical and insulting accusation disguised as a question anyway.

Because womxn aren't really told they *can* speak up. Womxn aren't told they *should* either. So when womxn *do* speak, they are putting a *lot* at risk in order to tell their stories. They're risking their reputation, they're risking their jobs, their future in their chosen professions, their families, the reputation of those family members, their relationships, their place in society, their social groups, their online presence, their dignity, their stability, and their freedom.

When womxn finally voice their stories, they are risking *everything* they have. They're risking *everything* they've worked so hard to build. Because *women are shamed for being assaulted.* Hence, most women just don't share these stories.

How can we know? Because women aren't telling you they were assaulted *for fun.* Most of them don't even speak about it, and the reason they don't speak is because *it's too much trouble.*

In a world where womxn were to speak, almost every womxn you know would speak of assault. It would begin with the way they were picked up and made to sit on an uncle's lap when they were less than ten years of age. It would be their own relatives, often their own fathers, that touched them inappropriately under the pretence of parental love, and the pressure of an entire family's happiness and future would be the responsibility of a ten-year-old sexual abuse survivor. If women were to speak, it would begin with their cousins trying to forcefully finger them under blankets, their brother's friends, their sister's boyfriends, the male teachers at school. It would be her neighbours, claiming to let the kids play in their houses and babysit them after school while making her touch his penis, asking her if she *liked it*—a girl of 11 years old, who *didn't know what was happening, but knew she sure as hell didn't like it.* The man on the bus that kept rubbing himself on her until she finally saw a wet patch on the back of her dress. The man on the train that put his finger up her underwear as she struggled to find a safe place to stand in peak rush hour. The man in the autorickshaw that kept pressing her breasts in the dark, but she didn't say a word. *Her silence was not her consent, it was her fearing the threat of violence and murder, her fear of shame.* The shopkeeper at the end of her street that stares at her chest every time she buys eggs, licking his lips and winking at her. The man at the bar who pinched her butt when she leaned in to order a drink, and by the time she turns around, she can't tell who it was within the herd of hundred men.

It would be the cab driver that wanked off the entire time while dropping her home from work, all along watching her in the rear-view mirror. The colleague at the office that casually touches her thigh while talking and the hairdresser that puts his hand far too deep down her neckline during the head massage. The boy she liked at 15 who forced her to give him a blow job, and when she cried, he accused her of being a slut, challenging her to go tell someone what she had just done for him. The boyfriend who raped her because she was in love with him and demanded she prove her love in bed. The boss at work who told her she was so talented that he saw her going many places, and he'd love to discuss those opportunities further over dinner. The husband who lets his friends come over and flirt with her, in hopes of having them invest in his business. The husband that thinks marriage is consent and a free pass to lifelong sex. The ex-boyfriend that uses her naked photos to threaten her into having sex with him. The stranger that grabbed her breasts in the crowded Durga Puja. The friend that raped her in her sleep, *accusing her of being too drunk to control her own self.*

In a world where womxn began to speak about their stories out loud, you would hear about my father. And you would hear the stories that I hear every day from womxn all over the world. You would maybe then stop wondering if we are *exaggerating, delusional,* or *seeking attention,* as you do today.

Most womxn do not speak about their own stories of abuse because raising your voice against assault is the same as saying *men need to change the way they live in this society.* Raising your voice against assault is often the same as raising your voice against the privilege men hold in this society. It is asking for men to be more accountable, more answerable, more responsible for the safety and well-being of others—and let's not forget that if you bite the hand that feeds you, you will begin to starve, until you can find a way to feed yourself.

My male friend was unfortunately right, far too many womxn are confused about what *assault* is. They underplay the abuse they've experienced, and they blame themselves for the horrid acts of others in order to have a sustainable life in our society. Because speaking up is *too much trouble,* and when the few that do take that trouble and *raise their voice,* we begin to wonder if it was all in their head. We make them doubt their stories, and we ask them if they're delusional. And *that* is precisely how you raise a generation of young, modern, independent, wonderful, ambitious, educated, smart women, who sit together on a Friday night and talk about how they were touched and groped and abused by men at the age of 7 to 17, but think they've *never been assaulted.*

Go on, write down any/all the memories you have of assault. Do it slowly, take all the time you need. It could be as little or as big as you remember it to be. Please don't compare your journey with anyone else's. Your pain, your growth, and your story don't matter any less based on what other womxn in the world have been through. This is about you.

My Notes

My Notes

CHAPTER 31

ADJUST

/əˈdʒʌst/

Alter or move (something) slightly in order to achieve the desired fit, appearance, or result.

Precisely what we're asking womxn to do on an everyday basis – adjust.

Don't be fooled though, there are a hundred different ways it's implied. The word varies, while the outcome required from them is identical.

Why can't you just *understand* why my family hates you?

Why can't you just *let it go?*

Yes, they hated you once. No, they never apologised, but they've *stopped* saying horrible things to your face, haven't they? Is that not enough?

He got promoted this time because he could work the extra hours every day. You're not going to make a *big deal* out of it, are you? *Relax, go home, and enjoy being a mother.*

All you have to do is change yourself when my family is here, is that *too much to ask for?*

He cheated on you, beta, but he's so sorry. He's begging you to forgive him. *What more do you want?*

Obviously, after a few years, you'll have to quit, when we have children, when *you* become a *mother*. Who else will raise the child? Why are you being so *unfair?*

You want him to be loving, be stable, be open to accepting your independence, and have a good family also? *You can't have everything.*

I'm just asking you to change what you're wearing. Why are you acting like I've slapped you or something? *What is wrong with you?*

It was one slap—and I've been apologising for weeks. *Don't you care about the children? Don't you care about the pain you will cause our families?*

Oh, so if we're not having sex, then you want to leave me. Why are you such a *slut?*

Why do you need my family to validate you all the time? Why do you care what they think of you? *You are being so selfish.*

I'm sure you know if you decide to have a baby, you can't be promoted for the next five years. *That's obvious, isn't it? I'm not sexist. I'm just doing what's best for the business.*

He's paid more because he also has more screen time. That's *fair,* right?

You can't start a family and keep working your job and also cook for everyone. You'll have to *choose your priorities.*

You are so arrogant. Why is your self-respect more important than *anything else?*

Your brother hasn't eaten yet. How insensitive is it of you to not offer him food first?

Your husband hasn't eaten yet. What values did your mother send you with?

If you can't even handle this much, how will you live with your husband and his family?

Adapting is a woman's job—we adapt and we keep the family together. It's *who we are. God made us flexible so that we could look after everyone.*

When you become a mother, you will understand.

What do you mean you don't want to be a mother? You're being disgraceful. It's a woman's *duty.*

Why are you being so difficult?

What is your problem?

Why are you being so stubborn?

My mother held our whole family together. Women in my family are respected. Be like her.

He doesn't take time off from work to take care of sick children, but you do. So, what equality do you want from us at work?

Why are you so demanding?

Why are you so dramatic?

Why are you so sensitive?

Why are you putting our entire family's respect at stake so publicly?

Why can't you just wear something else?

Why can't you smile more?

Why can't you cook?

Why can't you just be what I want you to be?

Hey, you got some of your own?

Tell me the thousand different ways you have been asked to adjust. Tell me so that we can make sure we remind each other not to allow it again.

My Notes

My Notes

CHAPTER 32

CHOICE

I want you to know that if you've ever had an abortion, *it is not your fault.* I also want you to know that I have had one too.

Letting a foetus grow or not is a choice that is *yours,* nobody else's. Choosing to bring a life into this world (or not) is a choice that is *yours,* nobody else's. Yes, creating a pregnancy usually involves two people, and in most situations, I'd tell you to consult, talk, discuss it with the other person, if there even is another person in the equation. But eventually, this *potential* life grows inside *your* body and no one should have the right to take a final call on what *you* do with *your* body. I've seen womxn be forced to abort their pregnancy, and I've seen womxn be forced to go ahead with the pregnancy. In both instances, it saddens me that *the decision of what happens to a womxn's body is taken away from the womxn herself.*

Your views on abortions might be the opposite of mine, and that's okay because we are supposed to choose for ourselves. Our views should define our own choices, not other people's. I'm not at all *pro* the idea that a country, a government, a society, a family, or another human being should have the right to *choose* on behalf of a woman what she should do with her body. It's easy to yell out *"abortion is murder"* and act like you really care about *human life* even though you as a person will have zero stake in that foetus once it's born. You aren't educating this life, you aren't making sure if it has a home, money, clothes to wear, food to eat, or even a sustainable home. Even a government doesn't contribute enough to the upbringing of this child, to make that decision on a woman's behalf. If you actually cared about human life, then you would be investing all this time and effort into *saving the children that are already alive.* You know, the ones that are *breathing*, homeless, abandoned, living on the streets and in orphanages. Those are lives, the same foetuses that were *saved* and are now left to die, homeless and in dire circumstances. *That* is murder.

People are so invested in the developing hands and fingers of a foetus but indifferent to the fully formed child that is sent to the orphanage after nine months.

You can stand outside abortion clinics and yell out abuses or judge womxn on the internet and call them murderers, but it doesn't make you any better as a person. It doesn't even make you *pro-life*. It just makes you an absolute asshole. Once a child is born, most anti-abortion protesters could not give a fuck about the life it's going to live. If they did, they would be at the orphanage instead, not an abortion clinic.

And this isn't even *"whataboutism"* because this is very much a *"why someone else's abortion is none of your business—you are not raising the child that that foetus will one day become."*

When I had my abortion, a few days prior to getting it done, I made the mistake of googling things and found a horrible quote about how abortion makes a womxn the mother of a dead child. I cried that entire night. I cried for hours, until eventually, I realised what a load of *bullshit* I was being sold in the name of humanity. There is so much *hate* and a desperate need to *control* women in our society, and it's powerful enough to make *you* want to blame yourself too. Abortion doesn't make you a murderer. You're not even killing a real *person*. A foetus isn't a person—it can become one, but it isn't. It's not *alive,* and I refuse to let a bunch of bored, insecure people that have nothing better to do than to be misogynists control how I feel.

I need you to remember that it is *not your fault. Your rights come before anything else growing within your body.* Only if there is you, is there anything else.

Equal responsibility

We often hold absolutely zero responsibility and judgements towards men when it comes to pregnancies, as though the womxn magically impregnated herself (I mean, not all womxn are Mary, nor are all men God). The blame, the shame, and the responsibility—everything ends up being a womxn's problem, and despite popular belief, it's actually not *always* easy for womxn to choose abortion. Abortion is one of the hardest decisions most women (if not all) make, I think mainly because of how stigmatised it is. *Why* womxn choose to have abortions does not need approval from us. Who are we to have opinions on another woman's decision if she's perfectly fine with it? *Their reasons don't matter.* It doesn't matter if she did it out of helplessness, or because she accidentally got pregnant and she's not ready, or she actually, truly just never wanted to be a mother—abortion is still a tough decision and the *least* we could do is let womxn make independent choices about what they want to do with their own goddamn bodies.

Apart from the mental stress attached with terminating a foetus, our entire bodies change so drastically in the process. Unlike men, who ejaculate and have there onwards done their part, womxn go through ridiculous amounts of hormonal imbalances and end up with so many side effects, including weight gain, weight loss, hair loss, haemorrhoids, swelling, depression, anxiety, eating disorders, excessive bleeding, and other side effects that leave lifelong impacts.

After I had mine, I went into extreme depression. I gained a lot of weight, and the stress of being blamed and questioned made me want to isolate myself as much as possible. It was only with the help of my family and my friends that I was able to heal properly and realise that *it's okay to do what's right for me.* I don't have to be guilty for wanting control over *my own body.*

I'm here to remind you of the exact same thing. It is not your fault. You haven't done anything wrong. Whatever your reasons were at the time when you decided, even if you regretted it afterwards or felt guilty due to your surroundings—*remember that you made a choice, based on what you needed to do for yourself at that moment. Nothing else matters.*

Don't listen to people that say *"what if your mother had aborted you"* because that argument doesn't make *any* sense. A lot of womxn have abortions and miscarriages, and honestly, I guess if she had made a choice to abort you back then, you wouldn't be *you* today—*it's really that simple.* It's nothing to get overly emotional about. Many of our mothers have had abortions, and that foetus didn't make it, but here we are, we did. If your mother had married another man, you still wouldn't have been *you* today. You'd be a different life, a different egg with an entirely different sperm… and it wouldn't have been *you.* The same way that you turned out different from your siblings too. It's as dumb as someone yelling out *"what if your mother had been with another man, that would've been murder because you wouldn't be you!"* To which I can't wait to scream back *"wait, but would that me at least have had green eyes?!"*

People should have a child when they are financially and mentally stable and actually *want* a child, not because they accidentally got pregnant and are now forced to keep it. There are enough children in this world being born and thrown outside orphanages, not being adopted because everybody wants a child but nobody wants someone else's child. Do you know how much worse it is to have a child when you cannot give them the life they deserve? A foetus is not human enough, but a child that's alive in this world *is.*

If people really cared about children or life as much as they claim to, we wouldn't have so many orphans in our world… everyone that's anti-abortion would adopt a child instead. And the governments and policies that restrict women and want to make abortions illegal would have laws in place with facilities that *help* women and children in need all over the world. Except, none of that exists. What does exist is the guilt they put you through for deciding what you want to do with *your own body.* Which isn't so surprising when you realise that society just wants to constantly control everything a womxn does.

I want to tell you 101 times, it isn't your fault. You haven't done anything wrong. You aren't *about to* do anything wrong either. You didn't make the wrong decision. You have to stop telling yourself you made a mistake once it's done and instead remind yourself that you had your reasons. Stop reciting the toxic narrative that society feeds you.

If you were pregnant again and wanted to make the *same decision all over again,* you still would not be wrong.

Trust me when I say this: if men could get pregnant, we would be promoting abortions instead of banning them. Because it would be a horrendous crime to let men get pregnant and then go through involuntary labour for nine months. That's when we would be sensitive about all the health issues, side effects, and the loss of job opportunities that take place. Womxn would be forced to take birth control. *Oh wait, we already are.*

The lack of birth control options for men is a perfect example. We live in the 21st century, and yet we don't have a single contraceptive pill that can be taken by men to avoid pregnancy. Reason? Because studies show that birth control pills that were being tested on men were causing side effects like depression and anxiety, so they temporarily shut it down. Even though one of the biggest reasons behind depression in womxn happens to be the same birth control pills. Womxn also suffer from premenstrual syndrome, popularly known as *PMS,* and yet, we haven't acknowledged the hormonal imbalance they go through during their period, let alone discover better medication to deal with it.

As womxn, as half the population of this world, you deserve *better,* you deserve *more,* you deserve equal treatment. The world, unfortunately, is not going to offer it to you on a platter, but it's okay to get up and grab your rights yourself. Just because they tell you to shut up and obey, does not mean you have to. This is your life, your choice, your story—why should anyone else have the right to write it?

I can't give you equality, or a life without guilt and unfair treatment, but what I can give you are my words, my own experiences. When I found out I was pregnant, I was in the process of breaking up with the man, and I had no idea *how* to deal with this new information. I took all the precautionary steps and still, here I was. The abortion was *my* choice. It didn't work out the way I wanted it to, and they left a piece inside me, and due to the amount of excess bleeding, I had to go in for another termination—twice in two months. Eventually, my body healed. My mind, however, didn't for a very long time.

I remember the amount of guilt I felt; it was inexplicable. I woke up bawling my eyes out every day, and I cried myself to sleep every night. I remember knowing rationally in my head that I hadn't *done* anything wrong, and yet I felt so disoriented. A lot of what I felt was because I spent an awful amount of time on the internet and read terrible things people said, like I was a murderer. I hated having to live through the abortion twice. My hormones were hitting the roof, and my breasts used to ache. My horribly insensitive ex-boyfriend at the time, the same one I was trying to break-up with before I found out I was pregnant (the *"stop your randi rona"* mansplainer), told me I could only stay with him *without* my dog. He refused to live with me for the time being when I felt mentally unable to cope because he said his *gym was too far* from my house and that he found it *difficult to drive the 9 km distance*. The evening I got the second termination done, he turned around and told me he wanted to have a child of his own. I couldn't believe that he chose the one day when I was drugged, half-conscious, in excess pain, bleeding after my abortion, as the day to tell me *he wanted to have a child*. I let it go, knowing very well that I didn't have the energy for anything else.

The next few months were extremely hard for me. I tried to hurt myself once—that's when I started therapy because I didn't want to die; *I really wanted to live*. I didn't know what was happening to me. I would have strange blackouts, and *it hurt so much*. I just wished that someone would tell me that it was *okay*, that I hadn't done anything wrong. I have always had an extremely supportive family, so my brother told me that he would stand by whatever I decided. But this strange guilt… of knowing that I had to *"hide"* the fact that I'm getting an abortion from the world made me feel so sad and suffocated. I wanted to talk about it. I wanted people to know that I was suffering right in that very moment and I was going through a really tough time emotionally and I needed a break from expectations. But we don't talk about abortions. Abortions are stigmatised in our misogynistic society. Womxn are expected to deal with it in isolation *so that we don't end up uniting*. I say it's time we do.

You feel wrong, *even though you're doing nothing wrong.*

In your head, you don't hear the voices of other womxn like you. You only hear the accusations made by society, and it destroys you from within. That's what they want—for us all to believe that we're wrong, which is why they divide us from each other. You are *not wrong.*

Was it hard for me? Yes. Would I do it again? I absolutely would if I still didn't want to have a child at that time (or at all).

I could be with someone I loved to bits and pieces, I could be in a place in life where I was maybe even financially stable, in love, ready for a family—but if I wasn't *ready to bring another life into this world,* I would terminate the foetus all over again. That decision would be no one else's but mine – because it's my body that bears all the changes in order to turn a foetus into a child, and my body is not a political playground. My body is not up for debate.

If people in this world care so much about the foetus, maybe they should focus more on having better contraceptives, preferably for men and women *both*, with fewer side effects, vastly spread sex education with less stigma and more awareness. Focus on making men more accountable for the outcome, and women less attacked, while simultaneously minding their own damn business.

As for you, I need you to remember that *you didn't murder anyone.* If anything, *you gave yourself the life you absolutely deserve.*

I won't tell you what to write this time…

My Notes

My Notes

CHAPTER 33

ROMANCE HAS GOT NOTHING TO DO WITH IT

One of the most *outwardly romantic* relationships I've ever had was based on an immense amount of physical and emotional abuse. I always saw movies and books talk about *toxic love,* the power of abuse, the relationship between narcissists and empaths… and don't get me wrong, I don't think all romantic relationships are abusive, or that all abusive relationships are romantic, or anything else that seems as black and white.

All I'm saying is that in my own personal experience of abuse, I noticed that there was enough intense romance and public display of affection to confuse me. There was a lot of *"without you, I would die"* and so many *"I want to burn the hands that dared to hit you, my chanda (moon)"* and uncountable *love letters written from the edge of the world…* and I felt so exhausted, so unstable, and perpetually gaslit in such a way that I thought I was losing my mind.

One minute, I'd be swept off my feet, held in the arms of the man that swore he couldn't breathe without me, and another moment, I was lying on the floor, dragged, bruised, howling into the ground beneath me. I realised that nobody—not your parents, teachers, friends, siblings, your first love, nor your grandmother—teaches you *how* to deal with that kind of abuse. If you're lucky, people will warn you about abuse at an early age. You'll be told to "*never let a man hit you*" and to "*walk away if it's abusive and he ever raises his hand or curses you.*" I wasn't directly told any of the above, but I did grow up watching a lot of abusive men around me, and I knew, *I knew it wasn't right.*

The thing this world fails to warn you about is that there's a huge chance *that the person causing you a lot of physical and emotional harm will also constantly try to sweep you off your feet.* They don't warn you that these toxic relationships aren't black and white. They're never as simple as being beaten up and then never being apologised to—*that* would have been easier to spot and flee from. Abusive relationships are often the hardest ones to understand and cope with because your abuser *convinces you* that they *didn't mean to harm you,* that *you need them in your life, and you are the only person that can save them,* that *you've done something to trigger this monster within them,* and *without you, they would die.*

For some womxn, it first begins with a fight; for others, it begins with sex. Either way, it's abuse. I would've left after the first time, and the second time, and the third—if I wasn't then made to also believe that every day, *I* was doing something wrong. Every day was a new opportunity to *fix him,* to *save him* from his demons that were perpetually triggered *by* me. Yet, every day, he reminded me that I had failed to save him once again. Instead, I made him *hate himself, for hitting me.* Every day, he made me feel like *he* was all I have, *he* was my safe space, even though I was petrified that he would choke me or hurt me again. Every day, he would promise to be a new man, a better man, the man that I deserved to spend my life with, and *every day,* he would fall on his knees and beg for my forgiveness because without me, *he could not breathe.* I would've left if they'd warned me that after every time he wept and swore to burn those hands, he would use them to hit me with them, *all over again.*

Then one day, I was watching *Saath Khoon Maaf* and it felt like the ground beneath my feet had shifted. The story, the poetry, the love letters, the songs, the romance—the same abuse that followed.

It made me realise that romance has got nothing to do with it.

I decided I was going to make sure I tell *as many young womxn as I possibly could.* While I couldn't decide for others what they do and how long they choose to stay in abusive relationships, the one thing we can all do is create as much awareness as possible. Remind as many young womxn as possible, let them *know* that they're not alone and they're not at fault and they're not *the only ones* living that life. Many more of us have lived it.

No one tells you this growing up, and absolutely nobody warns you, but *romance* has nothing to do with *respect.* You can be in the *most romantic relationship in this world,* it can be the absolute *fairy-tale romance, straight out of the books,* and it still won't guarantee you any *respect.*

We spend far too long telling little girls fairy tales and stories of princesses. We glorify love stories and sing songs about romance, enough for *most girls* to grow up to desire *romance* over everything else. I know it made me weak in the knees too. I know that all I ever wished for in a man when I was a kid was that he be *romantic.*

Today, I demand honesty, compatibility, companionship, patience, tolerance, love, and above everything else, *respect.*

Do I still have romance in my relationship? Of course, I do. We write love letters to each other and leave notes around the house. We have dinner dates, and we drink wine and stare into each other's eyes… but I made a very conscious decision to demand *respect* above anything else in my relationship. It is *because* we respect each other that there is romance—not the other way around.

To tell young children that people who are romantic towards each other are also automatically kind to each other is an outright lie. Unfortunately, we're telling the narrative of love stories through fairy tales *completely wrong.* The world doesn't tell you *any* of this when they're preparing you to deal with life, when you're hormonal or falling in love, and I think it's about time we start *actively talking about it.*

Say it out loud.

Say it to girls when they are young enough to learn from it.

Say it without stigma and without any shame.

Say it so we can raise a generation wherein womxn *know* to look for equality, dignity, respect.

Say it so we can educate them of the signs to look out for before it's too late.

Say it so we can finally begin to hold our men accountable for their actions.

There is a 99% chance that Snow White, Barbie, Rapunzel, Cinderella, Juliet, Jasmine, Ariel, Sleeping Beauty, and honestly, far too many other characters of love stories in the *real world today* would've ended up making a million sacrifices and being in an abusive relationship shortly after the story ended for us at their *happily ever after*—because when we tell womxn what to look for in a real, healthy relationship, we're not telling them to look out for themselves at all.

Maybe we can save all the womxn to come, and maybe we can't, but we can at least *try* our best to let every little girl know that *real love* isn't necessarily forever, and real love isn't when a man claims he'll die if she leaves him—that's an abuse of power, it's controlling, and it ought to be called out for what it really is. Love, instead, is when he wants to be the man she deserves to be with and lives up to becoming one.

Romeo and Prince Charming aren't worth your time if they can't get their shit together and learn to respect you.

Tell me what respect means to you.

Tell me if you've ever been in or come out of an abusive relationship.

Tell me anything.

My Notes

My Notes

CHAPTER 34

BECAUSE I DON'T HAVE A FATHER

I often wonder what people mean when they claim that I am *the way I am because I don't have a father.* The strange, overtly sexist statement is not only insulting but also reconfirms my belief that men in families exist to control and inject fear. A blanket statement such as this one endorses patriarchy and shames the independence or self-worth a womxn may hold. After all, *"she only has all this freedom to do as she pleases because she doesn't have a father."* What happens then if a girl *with* a father has freedom? Would that be considered *bad upbringing?* Is the bottom line that womxn should be controlled and put back into their place?

When someone turned around and sympathetically told my mother, *"It's not Saloni's fault that she's like this. I guess it's because she grew up without a father,"* as though not only was something *wrong* with my way of life, but they also *felt sorry for my childhood.* I was furious. I couldn't believe that people thought it was *okay* to speak to a womxn like this about *her* family and her children. After all, I have first-hand witnessed kids *with fathers,* and if that is the way to judge how a person would turn out, then I think I prefer how I turned out, over far too many people *with fathers.*

What bothers me the most is the way we attack single mothers, yet would absolutely clap for a single father. Regardless of how a child turns out, we will constantly appreciate the hard work and the efforts a single father may put into raising a child (even with the help of family members) because *we expect so little from men.* However, no amount of efforts made by a womxn is *good enough* as a mother. We say *not all men,* even though we shove them all into the same little box of stereotypical parenting and pathetically low expectations. Claiming that my mother raised a strong, independent, opinionated daughter was used as a way of insulting her. As though if only there was a man in the family, *I would've been slapped into behaving like a woman at the right age.*

This obviously shows that we're raising men to control womxn, by example and by conditioning.

Not long after this statement was made, I was watching a show where a man tries to molest his niece, and when she screams, he tells her *she doesn't have a father, that's why she's reacting like this.* I keep wondering what he meant by it. Was he claiming that if she had a father, she wouldn't have had the nerve to be so violently vocal in the middle of the night, because she wasn't afraid of the consequences, because she didn't have a man that was ready to jump down her mother's throat to blame *her* for it all? Because she wasn't afraid of having a voice? Or was he outright gaslighting her—that because she didn't have a father, she didn't know what his affectionate touch really meant? *All the outcomes made me sick in my stomach.* It made me sick to think about the kind of world we are raising our children in.

The kind of world where mothers would rather *"save"* their daughters by keeping them locked away after a certain age because they know that there are men in the family that are predators. *Protect their daughters by caging them instead of raising their voice against the abusers.* The kind of world where womxn hush-hush over the mamas, the chachas, and the uncles that are *too touchy.* Slap the daughter and ask her to put on some decent clothes, instead of addressing the problem: *the uneven, toxic distribution of power that men have and are never threatened for abusing.*

From being told that I wear these *indecent* clothes and speak the things I do *because I don't have a father* to constantly being asked to go show my nipples to my *father* if I'm such a *feminist*, I always wonder—*where does it come from?* Are we saying that a man cannot see the body of his own child because he will get aroused from it? Are we saying that there is something wrong with a man seeing his own daughter? Should the womxn of a household be scared of the men in their *own family,* because *men will always be men?* Are we accepting that we expect men to behave in such ways, and are we also, therefore, encouraging it as a society? Why do you think people on the internet ask womxn that if they care so much about #freethenipple, then they should take their tops off in front of their fathers? What's that supposed to do? Shame us? Shame our families? Get us raped? I fail to understand what the consequences of those actions need to be. By claiming that a woman could never be topless around the men of her family, are we not actually perpetuating the popular belief that *men are controlling their women, however, they cannot control their own sexual desires?*

Men rape. Men rape men, men rape womxn, and they rape children. Uncles, brothers, fathers, partners, husbands, strangers—I know it's hard for you to hear it out loud, but it's the truth. Womxn rape too, but statistically, men rape far more. I guess because I was raised *without a father,* I will tell you this. After all, there's no one to shut my mouth and *put me back into my place.*

Instead of applauding the womxn that raised me into the human being I am today, we dissect her every effort and blame my independence and strength on the lack of a male father figure. Rarely do I see a society that questions and rejects *men* for having walked out on their wives and children. We don't shame the men that abandon their families. Instead, we shame the women and children that they walked out on—as if it's *their fault.*

When I was barely a year old, my father tried to throw me out of the window. He held me out and told my mother that if she didn't do exactly what he wanted, he would throw me outside that very moment.

Today, *I am alive because I don't have a father.*
I am independent *because I don't have a father.*
I am fierce, I am strong, I am vocal, and I am free because I don't have a father.
I am lucky enough to be raised by the bravest and strongest woman I know because I don't have a father.
I was given the opportunity to make my own life decisions and learn from my own mistakes because I don't have a father.
I am aware of the patriarchy and its disadvantages, of the ways in which we abuse and confiscate the rights of womxn because I don't have a father.
I am capable of seeing the difference between love and ownership because I don't have a father.
I am proud because I don't have a father.
I have so many things today, but most of all, I am here, writing this to you, I am alive, and it is all because I don't have a father. So, if there is anything in this world I must thank the man for, it is for leaving before he killed me someday.

My Notes

My Notes

CHAPTER 35

YOU DON'T HAVE TO BE AN ACTIVIST

Feminism, like many other movements and ideologies, is constantly evolving and growing. What probably began (most likely by womxn) as a fight for simply their right to live with freedom, then morphed into a civil rights movement in the late 1800s, culminated in a political and legal debate at the turn of the 21st century. A movement that may once have been political has started to become broader today—more intersectional, catering to a wider range of people and cultures. *Feminism* and what it means is constantly evolving. I have friends who believe that *it isn't feminism if it isn't vegan*, others that say *it isn't feminism if it isn't intersectional*, and many that claim *it isn't feminism if it isn't taking into consideration men's rights as well.*

What is feminism to you?

I've spent a long time thinking about what *feminism* means to me. My idea and definition of the term are *constantly evolving.* As of today, through conversations, essays, articles, and movements, I have realised that the term more often than not is criticised, scrutinised, looked down upon, and very easily sets you up to fail—maybe because we live in a society that still benefits from the failure of feminism? After all, feminism truly *doesn't* promote family first traditions that have been inherited by a patriarchal society.

Feminism for me was a simple act of demanding space for my own identity. Long before I even knew that there was a *term* for it, I felt a certain kind of *discomfort* every time society demanded more from me than they did from the men around me, starting right at home, with my brother. Time and again, it felt *unfair,* but I couldn't understand what it was or *why?* It was years before I actually thought, *this is because I am a womxn...* and strangely, while some were things I fought for, others I simply accepted as a *way of life.* The older I got, the more *normal* it seemed that men and womxn have different sets of rules, and you must obey the rules in place for you in order to live in society. When in intervals I couldn't take it anymore, I rebelled. And when I did, I noticed there was so much rage towards my right to voice, but what I *also noticed* were *the voices of other women all around me, whispering for help.*

Feminism for me was as simple as *living my life.* The act of watching TV on the sofa lying down, drying out my lingerie, wrapping myself in a towel, wanting to go outside instead of helping in the kitchen, playing games with boys in the garden, having period stains, not folding my legs, and going for a walk with my girlfriends. Even the very first time I fought to stay out late at night, I remember so well not understanding *why* my brother could do the things I couldn't. At first, it felt like age, but as years went by, I was one day as old as he was a few years before me, but the rules weren't changing. Instead, it felt like my box of freedom got narrower and narrower, *even with my privilege.* We live in a society where a young girl's body is objectified and sexualised before she even knows what sexual desire is. I didn't even know what sex was when *I* first wanted to wear a bra.

I see little girls on the beach in bikinis today, and I don't know if six-year-old girls even know anything about the breasts that they don't have, or that their bodies would grow into looking different to a man's. Or that they will be slut-shamed for it. But there they are, in two-piece bikinis.

Feminism for me was… an extremely strange, steep curve in this journey of life. For far too many years, I didn't even know *why* I was treated differently. All I knew was that it's frustrating and exhausting being *me*. Being picked on and blamed, being touched, being restricted, and *I just wished I could wake up and I wouldn't be me anymore.* The thought that my gender or sex had *anything to do with it was a crazy thought that sure as hell never crossed my tiny brain.*

So, I often sit in parks and wonder how many millions of women would have arrived here before me, before us, before the term *feminism or womxn or equality* was ever invented, women who simply felt a disconnect with the way they were treated in our society. Women that knew there was injustice, that it *didn't feel right,* but still couldn't understand *why.* Women who wanted *a room of one's own,* who secretly wrote anonymous poems for newspapers and wanted to have orgasms without being electrocuted or told they're hysterical. Women that wanted to fall in love, women that loved other women, women that couldn't understand why they didn't desire to be mothers just like the others…

If you keep a bird caged from the moment it's born, legs tied, wings clipped, unable to see the sky, *maybe it will never even know that it was ever meant to fly.*

Being a womxn of many privileges and ignorance too, I didn't really realise *what* feminism was until I was in my mid-twenties. For me, it wasn't about having rights to be educated, or property rights, or the pay gap. Instead, it was about the smallest of small things. I wanted to spread my wings, to laugh, speak, run, and dance. I wanted to take up more space, and at every step along the way, *I was told to take as little of it as possible.*

As I became more vocal, more loud, more influential, I was then told that I didn't even understand what *feminism* was. I wasn't helping womxn in villages, nor was I educating young girls, and I sure as hell wasn't distributing sanitary pads, *so what kind of a feminist was I?* When that didn't work, I was told to *stop calling myself a feminist* because I'd only be pulled down and disliked by the people I want to work with. Women's bodies are controversial, whereas brands, production houses, and companies are all run by conservatives (insert: sexist and regressive), so they won't want to associate with you if you're talking about *women*. They'll say you're "*that feminist,*" and believe me, when they say it out loud, *it really starts to feel like an abuse.* I was warned to stop talking about womxn's bodies if I wanted to have *anything* to do with the Indian film industry; "*no one wants to work with a feminist,*" people would advise. "*If you care about women, go become an activist instead.*"

I'd laugh, genuinely never getting the connection between the two. I'm constantly told that wanting to wear whatever you want, exposing or liberating your body, not lying about losing your virginity, travelling the world, loving your skin (or another human) as openly "*isn't feminism*" and every single time I'm so confused because no one really seems to explain what *feminism is.*

I was under the misconception that feminism began with womxn demanding to have equal rights? Did only activists deserve to speak up about that and/or be treated equally? And if so, are *all* men activists? What about the couch potatoes, or the ones still living with their parents, the divorced, the ones in college, or travelling the world, or bodybuilding, or living like nomads?

Because from where *I* stand, I see a world full of men being treated with privilege for simply *being born men.* Not for being doctors and pilots, or becoming scientists, or giving birth, or being in the Olympics, or educating a whole nation, or even being activists—men are simply treated with respect, *for being men.* Nobody asks a man if he's saving lives or not when he takes his shirt off at the beach. Nobody asks if he's doing anything for prostate cancer when he's busy living his life, juggling multiple relationships. Or why he's not doing TED Talks about male suicide rates and mental health. Nope, he can simply go to the gym, upload topless selfies, get offended and say "*but I respect women, so not all men*" but still get a job that automatically pays him more than womxn, hop onto the internet and leave toxic, harmful, misogynist comments, and be proud of himself, without ever having once spoken about men's health.

The standards we hold men to are *so fucking low.*

As for womxn, the standards are unattainable.

Women are deprived of respect for *being women.* While I don't demand that the world respect a woman for simply being a woman, I sure as hell demand that we stop *disrespecting women for being women.*

Feminism for me is as minuscule as a girl demanding to wear shorts at home, or spreading her legs as she binge-watches TV with her brother who does the same. Feminism is a girl demanding that she be allowed to play volleyball, football, or whatever the hell she likes, instead of being forced to learn to make round rotis. Feminism is her desire to feel an orgasm, to learn more about her vagina and what turns her on. Feminism is about her right to education, her own body, as well as her contraceptive rights. Feminism is her basic right to life—the same right to life that we celebrate when it's a boy.

Yes, feminism is intersectional and racial and political. Feminism is radical, and feminism is the equality of sexes. Feminism is educating womxn and eradicating female foeticide. Feminism is body positivity and sexual awareness. But in which world did we decide that feminism can only be one or the other?

As I see it, *you don't have to be an activist to be a feminist.* You don't have to save the world; you don't have to dedicate your life to saving womxn. It would be wonderful if we all did whatever we can do for this world, but being a feminist doesn't obligate you into being an activist. You could never lift a finger towards *changing* the world in any way for womxn *and still be a feminist.* You won't be changing a lot of lives, and you sure as hell won't be an activist, but remember, *you don't have to be an activist to be a feminist.*

The same way that you don't have to run an orphanage to be a parent or save all the animals in the world to be an animal lover.

I'm tired of people being held up to such a harsh standard of life and choices when they identify themselves as feminists. *Do you help womxn? Do you care about poverty? Are you educating the underprivileged? Are you donating? Are you empowering womxn to become doctors and engineers instead of being naked? Or are you just vacationing and writing books and living your life? Are you saving any lives? Are you talking about animal rights? How are you a feminist if you eat dairy? Are you speaking about the LGBTQ+ community? Are you fighting for men's rights? Or for other womxn's rights that aren't as privileged as yours?*

As I said, in an ideal world, human beings should speak about all of the above and another hundred things that I have probably forgotten to add. In fact, even in this *not so ideal world,* we should promise ourselves that we will try to do better and we will be more aware, we will use our voice and our influence for the things that we care about, regardless of what we identify ourselves as.

Society goes *out of its way* to discourage you from associating yourself as a *feminist.* They make it so bloody hard and so impossible to be *a feminist.* At first, you're a *killjoy,* a threat, a man-hater, then they wait for you to make *one* mistake—because, on their terms and conditions, you are bound to fuck up. *You will often behave as per your conditioning, you will bounce to derogatory hip hop lyrics, and you will probably judge and complain about other womxn too, and you will fail.* And when you do, *you will take down feminism with you, because that's what they want.*

"Why feminist? Why not just equalist?" even though no one questions why our entire species is called *mankind.* You'd be a *drama queen* then. They want a world where people are afraid of calling themselves a *feminist* in order to *avoid as many conversations as we can that threaten the space a man holds.*

If you want to stand for the cause, regardless of who you are, *say it out loud. If you care about equality, say you are a feminist, not just a humanitarian but a feminist.* And remember that it doesn't really matter *what* you fight for in life, as long as you're fighting for the things you are capable of fighting for—the ones you have the *strength* to face.

If you think that people deserve the same opportunities, and womxn deserve to be *uplifted,* and men take up too much space in this world, and that LGBTQ+ rights are as important as everyone else's rights, and womxn deserve to be paid for the work they do, *then congratulations! You're a feminist.*

If you think men should be able to express themselves instead of being forced into a little box labelled toxic masculinity, then *you're a feminist.* If you think, just like men, everybody else equally deserves the right to sit on their couch and watch Netflix all day, go to the beach to do nothing, and later spend time with their partner, all along without being judged, controlled, limited, assaulted, raped, or threatened, then *you're a feminist.*

If you believe in live and let live, you're a feminist.

And guess what else? You don't have to actively *fight* for any/all of the above in order to be a feminist either. You really don't. *All you have to do is believe that everybody deserves the same rights, that equity is more important than equality, and let people fight their fights, help them by listening, supporting, and allowing them their space whenever the opportunity arises.*

You don't have to be an activist to be a feminist.

Do you call yourself a feminist? If you do, when did you begin? And if you don't, what's stopping you?

My Notes

My Notes

CHAPTER 36

WHAT I LEARNT AS A FEMINIST

That you aren't born one, but you become one.

That womxn deserve equal rights, and before that, they deserve equity.

That *people* should be allowed to coexist with an equal amount of respect and space to occupy, regardless of their gender, sex, and identity.

Not everybody is a *he* or a *she*.

That if people want to be identified as they/them, then that's *their choice.*

Not everybody is heterosexual either.

Not everyone actually even knows or has figured out what/who they are.

Womxn, children, and the LGBTQ+ community lack opportunities and are penalised for simply being who they are.

Womxn do most of the unpaid labour in the world.

Womxn are also the poorest in the world.

Womxn are paid less than men, not because they *work* less, but because womxn in our society are expected to make different life choices than men. So, technically, they are being penalised *for being womxn.*

Most caretaker roles are fulfilled by women and are usually also unpaid roles.

Our medical and health system doesn't cater to women's health as much as it should.

There is a gender-based data gap in almost *everything*—from medicine to virtual reality to public transport—because surveys and studies aren't segregated by gender, and we assume that the *default* is *man.*

That *Invisible Women* by Caroline Criado Perez should be part of the school curriculum, for *all children.*

Being angry and pissed off with injustice is a good thing—as long as you know what to do with that anger.

A lot of womxn around the world prefer to use the term womxn because they don't want to be identified as an extension of a man, and the etymology of the word man is *"thinker"* while the etymology of *woman* is *"the wife of man." Not all women want to be identified with a word that originally derives from "wives of thinkers."* Womxn should be allowed to choose for themselves what they prefer. To me, a lot like Miss, Mrs, and Ms, one doesn't have to take away from the other and womxn can be women, or womxn, as and when they please to be, without telling others what they should pick for themselves.

Not everybody that is privileged is against us. Sometimes, they're just ignorant and naive, sometimes they need your help in being educated, and sometimes they're actually on our side. Having privilege is not an individual's fault; *choosing not to acknowledge that privilege most definitely is.*

Womxn empower womxn, but womxn also bring other womxn down. Just like men.

Women are often co-enablers of patriarchy.

Empowerment doesn't necessarily mean that you deprive a womxn of her culture or her identity. Forcing a woman to remove her dupatta, her hijab, or her saree from her identity is *as wrong as asking a woman not to wear short clothes.* The aim should be to raise women in an environment where *they can choose for themselves.* Work towards educating and empowering women in ways where *they have freedom of choice.*

Changing the world isn't an overnight process. We must accept that we're working towards a change that we may not even live long enough to see, but there *will* be men and womxn that benefit from it.

Opportunities for *equal* amounts of education is *equally* important.

In order to create a society that works, we apply a damaging amount of pressure on men to be financially independent and womxn to be dependent... except it's not working, *it's failing.*

LGBTQ+ rights don't need your opinions and approvals if you're not part of their community. What you *should* be doing from your place of privilege is supporting them in their fight *for their rights.* If you can't find it in your heart to support the cause, then shut up and mind your own business. This isn't about you, and whether *you* like it or not, isn't important nor is it relevant. This is about their lives, it concerns them, and if you can't join their protest, then go home.

Go back and read that last paragraph, and replace LGBTQ+ with human rights and reread again. Anything and everything that doesn't concern you because you come from a place of privilege and it doesn't affect you doesn't require your opinion either.

When womxn say *"my body is not a political playground,"* what they're really saying is *what they do with their bodies shouldn't be up for debate.* Just like governments and its citizens don't decide what a man does with his body, no one should have a say in what women do with theirs either. Whether that's related to their period, abortions, birth control, sexual desires, their bodies, or their nipples—everything seems to be up for debate and be *voted for/against. Our bodies are not a playground for politics.*

Society is threatened by anyone other than a straight man occupying space in this world, *especially* when that anyone is a womxn.

There is a very subtle difference between patriarchy and misogyny. I've come to realise that to be a patriarch, you don't have to be a misogynist. However, you cannot be a misogynist without being a patriarch too. Misogyny is the act of hating women, and unfortunately, *very often,* the presence of one indicates the existence of both.

Womxn are not born wives and mothers but are conditioned to become one.

As a woman, your voice will be silenced, but you can, if you choose to do so, *scream.*

They don't teach you inequality in schools (not yet anyway), but you will learn about it through toxic abusive relationships, through the way you're treated in society simply for being a womxn, through the way your families differentiate between you and the men (often sons) in your family, through the judgements and the name-calling, through the way they try to control, cage, and silence you, through every single time you stand up for yourself and your rights, and the way you are told *it's your fault.*

People that identify themselves as *feminists* weren't just born as one or happened to be strolling in a park and decided that *today onwards, maybe I'll try feminism.* No, they have actively been through/seen a hell lot of inequality in ways that made them acknowledge that there is a bias towards men and unfair treatment towards anyone that isn't a man.

"You are not a feminist if you are not vegan" is a lie. You can very well be a feminist, or identify with feminism, *without* being vegan. *Fun fact: You can also be vegan, or an avid animal lover, and not be a feminist.*

Not all womxn are feminists. Not all feminists are womxn.

We all make mistakes, and because we make mistakes, we have the opportunity to learn new things. Nobody is perfect, and sometimes people are sexist, even the ones that claim not to be. It's what we are conditioned and raised with, and so we make mistakes. Never let people, or a person, be the definition of your cause. Feminism is a cause; people that identify themselves as feminists, including me, are just people who believe in that cause… but that doesn't mean we, you and I, don't fuck up. Of course, we fuck up; everybody does. Even the men and women you admire, the ones you swear by, the ones you idolise—they've all done/are capable of doing things you do not respect or agree with. Please don't let the people damage the cause.

It doesn't matter what I (or other people) want or say, equality and equity are the cause.

That's what we must fight for.

What have you learnt, as a feminist?

My Notes

My Notes

WOMXN

The word "womxn" was impactful enough to initially make me uncomfortable, before making me extremely curious. To me, the word is broad enough to include the people that have often felt neglected and left out in our communities, the people we should be *listening* to, instead of speaking on behalf of. Not all womxn can give birth, not all womxn become mothers, not all womxn fit into the little box of gender roles, and not all womxn are *female*. But all womxn belong *here*, with *us*.

While some women want to be referred to as just *women* because they've fought so hard to achieve that title, others (including myself) are looking for a better word that they can relate to without the word *man* in it. I don't want to talk on behalf of other womxn, but the word *womxn* makes me more self-aware, it makes me ask questions, and it makes *me* feel included. To me, it simply means that womxn everywhere can *choose* what they want to be identified as instead of being forced to just use one universal word.

I'm still trying to understand what the word means to me, hence I've used both in this book. I'm glad you could join me on a part of this journey. Together, we've sparked a fire, and I hope it helps you light the path of self-discovery of how you would like to be identified.

ACKNOWLEDGEMENTS

We are made up of our experiences. Of the people we love, the things we learn, the ones that hurt us, break us, and shake us. We are made up of our victories and our mistakes. In the moments when you think you cannot take it anymore… when it hurts so much that you think *this is it, it's over* - is when you grow. You unlearn, you evolve, *you become.*

I hope this book helps you heal, but know that this fight for our rights doesn't end here – this is only the beginning. There is no magic potion that can save you. You and I, cannot *eradiate* patriarchy, we cannot *undo* it. We can only change the way we respond to things and situations. The only thing in *our* control is how *we behave.* You will still disagree with your families; you will often feel like *there's no way you could be related to them.* You will wonder how someone you love so much, could be so oblivious to your rights. You will want to pull your hair when you often realize how *far* we are from equality. You will break down, but you will also get back up again. You, my love, are brewing.

I want to thank everyone that has been part of *my* journey, the people that have helped me get up every single time that I have fallen down. Those that have encouraged me to write this book.

The first thank you was always safely kept for my womxn. My beautiful, kind, self-aware womxn that have followed me on social media for so many years and bumped into me with tears on the street… my army of Cupcakes. You make me feel like my words matter and my voice is needed. Without you, I may have never thought of writing a book. Thank you for always asking me to write more, for sharing my words, for spreading awareness, for telling me that my words have helped you grow and made you stand up for yourself. Thank you, for letting my words have an impact in your life, it is the only reason I write.

The most important thank you, is for my mother - who has been and always will be the strongest womxn I know. The womxn I grew up watching and admiring (even though we cannot stop arguing). If there is anyone in this world that pushes my buttons like nobody else can, it's her. Maybe it is directly linked to how much you love someone. It is also her, who has taught me to be the womxn I am today. It is her that I have watched my whole life, fighting every battle with so much ease. My mother, Bindiya Chopra, who may not agree with my opinions very often, but will *always* fight for my right to speak. I love you. I want you to know that you *can* and *should* wear whatever you want to wear without worrying about whether future-in-laws or relatives or this society will mind or not – anyone that minds, doesn't matter. You are beautiful, and you deserve all the happiness in the world. Along with happiness, you also deserve an amazing, dashing, gorgeous man. (If you're reading this and are/know an eligible man, feel free to apply. He *must* be a feminist, must love old Hindi music, and will most definitely have to first be approved by me.)

I would like to thank my grandmother, Padma Chopra, who I've promised to read the whole book out loud for. My Nana, Susheel Chopra, who I wish so much was still here with us, he loved me more than anything else in this world. My whole childhood after he passed away became a blur and I miss him every day. Nani, I know you do too. I love you. *Dekho, aapki Tina "Mrs" nahi but at least "Author" toh ban hi gayi ;)*

Mama and Mami, Deepak Chopra and Jasmeet Chopra - thank you, I know no matter what happens, I can always fall back on you.

My best friend Ambika Acharya, she was the first person to tell me that she likes this title because she was rescued by me, and so she knows that the world will be too. You, my love, are *my person*, and you always will be. Thank you, for sharing this last decade with me and making it half bearable. I cannot wait to grow old with you.

My go-to boy, Eshaan Roshan – for all the times you've laughed at my angry messages to you that are the "size of a novel" - here's a book, *finally*. You are and always will be my Tom, and I, your Rachel.

My first and last housemate, Manisha Mondal, who has spent endless days and nights ranting with me for three years dissecting political speeches and ingrained patriarchal behavior. You were such an important part of my journey as a feminist, thank you.

My little *hathi parinda*, Anchal Goswami, I am so lucky to have you. You make me question the world while simultaneously showing me the beauty in it. You were the first human that made me feel like my words matter enough to save a life. You give me hope, and you make me believe in the deepest place of my heart that there is kindness and love out there, thank you.

My partner, Rahul Bhattacharya. I do not know anyone in this world who could have lived with me through this last year while I've been writing (especially when we often slip back into our gender roles and then I have a break down). Thank you, for all the times you've patiently listened to my objections and my opinions. Thank you, for being open to unlearning the patriarchy, for making me breathe and smell lavenders through my many panic attacks, and for always encouraging me to follow my dreams, however big or small. You make me a better person every day. I love you.

Last but not the least, I'd like to thank the only human being in this world that has actually made this book possible. My brother, Sahil Choujar. He is the *only* person that has read each and every word of this book, edited it, guided me when I felt lost and corrected me when I went off track. You have always been my support system. Today, I am a feminist, because of *you*. My role model, my favorite human being, my big brother. No amount of words are enough to say thank you for everything that you have added to my life… Without you, I truly do not know what I would've done. Thank you, for putting up with my mood swings, my hectic texts, and my break downs. Thank you, for always demanding better from me. I cannot imagine my life, or this world without your presence - that is how precious you are.

To my Notion Press team,

Vishal J. Menon, my Senior Publishing Consultant, my go to for everything from the day I signed up with Notion Press. Thank you for believing in me, for reading my captions, for having all the solutions and always being a phone call away. You're an absolute legend.

Gabriela Kristen Caster, my Senior Publishing Manager – thank you for being there for me, you've given me honest feedback whenever I've needed it, you've calmly listened to me when I've been in a state of panic while also reminding me to stop and feel the excitement.

Susan Linda Rajkumar, my Editing Team Manager, we got along from the moment we spoke over Australian universities and the use of the term "womxn" – you have enhanced my book in ways I am extremely grateful for. Thank you for all the suggestions, the advice, and for telling me that my book is the need of the hour.

Thank you to the entire team at Notion Press that has worked so hard day and night to make this book possible. I can't imagine how chaotic this would have been, especially through a cyclone, thank you for all your support and hard work; Naveen Valsakumar, CEO. Subbhaiya Perumal, Senior Manager – Operations. Surekha Thammannan, Senior Manager - Publishing Services. Pratheeksha J, Editor. Gokul Ramaraj, Senior Graphic Designer. Sathish Kumar & Karthikeyan, Senior Interior Designer.

Made in the USA
Monee, IL
25 March 2021